MODERN PERSPECTIVES IN BIOLOGY

Under the Editorship of

HARLYN O. HALVORSON *The University of Wisconsin*
MOLECULAR BIOLOGY
HERSCHEL L. ROMAN *University of Washington*
GENETICS
EUGENE BELL *Massachusetts Institute of Technology*
DEVELOPMENTAL BIOLOGY

edited by

John M. Allen
The University of Michigan

MOLECULAR ORGANIZATION
and
BIOLOGICAL FUNCTION

HARPER & ROW, PUBLISHERS · NEW YORK, EVANSTON, AND LONDON

MOLECULAR ORGANIZATION
AND BIOLOGICAL FUNCTION
Copyright © 1967 by John M. Allen

LIBRARY OF CONGRESS CATALOG CARD NUMBER: 67-10112

56433

CONTRIBUTORS

THOMAS F. ANDERSON
The Institute for Cancer Research
Philadelphia, Penna.

CHRISTIAN B. ANFINSEN
Laboratory of Chemical Biology
National Institute of Arthritis and Metabolic Diseases
National Institutes of Health
Bethesda, Md.

LAWRENCE BOGORAD
Department of Botany
The University of Chicago
Chicago, Ill.

JOHN E. DOWLING
Wilmer Institute
The Johns Hopkins University School of Medicine
Baltimore, Md.

I. R. GIBBONS
The Biological Laboratories
Harvard University
Cambridge, Mass.

ALBERT L. LEHNINGER
Department of Physiological Chemistry
The Johns Hopkins University School of Medicine
Baltimore, Md.

ALEXANDER RICH
Department of Biology
Massachusetts Institute of Technology
Cambridge, Mass.

J. DAVID ROBERTSON
Department of Neurology and Psychiatry
Harvard Medical School
Research Laboratory, McLean Hospital
Belmont, Mass.

CONTENTS

PREFACE

This volume presents papers derived from a lecture series sponsored, in the spring of 1965, by the Institute of Science and Technology of The University of Michigan.

One of the more pervasive developments in biological science over the past decade has been the progressive "molecularization" of the approach to cellular organization and cellular function. It has become increasingly clear that there is an essential unity between the organization of cellular structures and their function. A significant feature of this organization is the association of molecules into macromolecular aggregates with unique functional properties. These aggregates, in turn, are organized into higher orders of structure and function with properties unique to this level. The higher orders of aggregation, the functional modules of the cell, form interdependent systems, and a complex series of interrelations exists between them. The regulated interplay between modules makes possible the integrated function, indeed the very existence, of the cell. Thus, it is no longer realistic to expect that the properties and behavior of isolated molecules will serve to explain cellular function. It is, rather, the properties of molecules acting in association with other molecular species that furnish meaningful clues to the nature of cellular activity. An approach to cellular function that embraces not only properties of individual molecules but also the properties of these molecules as they are integrated into progressively higher orders of structure and function offers great promise for the eventual elucidation of the life process.

In organizing the lecture series from which these essays were derived, an attempt was made to provide breadth of coverage ranging from a consideration of individual protein molecules through intermediate levels of molecular organization to highly complicated and integrated systems which could, however, still be viewed in essentially molecular terms. In the choice of material, special attention was paid to the "visibility" of a particular system; for the quality of "visibility" is one of the great attractions of this area of endeavor and is one of the reasons for its success in the analysis of biological activity.

In this volume we begin with the properties of proteins and the ways in which these properties define the spatial characteristics of the molecule, its function, and its interaction with other molecular species. Next we examine the structural basis for protein synthesis and, from this point of departure, the molecular organization of "simple" biological systems, using virus particles as an example of molecular aggregates with a high degree of predictability in their organization. From this intermediate level of organization, we move on to functionally more complicated systems, and, by way of introduction, examine the molecular organization of cellular membranes. Finally, highly integrated and complex systems, as typified by mitochondria, plastids, visual receptors, and cilia and flagella, are considered. This progression through increasingly higher orders of complexity provides an oversight view of the essential features of cellular organization.

JOHN M. ALLEN

Molecular Organization and Biological Function

1

MOLECULAR STRUCTURE AND THE FUNCTION OF PROTEINS

Christian B. Anfinsen

Stated in its most elementary terms, the process of evolution involves the natural selection of organisms whose integrated functions are most highly adapted to environmental pressure and which serve to support individuals in the population to that point in life at which procreation has ensured survival of the line. Although we cannot speak of the "natural selection of proteins" since they are, after all, nonreplicating, the fundamental mechanism of evolution does appear to be heavily involved with the selection of mutants on the basis of the functional potentialities of the protein chains for which their deoxyribonucleic acid (DNA) codes. To the best of our knowledge, a mutation expresses itself at the molecular level only by the synthesis of a modified protein molecule. The protein that results is then either as adequate, more, or less adequate than that produced prior to mutation and the perpetuation of its kind depends upon the resulting suitability of its organismic host.

The sequences of nucleotides in DNA molecules code for amino acid *sequence*. As we shall discuss below, available experimental evidence indicates that this primary sequence contains all the information necessary for the spontaneous determination of three-dimensional structure. Both molecules and organisms are selected on the basis of function. Since function in proteins is not determined by linear stretches of amino acid sequence, but generally by groups of distant residues brought together in space by specific interactions, it becomes clear that we must consider the chemical basis of biological function as a three-dimensional problem.

We tend to accept as truisms hypotheses that were daydreams only a few years ago. It is hard to believe that the major advances in the three-dimensional analysis of protein structure (35,44), in what has been termed "chemical paleogenetics" (17,38,43), and in the study of

1

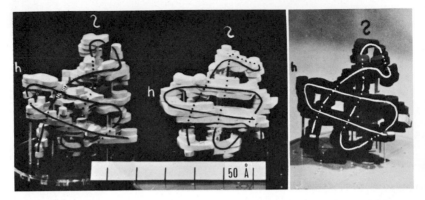

FIG. 1. The similar spatial orientations of the polypeptide chain of myoglobin and of the two chains of hemoglobin.

protein function by chemical manipulation (4,40,48,50), have been made in less than a decade. After this short but productive period, we may propose with some assurance a general hypothesis: Once Nature has reached a satisfactory geometric solution to a problem in protein function, a large amount of variability in structure is permissible so long as the resulting primary amino acid sequences determine the same general macromolecular conformation and allow the formation of an identical or very similar functional center with its limited but all important amino acid constituents. The nearly identical spatial orientations assumed by the chain of myoglobin and of the evolutionarily related hemoglobin chains are direct evidence of this hypothesis (Fig. 1). Considerable further support comes from the study of species variations in protein structures (the cytochromes, insulins, ribonucleases, fibrinogens, and so on) where identical functions are subserved by molecules retaining a major chemical pattern but differing markedly in the details of sequence.

CLASSIFICATION OF STRUCTURE IN RELATION TO FUNCTION

The detailed study of a number of enzymes and hormones suggests that proteins contain three major categories of three-dimensional structure: the *components of the functionally active centers*, the individual residues or groups of *residues which support and stabilize these active centers*, and the portions of sequence which act, in a sense, as *structural frameworks* on which the functional portions are arranged. The latter

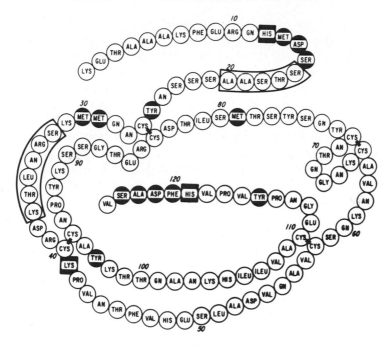

FIG. 2. The covalent structure of bovine pancreatic ribonuclease. Three residues that are almost certainly involved directly in the active center are enclosed in black squares. Residues known to be involved in the stabilization of the active center are indicated by the partially filled circles around each residue. Groups of amino acids that appear to be unessential for function or for stabilization are encircled. Hofmann and his colleagues [Finn and Hofmann, *J. Am. Chem. Soc. 87*, 645 (1964)] have shown that, of the entire portion of the sequence from residue 1 through residue 20, a synthetic peptide containing residues 8 through 13 is capable of restoring a small amount of activity to ribonuclease S-protein (see text). Lengthening this fragment by the addition of some or all of residues 1 through 7 increases this basal activity, suggesting that these residues contribute significantly to the association and stabilization of the active center.

category might be likened to the bailing wire that held together the working parts of many ancient Model-T Fords. Species variations in the bailing wire made little difference in the operation of the whole.

The unique function of a protein has been shown frequently to involve the close association in space of amino acid residues quite far removed in a linear sense from one another along the polypeptide chain. In bovine pancreatic ribonuclease (Fig. 2), for example, residues situated at positions 12, 41, and 119 (4,48,49,53,57) (in a total chain of 124 amino acids) appear to be brought into close proximity in the enzyme's active center, which in turn is locked into place by interactions between a number of other specific amino acid side chains. The functional importance and contiguity of the two critical histidine residues is suggested, in part, by the observation that specific chemical modification by bromoacetate or iodoacetate of the residues at 12 and 119 is dependent on having the native, functionally active form of the enzyme rather than the denatured form in which these two residues exhibit only the sluggish reactivity of ordinary histidines in a random polypeptide chain (10). The reaction of the two histidines to carboxymethylation with haloacetates is strongly inhibited by polyvalent anions such as phosphate or cytidylate much like the reactivity of the amino group on lysine No. 41 to dinitrofluorobenzene (29) or to N-carboxyaminoacid anhydrides (9). Since these polyanions bind strongly to ribonuclease, stabilizing the molecule to denaturation by such agents as heat or strong urea solutions (51), and also acting as competitive inhibitors, the inhibitory effects on reactivity to alkylation or acylation are strongly suggestive of involvement of these three basic side chains in the functional center of the enzyme. Interaction of the two histidine residues is particularly emphasized by the recent studies of Crestfield and his colleagues on the dimerization of carboxymethyl-histidine-12-ribonuclease and carboxymethyl-histidine-119-ribonuclease (11). These two derivatives, both enzymically inactive, complement one another by forming an active dimer with 50% the enzymic activity per mole of monomer. The repair appears to proceed through a mechanism in which the unmodified His-12 of one monomer is brought into close proximity to the unmodified His-119 of the other monomer, thus creating a cooperative active center.

The second category of structural components in proteins, those which help to stabilize and orient the more critically involved active center residues, may also be illustrated with examples from studies of ribonuclease. (This protein has received, perhaps, more detailed investigation than any other enzyme, and because of personal familiarity I shall lean heavily on its chemistry and function.) A number of amino acid residues in ribonuclease, other than those discussed above, must also be present in the molecule for normal enzymic function. However, a variety of experimental evidence suggests that this second group is more indirectly involved. Let us consider, for example, residues 13, 14, and 15 in the NH_2-terminal, 20 residue ribonuclease S-peptide portion of ribonuclease, originally prepared and studied by Richards and his colleagues (48). As is well known, the S-peptide portion and the S-protein fragment, both inactive in the cleavage of RNA, regenerate full activity when mixed at a molar ratio of 1:1 (Fig. 3). Full activity is retained, on mixing at a 1:1 ratio, when the ribonuclease S-peptide

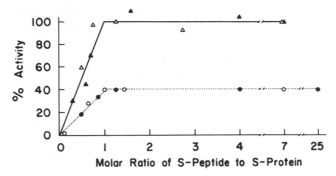

FIG. 3. Enzymic activity of reconstituted ribonuclease S and of several ribonuclease S derivatives. Upper curve: unmodified ribonuclease S-protein combined with
unmodified ribonuclease S-peptide (open triangles) and S-peptide lacking residues 16
through 20 (black triangles). Lower curve: unmodified S-peptide (open circles) and
S-peptide lacking residues 16 through 20 added to ribonuclease S-protein lacking
valine No. 241 and serine No. 123. All assays involved addition of increasing amounts
of the peptide or its derivative to 1 μg of the original or degraded S-protein in 1 ml
0.1% RNA in acetate buffer, pH 5.

portion is degraded to a pentadecapeptide with carboxypeptidase (45).
The synthetic tridecapeptide (residues 1 through 13) prepared by Hofmann et al. (30) is also capable of regenerating as much as 70% of
normal activity with ribonuclease S-protein, but only at molar ratios of
about 100:1. The catalytically active center may thus be regenerated,
but certain aspects of the catalysis such as substrate binding or the
intrinsic stability of the peptide-protein complex must be impaired.
Activity is lost upon conversion of the sulfur atom of methionine No. 13
in this derivative to the sulfone, although preparation of the tridecapeptide from the original 20 residue S-peptide by CNBr cleavage (producing
a COOH-terminal homoserine lactone) does not destroy the intrinsic
S-protein activating property (42). These observations, when considered
in the light of the full activity of the 15 residue carboxypeptidase
product, lead to the conclusion that residues 13, 14, and 15 are not actually involved in the catalytic center, but help to bind the region containing histidine-12 to the S-protein portion in an important but partially
dispensable way.

Similar deductions can be made for the COOH-terminal portion of
ribonuclease. Carboxypeptidase degradation of ribonuclease S-protein
causes the rapid removal of residues 119 through 124 (45). On the other
hand, carboxypeptidase degradation of native ribonuclease is extremely
slow, and only a partial removal of the terminal valine residue occurs
(without loss in activity) (50). If S-protein is carefully degraded, removal

of residues may be restricted to two COOH-terminal amino acids, serine and valine. The product is capable of regenerating 45 % of normal activity when added to S-peptide in molar ratios of 1:1 (see Fig. 3), but further addition of either S-peptide or the partially degraded S-protein does not enhance this value. We may conclude, therefore, that the serine residue at position 123 plays a role in the binding process but not in catalysis *per se*. When carboxypeptidase is permitted to degrade the ribonuclease S-protein molecule beyond the aspartic acid residue at position 121, activity is absent when tested by addition of S-peptide; this confirms the complete inactivity demonstrated in earlier experiments, which studied the rapid and specific removal of the COOH-terminal tetrapeptide by pepsin at pH 1.8 (2). Whether the carboxyl group of aspartic acid No. 121 is directly involved in the catalytic center as a participant in the covalent events of RNA cleavage cannot be deduced from available data, and this residue may be involved in a role more critical than mere stabilization of the active center.

The presumed *active center components* and *stabilizing residues* are indicated in Fig. 2. The latter category includes, in addition to those we have considered as examples, three of the six tyrosine residues of ribonuclease, which have been shown to exhibit anomalous ultraviolet spectral properties (58), and which also resist iodination in contrast to the other three residues, which behave much like free tyrosine in solution (7,8). Involvement of these unique tyrosine residues in active center stabilization has also been suggested by the correlation between activity in various ribonuclease derivatives and the presence of the anomalous spectral characteristics (51). Mention should also be made of the four methionine residues at positions 13, 29, 30, and 79. The sulfur atoms of these residues in native ribonuclease are quite resistant to conversion to the sulfonium form upon reaction with iodoacetate and only become reactive when the molecule is denatured by strong urea solutions or when subjected to higher temperatures (52). These findings support the idea that the side chains of the methionine residues are buried in the hydrophobic interior, and may contribute to the stabilization of native structure.

Surprisingly large portions of many proteins and biologically active polypeptides appear to be unessential for function, at least under conditions of *in vitro* assay. In recent work of Potts and Auerbach (46), for example, parathyroid hormone, containing 75 residues, was degraded to 45 by combined digestion with leucine aminopeptidase and carboxypeptidase with the loss of only about 50 % of the hormonal activity. Rasmussen and his colleagues (47) have reported on the preparation, by controlled acid hydrolysis, of other active derivatives of this hormone having molecular weights as low as 3300. The essentially normal activity of synthetic ACTH derivatives containing only two-thirds or less of the normal complement of 39 residues is another classical example of functionally unimportant sequence (50).

Residues 16–20 of ribonuclease were discussed above in relation to the chemistry of the ribonuclease S-peptide portion of the chain. Ooi and Scheraga (41) have reported that, after trypsin digestion of native ribonuclease at elevated temperatures, derivatives may be isolated lacking residues 32 and 33, 34–37, and 32–37, which show 25%, 21%, and 12% of normal activity, respectively. As we have mentioned, residues 123 and 124 may also be removed without inactivation. (It is possible that the simultaneous deletion of all of these residues might lead to full inactivation, but such a derivative has not yet been prepared.) Recent studies of Bernfield (6) have shown that ribonuclease S-protein, which has almost completely lost the ability to *hydrolyze* RNA without the addition of S-peptide, shows a relatively enhanced formation of di- and tri-nucleotides from uridine- and cytidine-2'-3'-cyclic phosphates. Thus, much of the catalytic center of ribonuclease and of its tertiary structure may be intact in this derivative, which lacks the 20 terminal amino acid residues.

AMINO ACID SEQUENCE DIFFERENCES AND HOMOLOGIES

The comparison of amino acid sequences of particular proteins isolated from various species and from bacterial mutants (62), and the study of similarities between proteins having possible common antecedents, such as trypsinogen and chymotrypsinogen, has become a very active branch of protein chemistry in the past few years. The results furnish us with considerable grist for the mill of protein geometry. Summaries of much of these data have appeared recently and I shall restrict my comments to selected illustrative examples and to the generalities that may be drawn from them.

With the recent elucidation of the complete amino acid sequences of trypsinogen and chymotrypsinogen it has become possible to make a direct comparison of these pancreatic enzymes (56). As illustrated in Fig. 4, a large part of the sequence is common to both, including those sections presumably involved in the catalytic centers, in two of the disulfide bonds, and in the activation site at which peptide bond cleavage leads to activation of the zymogens. The high degree of similarity in sequence makes it extremely likely that these proteins are derived from the same primitive precursor. Three-dimensional comparisons are

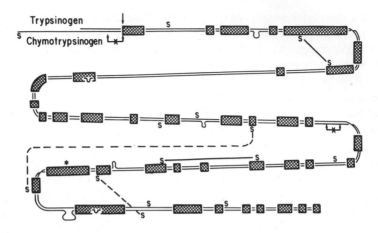

FIG. 4.   Sequence homologies in trypsinogen and chymotrypsinogen.

not yet possible, but it will not be too surprising if it is found that the spatial orientations of the backbone chains of these two proteins show strong similarities.

Even more striking similarities are evident from examination of the sequences of the cytochromes c, now completely elucidated for the proteins from a dozen or more species (39). Figure 5 summarizes the homologies in schematic form. Clusters of hydrophobic and basic amino acid residues are present as fairly invariant features of all the cytochromes examined. Although a portion of these may be involved as critical parts of the active center of the protein, it seems reasonable to assume that a large fraction of the invariant structure

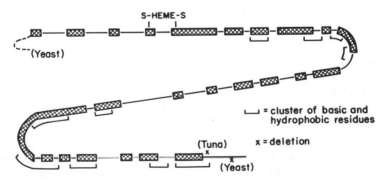

FIG. 5.   Areas of identity in the sequences of cytochromes c (from man, chicken, pig, horse, ox, tuna, and yeast).

is concerned with maintenance of a three-dimensional conformation, which during evolution has been modified in detail but not in broad outline.

DETERMINATION OF TERTIARY STRUCTURE BY PRIMARY SEQUENCE

In support of the hints obtained from the studies on structural and sequential homology discussed above, we have seen that large parts of biologically active proteins appear to be unessential for function. Therefore, it is of great interest to examine the nature of the critical interactions that guide the folding of polypeptide chains into specific, reproducible geometric structures and to attempt to relate these to the constant features of sequence observed in homologous proteins.

Reversible denaturation is a well-established phenomenon and has been carefully studied in several proteins not containing covalent cross linkages, such as tobacco mosaic virus protein (1,19) and myoglobin (28). In recent years a large series of proteins stabilized by disulfide bonds has also been investigated in terms of the ability of the reduced forms of these proteins, in which disulfide bonds have been converted to sulfhydryl groups, to undergo oxidation with the regeneration of the original half-cystine pairs and tertiary structure (16) (Fig. 6). By working under controlled conditions of low protein concentration, yields as high as 100% have been obtained in many cases (3,16). Table I summarizes a number of these studies. The over-all process, which has been discussed in detail elsewhere (16), appears to be driven solely by the highly favorable change in free energy of conformation in going from the random chain to the native form. The observation of extremely high yields of native protein indicates that the native state is the most probable conformation by a wide margin over other forms with different tertiary structure and half-cystine pairing. A direct demonstration of this principle comes from experiments on a ribonuclease derivative prepared by the oxidation of the reduced protein in the presence of urea, or under other conditions which destroy the clarity of the message contained in the amino acid sequence, such as low pH (26). When such a preparation, containing randomly paired (scrambled) half-cysteine residues (105 isomers, in theory), is incubated with low concentrations of β-mercaptoethanol, the theoretical yield of native enzyme is produced in a 10–20 hr period by internal disulfide interchange.

We have recently studied an enzyme present in the microsomes of several tissues which catalyzes the interchange reaction (21, 24, 25, 55). The

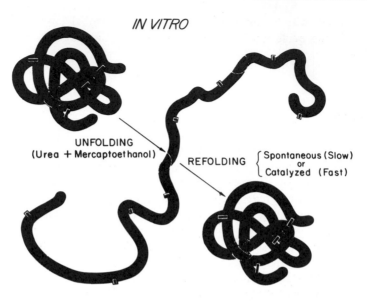

FIG. 6. Schematic drawing of the process of reductive denaturation and subsequent renaturation with the formation of correct disulfide bonds and tertiary structure. The cross-hatched region represents an active center, the components of which have become widely separated by the reduction process. As discussed in the text, reformation of the native structure proceeds spontaneously without catalysis but is greatly accelerated by the addition of an enzyme from microsomes.

addition of this enzyme, which has now been highly purified, catalyzes the conversions of "scrambled" ribonuclease, lysozyme, and soybean trypsin inhibitor to the native forms in a very short time. The requirement for β-mercaptoethanol during the rearrangement can be eliminated by previous partial reduction of the molecules, which, with other evidence, indicates that the enzyme does not catalyze reduction but operates purely by a sulfhydryl-disulfide interchange (21,22).

If the pairing of half-cystine residues is directed by information inherent in the primary sequence, we may ask whether interruption of this information by cleavage of the chain at one or more peptide bonds would seriously modify the message (22). Studies on the three-chained chymotrypsin molecule and the two-chained bovine or porcine insulin molecules have shown that these proteins are rapidly inactivated and converted to insoluble, randomly crosslinked networks under the action of the microsomal enzyme preparation. Chymotrypsinogen, the single-chain precursor of chymotrypsin, was, on the other hand, unaffected by similar treatment. Since the list of multichained proteins in nature is

TABLE I. *"Refolding" of Disulfide-Bond Containing Proteins After Reductive Denaturation*

Protein	Molecular Weight	Disulfide Bonds	Recovery of Activity (%)	"Random" Recovery (ca. %)	Criteria of "Nativeness"[a]	Authors
Ribonuclease (bovine pancreatic)	13,683	4	95–100	1	1–8	(2,59)
Lysozyme (egg white)	14,307	4	50–80	1	1–4, 6, 7	(23,32)
Taka-amylase A (Asp. oryzae)	55,000	4[b]	48	0.3	1–3, 8, 10	(33)
			100		1	(18)
Trypsin (bovine)	22,500	6		0.01		
CM-cellulose trypsin (insoluble)			4		1, 11	(14)
Poly-DL-alanyl trypsin (soluble)			8			(15)
Insulin (bovine)	5,734	3	5–10	6.7	1, 6–9, 11	(12,63)
Alkaline phosphatase (*Escherichia coli*)	40,000	2	80	33	6, 8, 11	(37)
Pepsinogen (swine)	41,000	3	50	6.7	3, 10, 11	(20)
Serum albumin (human)	69,000	17	50	?	6	(34,36)
T₁-ribonuclease	11,000	2	90	33	1	(61)
Soybean trypsin inhibitor	22,000	2	100	33	1, 10	(54)
Specific antibody (papain fragment I)	45,000	6–8	11–24	0.01–0.1	2, 6, 10	(60)
			50			(27)

[a] 1, specific activity; 2, optical rotation; 3, viscosity; 4, UV spectrum; 5, X-ray crystallography; 6, immunologic; 7, peptide-map; 8, chromatography; 9, crystal form; 10, sedimentation; 11, electrophoresis.
[b] 9 half-cystines.

unfortunately very small, we have also tested the phenomenom with the so-called "C-protein," which is a three-chained protein derivative prepared from ribonuclease by treatment with CNBr. This material is also rapidly converted to an insoluble aggregate of disulfide-bonded fragments by enzymatic treatment.

The studies with the enzyme suggest that meaningful information for any given three-dimensional structure must be coded into a single, uninterrupted polypeptide chain. As a corollary, it may be suggested that the two-chained insulin molecule, like chymotrypsin, can be derived from a single-chained precursor, which is converted to the commonly observed form by specific cleavage of one or more peptide bonds in a manner analogous to the activation of zymogens.

Humbel (31) has recently concluded, on the basis of pulse-labeling experiments of the type carried out for hemoglobin and lysozyme, that fish insulin is synthesized as *two* chains. If a similar biosynthetic process is found to apply for the mammalian insulins, another explanation must be sought for the apparent thermodynamic instability of the insulin structure as suggested by the SS-rearrangement data. For example, one or both of the separately synthesized A and B chain precursors may originally contain additional terminal residues or groups of residues [or, indeed, complexed proteins (5) or other cell constituents], which participate in coding for the proper disulfide bonding. After the removal of such postulated code-modifying materials, the disulfide bonds of the resulting insulin molecule would assume the metastable state suggested by the enzymic-induced rearrangement.

LOCALIZATION OF INTERACTIONS THAT GOVERN FOLDING

Since primary structure appears to determine tertiary structure and since the spontaneous folding process may be studied *in vitro*, we have available an experimental tool for the examination of essential and non-essential components in the process. The molecular model that results from the crystallographic studies of Kendrew (35) and his colleagues clearly illustrates that polar, hydrophilic groups are for the most part located on the exterior of the sturcture, in contact with solvent. Non-polar, hydrophobic side chains, on the other hand, are mainly buried within the body of the protein. A similar situation is indicated for the enzyme ribonuclease on the basis of experiments on the reformation of tertiary structure from the fully reduced polypeptide chain after chemical modifications of various charged amino acid side chains (16). As summarized in Table II, epsilon amino groups and carboxyl groups

TABLE II. *Reduction and Reoxidation of Chemically Modified Ribonuclease*

Preparation	Numbers of Amino Groups Covered (Average)	Chain Length (Average)	Activity of Protein (% of Native)	Activity After Reoxidation (% of Initial)
Poly-DL-alanyl ribonuclease				
PAR 4	8 of 11	5	100	95
PAR 5	8 of 11	7–8	65	40
Poly-DL-tyrosyl ribonuclease				
PTR 2	1 of 11	3	100	100
PTR 3	2 of 11	3	100	60

Preparation	Group Covered	Number of Groups Covered (Average)	Charge Substitution	Activity of Protein (% of Native)	Activity After Reoxidation (% of Initial)
Succinyl ribonuclease	-NH$_2$	6–7 of 11	– for +	15	62
Methylated ribonuclease	-COOH	7–8 of 11	0 for –	18	48
Phthalyl ribonuclease	-NH$_2$	3–4 of 11	– for +	24	75
Butyryl ribonuclease	-NH$_2$	5–6 of 11	0 for +	44	77
Caproyl ribonuclease	-NH$_2$	2–3 of 11	0 for +	96	70

may be treated with N-carboxyamino acid anhydrides (Equation 1), various acylating agents (Equation 2), or by esterification (Equation 3).

$$R \diagdown CH-C \diagup{O} \diagdown{O} + NH_2-Protein \rightarrow NH_2-CH-\overset{O}{\overset{\|}{C}}-NH-Protein + CO_2 \quad (1)$$

$$CH_2-C \diagup{O} \diagdown{O} + NH_2-Protein \rightarrow CH_2-COOH$$
$$CH_2-C \diagdown{O} \qquad CH_2-\overset{O}{\overset{\|}{C}}-NH-Protein \quad (2)$$

$$Protein-COOH + ROH \rightarrow Protein-\overset{O}{\overset{\|}{C}}-OR + H_2O \quad (3)$$

The resulting active materials can then be reduced to form the random polypeptide chain which can then be subjected to reoxidation. The data in these tables show that large variations in molecular weight and in net charge can be introduced without serious impairment of the reformation of a functionally competent active center. For example, fairly extensive acylation with agents which, after attachment to the epsilon-NH_2 groups of lysine residues, cause either no change, an increase, or a decrease in net charge on the protein, leads to only minor losses in the ribonuclease activities of the products (13,16). These acylated materials may be fully reduced, and their ability to reform three-dimensional structure compatible with activity may be studied by oxidation of the SH groups to disulfide bonds. As shown in Table II, a large fraction (nearly all in some cases) of the original activity of the acylated derivatives is regenerated by such treatment, indicating that the added groupings do not cause steric or electrostatic interference during the process of internal organization of the protein molecule during sulfhydryl group oxidation. A typical situation, intended to emphasize the unlikelihood of fitting long polyalanine side chains into the interior of the molecule, is illustrated schematically in Fig. 7. On the basis of such experiments, and taking into account the myoglobin results, we may conclude that hydrophobic side chains and other uncharged groupings must be, by far, the major determinants of interior conformation.

A similar conclusion may be reached from a consideration of what have been called permissible and nonpermissible replacements, observed in studies on species variations in structure and of structural variations

POLY–DL–ALANYL RIBONUCLEASE

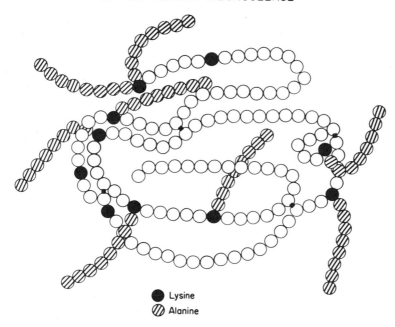

● Lysine
⊘ Alanine

FIG. 7.   In spite of the addition of an extensive "fur" of polyalanyl side chains, this sort of ribonuclease derivative is still fully active. It may be fully reduced and subsequently reconverted by oxidation to the disulfide-bonded form with essentially complete recovery of activity.

in mutants. Epstein, in a recent paper (17), has summarized a large number of such data from the literature on the hemoglobins, cytochromes c, and the other proteins. The collected data (a portion of which is shown in Table III) strongly support the argument that replacements are "permissible" generally only when polar residues replace polar residues and hydrophobic residues replace other hydrophobic residues. In the case of the cytochromes c, where a large number of species variations have been studied, the results clearly show that the residues in several clusters of hydrophobic and basic residues are, for the most part, not replaced or are replaced by residues of similar polarity (see Fig. 5). We may conclude that the invariant or relatively invariant parts of polypeptide chains are manyfold more influential and critical in the determination of protein geometry and of the functional center than are the variable residues that may be located mainly on the exterior of the structure or may subserve less critical stabilizing roles internally.

TABLE III.   *Analysis of Observed Amino Acid Exchanges*

Proteins		Type I "Permissible" (Polar Polar) (Nonpolar Nonpolar)	Type II "Possibly Permissible" (Polar Gly, Ala)	Type III "Non-permissible" (Polar Nonpolar)
Cytochrome *c*				
Horse/Yeast	39	26	3	10 (26%)
Tuna/Yeast	41	29	7	5 (17%)
Hemoglobin				
Human: α/β	72	48	15	9 (13%)
Human: β/γ	40	24	12	4 (10%)
α: Human/Horse	17	9	6	2 (11%)
β: Human/Horse	21	13	6	2 (10%)

ON THE PREDICTABILITY OF TERTIARY STRUCTURE

Although it is clear that the elucidation of three-dimensional structures of proteins will depend almost entirely on X-ray crystallography
during the next few years, the fact that primary sequence is apparently
fully competent to direct the precise folding of a chain makes it permissible to visualize a stage in protein chemistry where chemical, biological,
and thermodynamic data will permit us to program a computer rather
than rely on the X-ray camera. We can list a number of major factors
that can be taken into account in such predictive processes. (a) The
distribution of invariant and variant portions of proteins can give us
some idea of those segments of amino acid residues that are critical in
the determination of folding and of functional centers. (b) Structural
restrictions introduced by the steric properties of disulfide bonds, pro-
line residues, and the peptide backbone may, hopefully, be found to be
the same in most protein structures. (c) The apparent external location
of charged amino acid side chains, and the location within the interior
of protein structures of most hydrophobic residues, add a particularly
useful set of partial restrictions. (d) Van der waals approach distances
of side chains in the myoglobin structure, at least, are satisfactorily
close to predicted values and the relative absence of internal solvent
molecules may be general. (e) The experiences of Kendrew and Perutz
have shown that the presence of helical structure greatly simplifies the

crystallographic and model building problems in protein chemistry. The location of helical sections, when indicated to be present in a protein by such methods as optical rotatory dispersion, might occasionally be tentatively deduced from a consideration of the known chemistry of the protein, although in ribonuclease, for example, which is estimated to contain 20–25% α-helix, it seems extremely unlikely, when all information is considered, that this helicity can be located with any assurance.

Most important will be the accumulation of further generalities of protein structure from three-dimensional structures to be obtained by crystallographers, and the development of chemical and physical methods for the detection and location of such components as α-helical coiling and hydrophobic interactions. As our catalog of structural data accumulates, we may look forward to the spontaneous folding of tailor-made sequences that have been programmed by the synthetic chemist to yield biologically active macromolecules of predictable three-dimensional structure.

REFERENCES

1. Anderer, F. A., *Z. Naturforsch. 14b*, 642 (1959).
2. Anfinsen, C. B., *J. Biol. Chem. 221*, 405 (1956).
3. Anfinsen, C. B., and Haber, E., *J. Biol. Chem. 236*, 1361 (1961).
4. Anfinsen, C. B., *Brookhaven Symp. Biol. 15*, 184 (1962).
5. Antoniades, H. N., Renold, A. E., Dagenais, Y. M., and Steinke, J., *Proc. Soc. Exp. Biol. Med. 103*, 677 (1960).
6. Bernfield, M. R., *J. Biol. Chem. 240*, 4753 (1965).
7. Cha, C., and Scheraga, H. A., *J. Biol. Chem. 238*, 2958 (1963).
8. Cha, C., and Scheraga, H. A., *J. Biol. Chem. 238*, 2965 (1963).
9. Cooke, J., Anfinsen, C. B., and Sela, M., *J. Biol. Chem. 238*, 2034 (1963).
10. Crestfield, A. M., Stein, W. H., and Moore, S., *J. Biol. Chem. 238*, 2413 (1963a).
11. Crestfield, A. M., Stein, W. H., and Moore, S., *J. Biol. Chem. 238*, 2421 (1963b).
12. Dixon, G. H., and Wardlaw, A. C., *Nature 188*, 721 (1960).
13. Doscher, Marilyn S., and Richards, F. M., *J. Biol. Chem. 238*, 2399 (1963).
14. Epstein, C. J., and Anfinsen, C. B., *J. Biol. Chem. 237*, 2175 (1962).
15. Epstein, C. J., and Anfinsen, C. B., *J. Biol. Chem. 237*, 2464 (1962).
16. Epstein, C. J., Goldberger, R. F., and Anfinsen, C. B., *Cold Spring Harbor Symp. Quant. Biol. 28*, 439 (1963).

17. Epstein, C. J., *Nature 203*, 1350 (1964).
18. Epstein, C. J., Stepanov, V. M., and Goldberger, R. F., unpublished data.
19. Fraenkel-Conrat, H., and Singer, B., *Biochem. Biophys. Acta 33*, 359 (1959).
20. Frattali, V., Steiner, R. F., Millar, D. B. S., and Edelhoch, H., *Nature 199*, 1186 (1963).
21. Givol, D., Goldberger, R. F., and Anfinsen, C. B., *J. Biol. Chem. 239*, 3114 (1964).
22. Givol, D., De Lorenzo, F., Goldberger, R. F., and Anfinsen, C. B., *Proc. Natl. Acad. Sci. U.S. 53*, 676 (1965).
23. Goldberger, R. F., and Epstein, C. J., *J. Biol. Chem. 238*, 2988 (1963).
24. Goldberger, R. F., Epstein, C. J., and Anfinsen, C. B., *J. Biol. Chem. 238*, 628 (1963).
25. Goldberger, R. F., Epstein, C. J., and Anfinsen, C. B., *J. Biol. Chem. 239*, 1506 (1964).
26. Haber, E., and Anfinsen, C. B., *J. Biol. Chem. 237*, 1839 (1962).
27. Haber, E., *Proc. Natl. Acad. Sci. U.S. 52*, 1099 (1964).
28. Harrison, S. C., and Blout, E. R., *J. Biol. Chem. 240*, 299 (1965).
29. Hirs, C. H. W., *Brookhaven Symp. Biol. 15*, 154 (1962).
30. Hofmann, K., Finn, F., Haas, W., Smithers, M. J., Wolman, Y., and Yanaihara, N. J., *J. Am. Chem. Soc. 85*, 833 (1963).
31. Humbel, R. E., *Proc. Natl. Acad. Sci. U.S.*, in press.
32. Imai, K., Takagi, T., and Isemura, R., *J. Biochem. 53*, 1 (1963).
33. Isemura, R., Takagi, T., Maeda, V., and Yutani, K., *J. Biochem. 53*, 155 (1963).
34. Karusch, F., In *Immunochemical Approaches to Problems in Microbiology*, Ed. M. Heidelberger and O. J. Plescia, Rutgers University Press, New Brunswick, 1961, p. 368.
35. Kendrew, J. C., *Science 139*, 1259 (1963).
36. Kolthoff, I. M., Anastasi, A., and Tan, B. H., *J. Am. Chem. Soc. 82*, 4147 (1960).
37. Levinthal, C., Signer, E. R., and Fetherolf, K., *Proc. Natl. Acad. Sci. U.S. 48*, 1230 (1962).
38. Margoliash, E., *Proc. Natl. Acad. Sci. U.S. 50*, 672 (1963).
39. Margoliash, E., and Schejter, A., *Adv. Prot. Chem. 21* (1966), in press.
40. Neurath, H., In *Symposium on New Perspectives in Biology*, Biochem. Biophys. Acta Library, No. 4, Ed. M. Sela, American Elsevier, New York, 1964.
41. Ooi, T., and Scheraga, H. A., *Biochem. 3*, 641 (1964).
42. Parks, J. M., Barancik, M. B., and Wold, F., *J. Am. Chem. Soc. 85*, 3519 (1963).
43. Pauling, L., and Zuckerkandl, E., *Acta Chem. Scand. 17*, S9 (1963).
44. Perutz, M. F., *Science 140*, 863 (1963).
45. Potts, J. T., Jr., Young, M., and Anfinsen, C. B., *J. Biol. Chem. 238*, 2593 (1963).

46. Potts, J. T., Jr., and Auerbach, G. D., In *The Chemistry of Parathyroid Hormone. Parathyroid Hormone; Ultrastructure, Secretion and Function*, Ed. R. V. Talmage, P. J. Gaillard, and A. Budy, Univ. of Chicago Press, Chicago, 1965, p. 53.
47. Rasmussen, H., and Craig, L. C., *Recent Prog. Horm. Res. 18*, 269 (1962b).
48. Richards, F. M., and Vithayathil, P. J., *Brookhaven Symp. Biol. 13*, 115 (1960).
49. Scheraga, H. A., and Rupley, J. A., *Adv. Enzymology 24*, 161 (1962).
50. Schwyzer, R., *Ann. Rev. Biochem. 33*, 259 (1964).
51. Sela, M., Anfinsen, C. B., and Harrington, W. F., *Biochem. Biophys. Acta 26*, 502 (1957).
52. Stark, G., Stein, W. H., and Moore, S., *J. Biol. Chem. 236*, 436 (1961).
53. Stein, W. II., *Fed. Proc. 23*, No. 3, 599 (1964).
54. Steiner, R., De Lorenzo, F., and Anfinsen, C. B., *J. Biol. Chem. 240*, 4648 (1965).
55. Venetianer, P., and Straub, F. B., *Biochim. Biophys. Acta 67*, 166 (1963).
56. Walsh, K. A., and Neurath, H., *Proc. Natl. Acad. Sci. U.S. 52*, 334 (1964).
57. Westheimer, F. H., *Adv. Enzymology 24*, 441 (1962).
58. Wetlaufer, D. B., *Adv. Prot. Chem. 17*, 303 (1963).
59. White, F. H., Jr., *J. Biol. Chem. 236*, 1353 (1961).
60. Whitney, P. L., and Tanford, C., *Proc. Natl. Acad. Sci. U.S. 53*, 524 (1965).
61. Yamagata, S., Takahashi, K., and Egami, F., *J. Biochem. 52*, 272 (1962).
62. Yanofsky, C., In *Informational Macromolecules*, Ed. H. J. Vogel, V. Bryson, and J. O. Lampen, Academic Press, New York, 1963, p. 195.
63. Yu-Cang, D., Yu-Shang, Zi-Xian, E., and Chen-Lu, T., *Scientia Sinica (Peking), 10*, 84 (1961).

2

THE STRUCTURAL BASIS OF PROTEIN SYNTHESIS

Alexander Rich

Within the past five years our understanding of the mechanism of protein synthesis has increased to the point where we now have a fundamental appreciation of the major pathways by which amino acids are assembled into polypeptide chains. Our understanding of this process will certainly be refined by continued research, but it is quite likely that the major features of the process are now well understood. The information necessary to assemble amino acids into the specific sequences characteristic of proteins is found in the nucleotide sequence of the deoxyribonucleic acid (DNA) in the genome. We describe the events leading to the final assembly of protein molecules in two parts. *Transcription* is the name given to the synthesis of a specific ribonucleic acid (RNA) strand formed by using one of the two strands of the DNA as a template. This yields a linear polymer molecule of messenger RNA, which has nucleotides arranged in a sequence such that it can assemble amino acids in a defined order. The second step in this process, called *translation*, involves utilization of the nucleotide sequence in messenger RNA to form the polypeptide sequence of completed proteins. This process takes place on ribosomes, and the object of this article is to discuss various aspects of protein synthesis as it occurs on the ribosomal structures.

THE RIBOSOME AS AN ASSEMBLY SITE

When viewed by the electron microscope ribosomes appear as roughly spherical particles with a diameter near 200 Å. They have a total molecular weight of 3 to 4 million depending upon the species. The ribosome is composed of protein and RNA with the latter present in greater amount. The particle is built from two unequal-sized subunits, and the ribosomal RNA is likewise present as two large unequal-sized molecules. These molecules are believed to provide a core or framework around which the ribosomal proteins assemble to form the final functioning unit. The detailed nature of the ribosomal structure is unknown, and we have no understanding of the function of the ribosomal RNA. Nonetheless, it is known that the ribosome acts by assembling various macromolecular species to carry out protein synthesis.

The assembly of amino acids does not occur directly, but rather through the use of the soluble or transfer RNA (sRNA) molecules. These contain 70 to 80 nucleotides and act as intermediates between the nucleotides on the messenger RNA and the amino acids. The initial step in this process is the activation of the amino acid, which results in its being linked covalently to the terminal adenosine of a particular species of sRNA molecule.* This takes place on the activating enzyme, which is specific for both the sRNA and the amino acid.

Messenger RNA contains sequences of ribonucleotides that originate in DNA. Amino acid sequence data are encoded in the messenger RNA strand in triplets of nucleotide bases, each triplet representing a particular amino acid (4,9). The triplet of bases on the messenger RNA strand is called a "codon" and is believed to be matched by a complementary triplet of bases on the soluble RNA molecule, the anticodon. It is likely, however, that one of the three bases pairs together in an unusual manner (9).

The primary event in protein synthesis is an assembly on the ribosome of the messenger RNA strand, the activated sRNA molecule, and the enzymes necessary for peptide bond formation. The assembly is believed to be specific in that it allows for the interaction of codon and anticodon nucleotides. Ribosomes will bind one sRNA molecule; however, when they are involved in protein synthesis they contain two soluble RNA molecules attached to each ribosome (2,14). The growing or nascent polypeptide chain is attached to the ribosome through one of the sRNA molecules (5). The basic event is that of reading out information encoded in the linear polymer structure of messenger RNA. Since amino acids are added one at a time, it is reasonable that the ribosome must move along the messenger strand as amino acids are added.* Very little is known about the moving mechanism, but an idea of the type of mechanism involved can be illustrated in a diagram.

Figure 1 shows a diagram of the process. The hook-shaped form represents a soluble RNA molecule, the three prongs projecting

* Many of the general items related to protein synthesis are discussed in greater detail in the *Cold Spring Harbor Symposium*, Vol. 28 (1963).

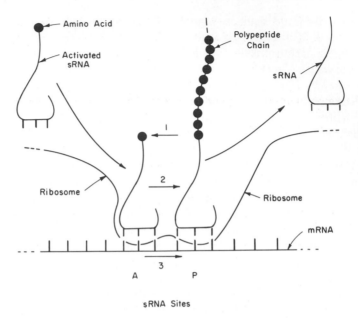

FIG. 1. A diagram illustrating a possible mechanism for translating the ribosome along messenger RNA during protein synthesis. Process 1 represents the addition of a single amino acid to the polypeptide chain, whereas processes 2 and 3 represent the movement of both sRNA and messenger RNA from site A to site P. The system is then ready to operate again.

downward represent the three anticodon nucleotides, and the solid circle represents an amino acid. We speculate that there are two sites involved, site A for the activated amino acids and adjacent to it, site P where the nascent polypeptide chain is found. The amino acid that is to be added next is attached to the sRNA in site A and the protein synthetic act thus involves the transfer of the growing polypeptide chain from site P to the sRNA chain on site A (Process 1 in Fig. 1). This step involves a transfer enzyme needed to form the peptide link. After that step we can imagine that the sRNA is released from site P and the molecule bound at site A with the codon triplets of the messenger RNA is then transferred to site P (Processes 2 and 3 in Fig. 1). Amino acid addition thus may involve a movement of sRNA and its complexed messenger RNA from site A to site P, a distance of slightly over 10 Å. This is necessary in order to set up the system once again, so that the addition of the succeeding amino acid can occur. As soon as site A is emptied, it can again be loaded with an amino acid attached to its activated sRNA.

This highly schematic diagram is presented not because it represents a mechanism which has been established but rather a convenient framework by which one can visualize the repetitive or iterative nature of the amino acid assembly which takes place on the ribosomal surface. The detailed nature of the sRNA binding to the ribosome as well as the moving mechanism is entirely unknown.

POLYRIBOSOMAL STRUCTURES

With the knowledge that three nucleotides specify each amino acid, it is possible to describe a quantitative relation between the size of the messenger RNA and the length of the polypeptide chain it specifies. If we take a protein such as hemoglobin, which is made of polypeptide chains containing approximately 150 amino acids, we anticipate a messenger RNA with about 450 nucleotides. In the stable form of nucleic acid structures, nucleotides are spaced 3.4 Å from each other, as this is the thickness of the unsaturated purine and pyrimidine rings. Accordingly, we would anticipate that the messenger RNA for hemoglobin would have a total contour length of approximately 1500 Å. Since the ribosome has a diameter of 220 Å, it is clear that more than one ribosome can be associated with the messenger at any one time. In the case of hemoglobin synthesis, polyribosomal structures are found as shown in Fig. 2(a) and (b). The platinum shadowed electron micrograph shown in Fig. 2(a) contains typical clusters of polyribosomes (polysomes) usually with five or six ribosomes per cluster. Figure 2(b) shows uranylacetate stained reticulocyte polyribosomes, many of which show the thin messenger RNA strand positively stained in the photograph (13). By measuring the center to center spacing one can see that there is a gap of approximately 50 to 100 Å between each ribosome on the messenger strand. It is important to recognize that one ribosome alone acting on a messenger strand is capable of producing a single polypeptide chain. It does not need the other ribosomes that are present. However, the existence of several ribosomes on the same messenger RNA strand makes possible a more efficient synthesis in that several polypeptide chains are being assembled at the same time.

The information in the messenger RNA strand is encoded in a linear polymer, and the polypeptide structure being assembled is also a linear polymer. Thus, it is reasonable to interpret the polyribosomal structure as indicating various stages of protein assembly. The ribosome attaches to one end of the messenger strand and begins to assemble first the N-terminal amino acid of the polypeptide chain. With further movement along the strand there is a continued addition of more amino acids and

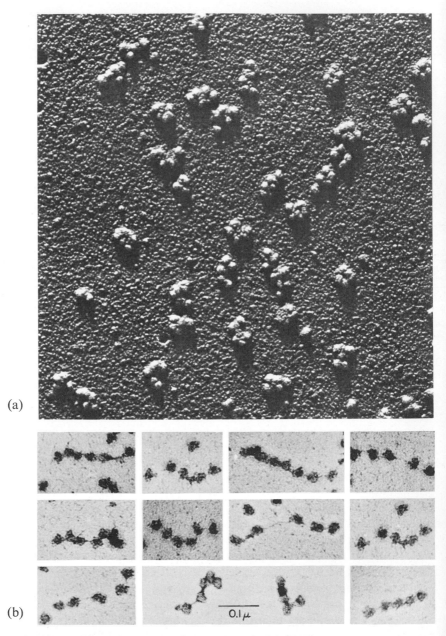

(a)

(b)

FIG. 2. Electron micrographs of recticulocyte polyribosomes. (a) Platinum shadowed preparation; (b) uranyl acetate staining, which shows a faint dark staining thread passing between the ribosomes (13).

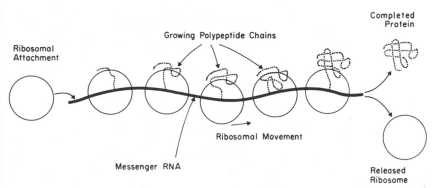

FIG. 3.   A schematic diagram of polyribosomal function.

the polypeptide chain is lengthened. Finally, when the ribosome reaches the end of the messenger strand, the C-terminal residue of the polypeptide chain is incorporated and the ribosome is released with the completed polypeptide. A schematic model of this process is shown in Fig. 3, where five ribosomes are shown attached to the messenger and likewise five different stages in the assembly of the completed polypeptide chain are illustrated.

Polyribosomal structures have been seen in a large variety of organisms and indeed, it is likely that they are used universally. However, the structures are delicate and break down easily during extraction. One of the most striking characteristics of polyribosomal structures is their great sensitivity to small amounts of ribonuclease, which has the effect of cleaving the messenger strand in between the individual ribosomes and therefore converts the polyribosomal structure into single ribosomes. Accordingly, a variety of gentle techniques has been developed to show their existence in different tissues. The universality or near universality of polyribosomal structures simply underlines the fundamental efficiency of protein synthesis as it is normally carried out. This suggests that, in general, ribosomes exist in abundance in living tissue and the limiting or controlling factor in protein production is usually the messenger RNA. However, polysomes are dynamic structures and they can break down *in vivo* under specialized conditions.

MONOCISTRONIC AND POLYCISTRONIC MESSENGER RNA

The example described in Fig. 3 for hemoglobin production is a typical representative of a monocistronic system in which the messenger strand codes for a single polypeptide chain and the ribosomes pass across the entire length of the strand in the course of making a single protein. However, we have, in addition to this, other types of messengers which code for more than one protein. There are, in general, two categories of polycistronic messengers. One of them is represented by the RNA viruses, which usually contain a large piece of RNA that codes for more than one protein. In addition, there are also naturally occurring polycistronic messengers found in the cell, which may behave in a fashion somewhat distinct from that seen in the viral case.

A typical example of a viral polycistronic messenger is that seen in the polio virus. It is a small RNA virus containing a protein coat which encloses a strand of RNA of molecular weight close to 2 million, approximately 6000 nucleotides. This has enough total coding capacity to make polypeptide chains totalling 2000 amino acids. It is clear in this case that the molecule is manufacturing a variety of proteins since, in addition to two coat proteins and an RNA polymerase, it is likely that there are at least two other components, which have been tentatively identified. Accordingly, we may imagine that the messenger strand codes for proteins A through H as shown in Fig. 4. In general, one can think of two distinct methods of reading this messenger strand as shown in Fig. 4. In one method ribosomal attachment occurs only at one end of the messenger strand and the ribosome then passes across the entire strand producing in serial fashion proteins A, B, C, etc. In an alternative method, each cistron has its own ribosomal attachment site and the individual proteins are made at rates which are not coupled to each other in an obligatory fashion. Thus, for example, protein A may be a polymerase molecule needed in a very small number, whereas proteins G and H may be the viral coat proteins produced in large numbers.

Experiments have been carried out in which the size of the polyribosome associated with polio virus infection of Hela cells has been measured, and it has been shown that the polysome produced is large enough (50 to 70 ribosomes) to be interpreted in terms of the entire RNA strand being engaged in protein synthesis at one time (11). This suggests that the viral RNA is not broken up into a smaller subunit during translation. There is some indication that the method of translation is the one shown in Fig. 4(a). One source of evidence is the fact that electron micrographs of polysomes obtained from polio-infected Hela cells typically show polysomal structures that seem to have gaps. The examples shown in Fig. 5(a) and (b) suggest but do not prove that the mechanism for polio virus protein synthesis involves the independent translation of individual cistrons rather than the collectivized translation of all of the cistrons.

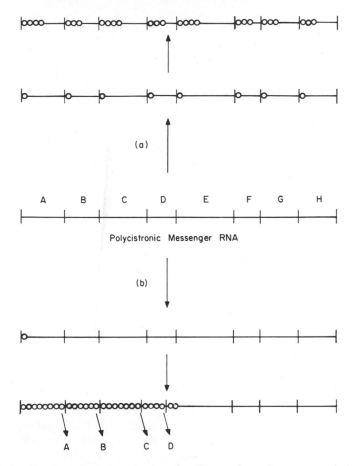

FIG. 4. Two hypothetical mechanisms for ribosomal attachment to a polycistronic messenger RNA strand. A–H represent eight different cistrons. (a) Ribosomes attach at the beginning of each cistron; (b) ribosomes attach only at one end of the messenger RNA strand (11).

POLYCISTRONIC MESSENGER RNA IN BACTERIA

When bacterial cells are disrupted by appropriately gentle methods the contents can be centrifuged in a sucrose density gradient and the polysomes sediment in a broad distribution moving more rapidly than the single ribosomes. In cells synthesizing a wide variety of proteins, polysome size varies from small clusters of two, three, or four ribosomes to large groups which may have in excess of 70 ribosomes sedimenting as a single kinetic unit. The polyribosomes contain nascent

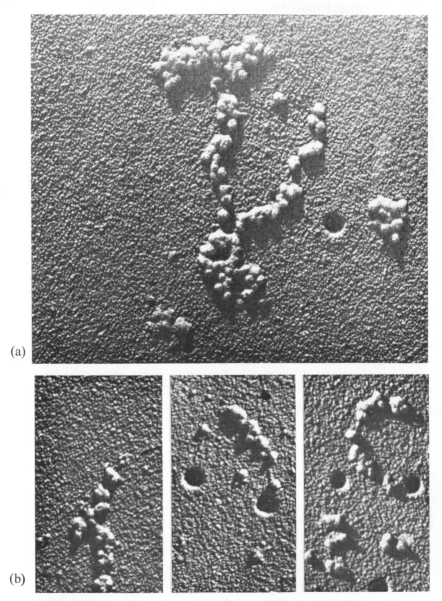

(a)

(b)

FIG. 5. Electron micrographs of polysomes found in polio-infected Hela cells treated with actinomycin D (11). (a) A large polysome fully loaded with ribosomes; (b) polysomes showing the ribosomes collected in clusters, suggesting the translation of individual cistrons.

protein molecules and, accordingly, if we have a way of detecting or differentiating these proteins from each other, we would expect to find them appearing at different positions in the polysome distribution depending upon the length of messenger RNA holding the ribosomes together. It has been possible to identify one class of polysomes in bacterial cells by measuring the enzymatic activity of nascent proteins attached to the ribosomes (3). The addition of β-galactosides induces the formation of the enzyme β-galactosidase in certain bacteria. In this system, studied extensively by Jacob and Monod (6), the β-galactosidase is used to metabolize the galactoside as an energy source. There are very few β-galactosidase molecules in the noninduced cell, whereas in the induced cell an astonishingly large proportion (up to 5%) of the total protein is found in this one enzyme.

Figure 6(a) shows the polysomal distribution from a noninduced *Escherichia coli* where the solid line represents the optical density and 70S marks the peak of single ribosomes sedimenting toward the left (7). Fractions from the sucrose gradient are analyzed directly for β-galactosidase activity. It can be seen that there is no enzymatic activity associated with ribosomes or polysomes, and only a small amount of enzymatic activity is found in the lysate at the top of the gradient. However, in Fig. 6(b), the cell contents are shown after 3 min of induction. A peak of enzymatic activity is now associated with the larger polysomes. Electron microscopic examination of this fraction shows that this peak is associated with very large polysomes containing approximately 40 to 50 ribosomes. The association of enzymatic activity with polyribosomes is probably due to the fact that some nascent chains are almost complete and have folded to make a protein molecule with a configuration very close to that seen in the intact native molecule. For this reason the schematic diagram of Fig. 3 shows the polypeptide chains folding as they are being synthesized on ribosomes. The β-galactosidase is a very large molecule with a molecular weight near 0.5 million, and it is made by the association of four subunits (16) each of which is somewhat complex itself. The asymmetric unit has a molecular weight of about 130,000, which means it has approximately 1000 amino acids. It is quite likely that some of these subunits, which have come very close to assembling all 1000 amino acids, are acting as the condensing site for three other completed subunits to form a molecule with enzymatic activity. In this system it has been shown that only the tetramer has enzymatic activity, but not the isolated subunit (16).

Subsequent to the addition of inducer to these bacterial cells, the amount of polysomal bound β-galactosidase increases steadily. An example of the kinetics during the early stages of induction is seen in

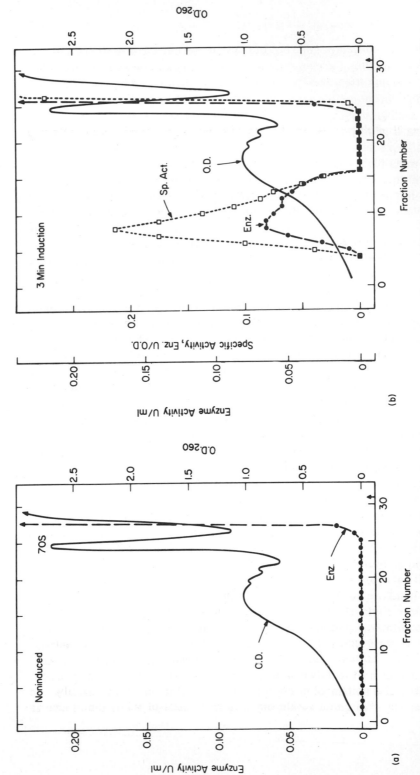

FIG. 6. Polysomal patterns from *E. coli* assayed for β-galactosidase activity (7). (a) The non-induced cell; (b) three minutes after the addition of an inducer.

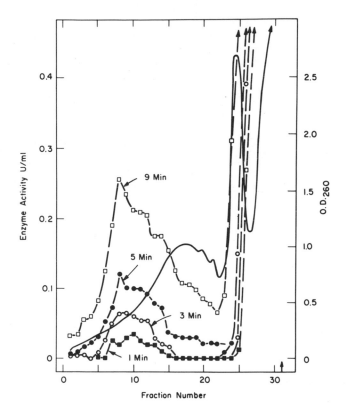

FIG. 7.   The change in polysomal bound β-galactosidase at various time periods following addition of an inducer (7).

Fig. 7 (7). There is a gradually increasing amount of polysomal bound β-galactosidase activity as a function of time of induction. This is in accord with the interpretation of Jacob and Monod, who suggested that enzyme induction is characterized by increasing the production of a messenger RNA for the induced molecule.

When the inducer for β-galactosidase is added, two other proteins are produced in addition, an acetylase and a permease, both of which are believed to be normally required in the utilization of β-galactosides (6). It is possible to show that these molecules are produced on the same messenger strand through the use of mutant strains of bacteria. This has been done by quantitating the sedimentation of the polysomal bound β-galactoside activity. An example is shown in Fig. 8, in which the distance traveled down the gradient by the peak of specific activity (*b*) is divided by the distance traveled down the gradient by the single 70S

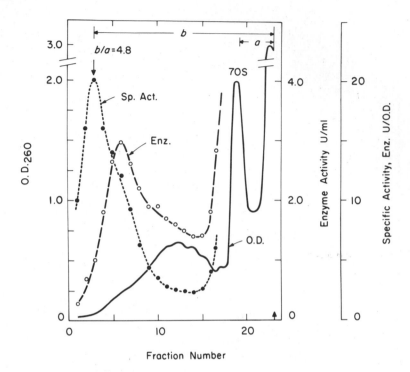

FIG. 8. Polysomal pattern from *E. coli* induced for β-galactosidase. The ratio (b/a) is constant over a wide variety of conditions (8).

ribosomes (*a*). The ratio (*b/a*) is 4.8 ± 0.2 in the wild type strain. This ratio does not change under a wide variety of altered experimental conditions, such as changes in temperature, bacterial nutrition, and polysome concentration (8). In surveying bacterial mutants, which are unable to produce permease and acetylase, it has been shown that in general the ratio (*b/a*) does not change providing there is only a point mutation in this region of the genome. However, this is not the case for bacterial mutants with a large deletion which removes the information required to make acetylase and permease from the DNA of the bacterial cell. The polysome is then much smaller and the ratio (*b/a*) falls as shown in Fig. 9. The wild type strain HFR 3000 has (*b/a*) = 4.9, whereas the deletion mutant A 381 has (*b/a*) = 4.0. Both strains have polysomal bound β-galactosidase activity, but the strain deleted in the acetylase-permease region makes a smaller polysome. This implies that the messenger RNA for that mutant is smaller than it is in the wild type strain. Hence, the induced messenger RNA is polycistronic.

Evidence supporting this interpretation is seen in a study of a

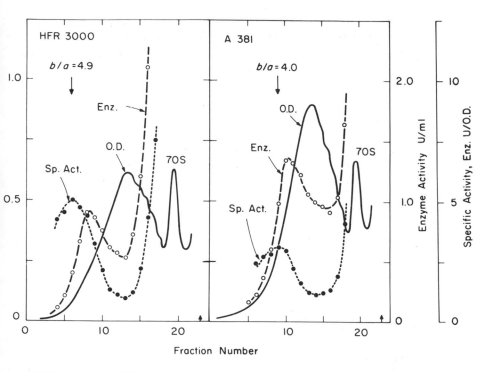

FIG. 9.   The size of β-galactosidase polysomes in wild type *E. coli* (HFR 3000), and in a mutant (A 381), which has a large deletion in the permease-acetylase region (8).

special class of point mutations in the acetylase-permease region, which are called "amber" mutations. These mutations are believed to produce shorter than normal polypeptide chains probably due to a premature release of the ribosome from the polysomal structure (12). Amber mutations in the acetylase-permease region yield smaller β-galactosidase polysomes than do those produced by the wild type. However, if the amber mutant organisms are irradiated with ultraviolet light, it is possible to isolate wild type revertants, which then have the larger wild type β-galactosidase polysomes (8). Thus, the change in the genotype is associated with the change in the size of the β-galactosidase polysome, supporting the interpretation that the messenger RNA is polycistronic.

THE FLOW OF RIBOSOMES ON POLYCISTRONIC MESSENGERS

There are many unsolved problems associated with the movement of ribosomes on polycistronic messengers. A generalized scheme showing

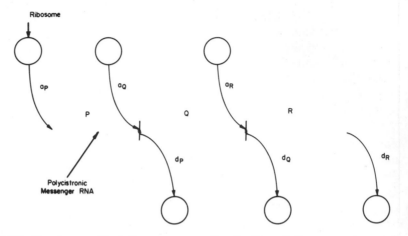

FIG. 10. A generalized diagram representing the flow of ribosomes over a poly-cistronic messenger RNA. P, Q, and R represent three cistrons coding for different proteins. The attachment process is represented by (a) and the detachment process by (d). Ribosomal movement is from left to right.

all possibilities of normal ribosomal attachment and detachment is shown in Fig. 10. An idealized messenger is composed of three cistrons, P, Q, and R, and ribosomes are shown attaching at three positions at the beginning of each cistron in processes a_P, a_Q, and a_R. Detachment at the end of each cistron is shown by processes d_P, d_Q, and d_R. It is not necessary that all of these processes actually occur. As discussed earlier, the system could function very well with only the attachment a_P and detachment d_R. This would represent a system similar to that shown in Fig. 4(b) in which the ribosome consecutively reads all three cistrons. In such an arrangement there would then be a stoichiometric relation in the number of proteins produced from cistrons P, Q, and R. This may occur in some cases; however, in β-galactosidase induction it has been shown that the ratio of β-galactosidase to acetylase is normally 10 : 1 in terms of the polypeptide chains that make up the asymmetric units of both protein molecules (10). This makes it unlikely that the ribosome attaches at one end and continues to the other end. It has also been shown that as one changes the incubation temperature for certain strains of bacteria, the ratio of these enzymes also changes. This suggests that the temperature dependence of ribosomal attachment or detachment may differ from cistron to cistron. It might be possible to explain these results by using one attachment process, a_P, and all three detachment processes shown in Fig. 10. This would lead to a gradient of production involving P > Q > R. This mechanism has been suggested for some systems but there is not enough evidence at the present time to state with assurance which of the various alternatives can occur.

We have as yet only a limited understanding of the physical parameters responsible for both ribosomal attachment or detachment. In work on the amber mutations mentioned above, two groups of workers have shown that the mutation involves the formation of a nucleotide triplet: uridylic acid-adenylic acid-guanylic acid in the messenger RNA (1,15). This triplet has the property of terminating the growth of polypeptide chains and has led to the possibility that the triplet UAG may be a normal chain terminating triplet. If this were true, it might play a role in the detachment of ribosomes as well as the detachment of growing polypeptide chains. Aside from this suggestion, however, there is no other information available about potential chain terminating mechanisms. Much less is known about the mechanism of ribosomal attachment. One conceivable possibility is that ribosomes only attach at the ends of messenger RNA strands, but this seems unlikely in view of the data available from work with the RNA viruses. It is possible that there exist chain initiating triplets, since at the present time a few of the coding triplets have not been assigned with great certainty (9). Alternatively, however, it is conceivable that the attachment of ribosomes involves a much longer stretch of the messenger RNA molecule. Thus, for example, a particular sequence of, say, five nucleotides might be needed to anchor the ribosome to the end of the messenger RNA strand. This sequence might then be used for determining the phasing of the reading of the messenger strand by the ribosome during protein synthesis. It would imply a specific site at which translation is initiated. This group of nucelotides might, of course, be composed of triplets that code for particular amino acids. However, if we postulate that the ribosome does not initiate translation before it has attached to these hypothetical initiating nucleotides, it rules out the possibility of translating those by mistake. Alternatively, this poses some restrictions on the types of adjoining codons found in the messenger RNA. It is thus possible to devise mechanisms of this type with specific attachment sites, which might be used to determine the attachment of ribosomes both in monocistronic as well as polycistronic messenger RNA's. However, further experimental work will be necessary before it is possible to decide which of the various alternatives actually occur in natural systems.

REFERENCES

1. Brenner, S., Stretton, A. O. W., and Kaplan, S., *Nature 206*, 994 (1965).
2. Cannon, M., Krug, R., and Gilbert, W., *J. Mol. Biol. 1*, 360 (1963).

3. Cowie, D. B., Spiegelman, S., Roberts, R. B., and Duerksen, J. D., *Proc. Natl. Acad. Sci. U.S. 47*, 114 (1961).
4. Crick, F. H. C., Barnett, C. L., Brenner, S., and Watts-Tobin, R. J., *Nature 192*, 1227 (1961).
5. Gilbert, W., *J. Mol. Biol. 6*, 389 (1963).
6. Jacob, F., and Monod, J., *J. Mol. Biol. 3*, 318 (1961).
7. Kiho, Y., and Rich, A., *Proc. Natl. Acad. Sci. U.S. 51*, 111 (1964).
8. Kiho, Y., and Rich, A., *Proc. Natl. Acad. Sci. U.S. 54*, 1751 (1965).
9. Nirenberg, M., Leder, P., Bernfield, M., Brimacombe, R., Trupin, J., Rottman, F., and O'Neal, C., *Proc. Natl. Acad. Sci. U.S. 53*, 1161 (1965).
10. Nishi, A., and Zabin, I., *Biochem. Biophys. Res. Comm. 13*, 320 (1963).
11. Rich, A., Pennman, S., Becker, Y., Darnell, J., and Hall, C., *Science 142*, 1658 (1963).
12. Sarabhai, A., Stretton, A. O. W., Brenner, S., and Bolle, A., *Nature 201*, 13 (1964).
13. Slayter, H. S., Warner, J. R., Rich, A., and Hall, C. E., *J. Mol. Biol. 7*, 652 (1963).
14. Warner, J. R., and Rich, A., *Proc. Natl. Acad. Sci. U.S. 51*, 1134 (1964).
15. Weigert, A., and Garen, A., *Nature 206*, 992 (1965).
16. Zipser, D., *J. Mol. Biol. 7*, 113 (1963).

3

THE MOLECULAR ORGANIZATION OF VIRUS PARTICLES

Thomas F. Anderson

INTRODUCTION

Virus particles represent forms of life in which, as nearly as we can tell, all biological activity has stopped at exactly the same stage. Purified preparations of any given type of normal virus, and there seem to be thousands of types, are therefore chemically homogeneous so that ideally the results of chemical analyses of large populations can be divided by the number of particles in the population to yield values that are significant for each particle. When examined with the electron microscope the particles in purified preparations appear identical except for recognizable artifacts of preparation. Furthermore, X-ray analyses of the many viruses that can be crystallized show that the identity extends to within at least a few tens of Angstrom units.

There are many reasons why the study of viral structures is rewarding. We might mention first that the highly symmetrical structures of the viruses are esthetically and, what might be the same thing, mathematically pleasing. But to a scientist the structures have a much deeper meaning for they reflect first the biological and physico-chemical mechanisms by which they were assembled and came into being. Much as a good mechanic can tell one by what means a given machine was constructed—this part turned on a lathe, that part filed by hand, or another part cast in a mold—so the student of viral structures would hope to deduce the principles and mechanisms that govern their manufacture and assembly.

Similarly, a good mechanic could tell the purposes which a machine or tool might serve. In the case of viruses, the organization seems to

This work was aided by grants GB–982 from the National Science Foundation and CA–06927 from the United States Public Health Service.

serve two purposes: protection and infection. Virus particles consist of two components, a protein envelope or capsid surrounding or enclosing a long, delicate, and biologically essential strand of nucleic acid. Like a computer tape, the deoxyribonucleic acid (DNA) or ribonucleic acid (RNA) contains the specifications for the component parts of the virus particle, the special enzymes necessary to make them, and any other components needed for successfully reprogramming the machinery of the host cell to make daughter particles. One obvious function of a viral structure, therefore, seems to be to protect this delicate strand of coded information from mechanical forces and enzymes which could alter the free nucleic acid fiber so as to render it useless to the virus.

When the nucleic acid is very carefully extracted from viral particles and delivered to host cells one can, in many cases, induce the formation of new daughter particles, but with an extremely low efficiency. This brings us to another function of the viral particle: to deliver the viral nucleic acid to susceptible host cells with high efficiency. The design of a viral particle anticipates the infectious role each of its elements will have to play when the particle encounters the appropriate organelle of a susceptible host cell.

A complete determination of viral structure would involve knowing the amino acid sequence in each of its proteins, the way they are folded, and the forces that hold the protein elements together. It would also involve a knowledge of the sequence of bases in the nucleic acid contained in the virus. So far, we are a long way from reaching these goals, but in the case of several viruses, there seems to be some hope of doing so.

Virus particles are put together in three main architectural styles or patterns. In one, the protein subunits are arranged in a helical pattern with the nucleic acid sandwiched between the protein elements in adjacent turns of the helix. Crane (12) was one of the first to show that the linear assembly of identical units would lead to a helical structure. The result is a rod- or thread-shaped virus particle. In the case of plant viruses like tobacco mosaic virus the rods are naked, but in the case of many animal viruses containing RNA, the threads are contained in a membrane envelope, part of which owes its origin to the host cell membrane and part to the virus itself.

In the second architectural pattern the virus particle has roughly the shape of a sphere, but higher resolution reveals that the protein subunits are arranged in five- and sixfold clusters or "capsomeres" on icosahedral patterns with the nucleic acid contained within the icosahedral shell or "capsid" (26).

A third pattern is a combination of the previous two: The nucleic acid is packaged within a protein envelope or head, which often has a polyhedral shape, but in addition the head has a special linear organelle or tail attached to it which seems to be designed for the injection of the nucleic acid into the host cell.

Here I could present an illustrated glossary of all these different types of viruses, but there would be space for only a fleeting view of each of them. Instead, it would probably be more interesting if I described only one of the virus types in considerable detail, for then we might begin to understand how complex, yet superbly organized, a virus particle is. I shall describe the last-mentioned class of viruses, the bacteriophages T2, T4, and T6 that have bacteria as their host cells.

STRUCTURE AND LIFE CYCLE OF THE T-EVEN BACTERIOPHAGES

One of the first electron micrographs of T2 bacteriophage (Fig. 1), taken 23 years ago with S. E. Luria (25), serves to illustrate the relative sizes of the watermelon-shaped bacteria and the tadpole-shaped virus particles. One of our first problems was to determine whether the phage particles attached themselves to the host cell by the head or by the tail. In this micrograph it would seem that some type of action at a distance had drawn the phage particles head first to the host cells. This, however, turned out to be an artifact of preparation. As illustrated in Fig. 2 the "action at a distance" appears to be the receding meniscus of the evaporating water, for the phage particles adhere to the supporting membrane by the tips of their tails and so in the last stages of drying for electron microscopy the meniscus tips the heads toward the bacteria.

When the meniscus of the evaporating water was eliminated, by passing the specimen through the critical point of the surrounding medium, it could be clearly seen in stereoscopic micrographs (Fig. 3) that the phage particles adhere to the bacteria by the tips of their tails. We thus arrived at the crude picture of the functional anatomy of T-even bacteriophages shown in Fig. 4 (5). The tip of the tail was viewed as the site of specific adsorption of the phage to the bacterium. The head was shown to contain the nucleic acid, for after osmotic shock had effectively removed the nucleic acid from the particles, the heads were emptied. As shown by Herriott (16), the viral "ghosts" left behind consist mainly of protein.

About this time, too, Hershey and Chase (17) showed that after adsorption of phage it is essentially only the nucleic acid that enters the

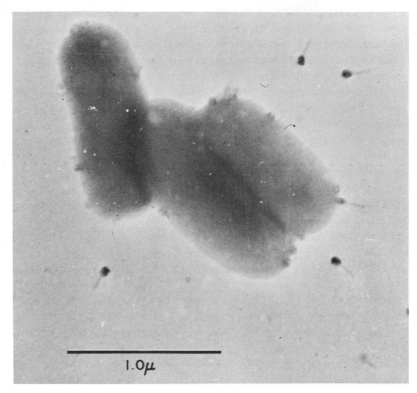

FIG. 1. An early electron micrograph of a mixture of T2 bacteriophage and its host, *Escherichia coli* strain B (1).

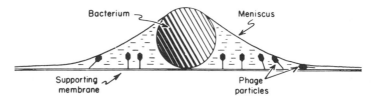

FIG. 2. A schematic drawing illustrating how the bacteriophage particles originally adhering to the supporting membrane by the tips of their tails are tipped toward the larger bacteria by the receding water meniscus in the last stages of drying to produce the orientation of particles about the bacteria seen in Fig. 1 (from 5).

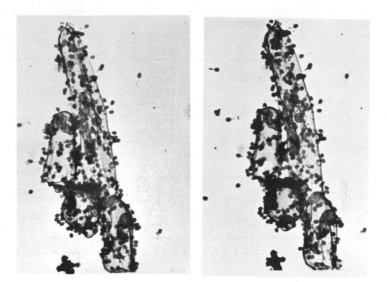

FIG. 3. A stereoscopic pair of electron micrographs of T2 particles adsorbed to host cell walls by the tips of their tails. The specimen was prepared by the critical point method to eliminate the surface tension artifacts observed in Fig. 1 and illustrated in Fig. 2 (4). ×20,000.

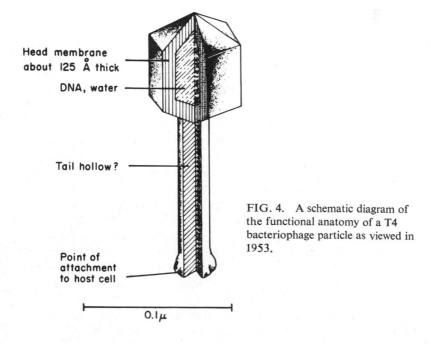

Head membrane about 125 Å thick

DNA, water

Tail hollow?

Point of attachment to host cell

0.1 μ

FIG. 4. A schematic diagram of the functional anatomy of a T4 bacteriophage particle as viewed in 1953.

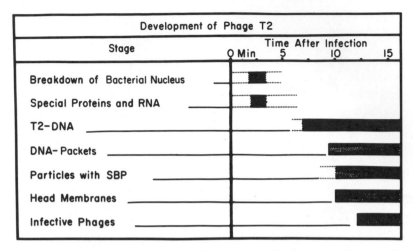

FIG. 5.   A chart showing the sequence of events in the development of the complex formed between T2 bacteriophage and its host cell (after Kellenberger).

host cells and that the phage protein could be sheared from the cells without influencing the normal development of the viral-host complex.

The sequence of events in the development of the viral-host complex is illustrated in Fig. 5. Within 2 min after infection, (a) an RNA complementary to some of the phage DNA is made within the cell, (b) a number of special proteins are produced, and (c) the bacterial nucleus breaks down (cf. 15,28). The distinctive DNA of the T-even phages, which contains the unusual base 5-hydroxymethylcytosine (31), begins to be formed about 7 min after infection. Then the T-even DNA begins to condense into packets with the shape of the bacteriophage heads as shown in sections of the virus-host complex made at this time (Fig. 6). These packets of nucleic acid become coated with the head protein and assemble into completed bacteriophage particles. Antigens characteristic of the head membrane appear at about this time, as well as antigens, presumably tail proteins, capable of blocking the ability of anti-T-even sera to neutralize the phage (serum blocking power, SBP). If one disrupts the virus-host complex at 12 min after infection, he can find the first complete infectious daughter phage particle; thereafter the numbers of daughter particles increase steadily until at 21 min a lysozyme is produced by the infection, which causes the cells to disintegrate and liberate the 100 or more daughter particles contained within the complex (19).

The released daughter particles are then free to infect other cells and repeat the cycle. Eventually all the cells in a liquid culture can

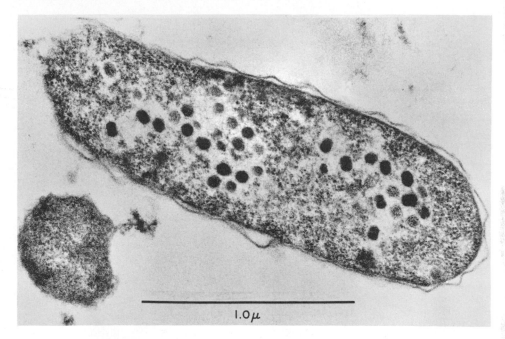

FIG. 6.   A thin section showing a stage in the growth of T4 in *E. coli* at which packets of DNA have been formed having the size and shape of mature phage heads (courtesy of E. Kellenberger).

become infected and lyse by a pandemic of this disease. On the other hand, if the cells are immobilized in nutrient agar in a petri dish, every phage particle or infected cell initiates a localized epidemic of the lytic disease, which spreads to produce a visible zone of lysis called a plaque. By counting such plaques one can make a precise determination of the number of free phage particles plus infected bacteria placed on the agar surface.

MOLECULAR ORGANIZATION AND FUNCTION OF THE T-EVEN BACTERIOPHAGE PARTICLE

In the last dozen years we have learned many details of the structure of phage particles, the roles their organelles play during infection of the host cell, and the way in which the phage nucleic acid programs the development of the viral-host complex. I'll concentrate mainly on the problem of structure and function, an aspect of virology that has advanced rapidly due to the introduction [six years ago by Brenner and

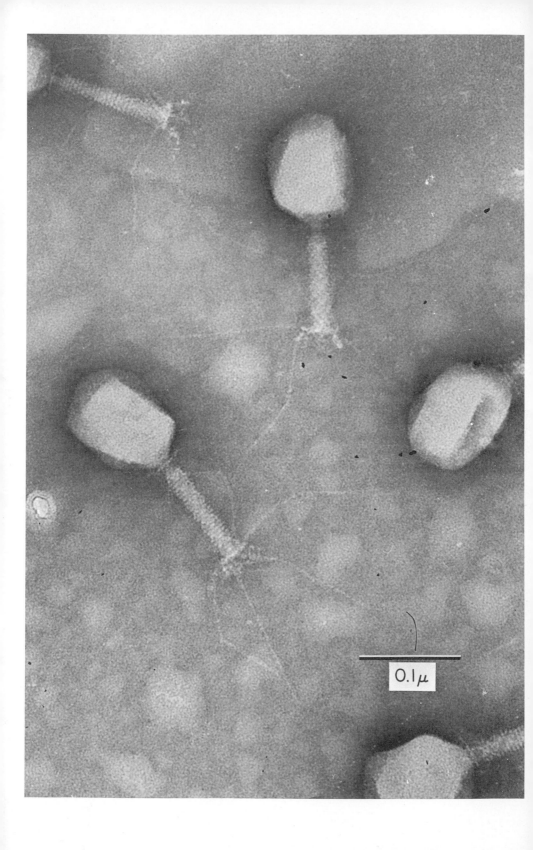

0.1μ

Horne (9)] of the negative-staining technique in electron microscopy. Figure 7 is a modern electron micrograph of T4 bacteriophage prepared by this technique. We note that the particles are essentially identical except for recognizable artifacts of preparation. In Fig. 8 one of these particles is shown at higher magnification. We note the polyhedral head containing the DNA of the particle; below the head is a collar surrounding a narrow neck; and below that is a 1000 Å long tail with 24 evenly spaced striations. The tail is terminated by a base plate to which six 1200 Å long and 20 Å thick tail fibers with kinks in the middle are attached.

Chemical analyses show that each particle has about 144 molecules of adenosine triphosphate (ATP) (22) and 6 molecules of folic acid, each with 5 glutamyl residues (24). As shown in Fig. 9 the tails of these particles can undergo a transformation (10,22). The tail is then shown to consist of a sheath surrounding a central hollow needle about 1000 Å long and 80 Å in diameter. Contraction of the tail sheath releases some 144 molecules of inorganic phosphate into the medium from the conversion of the 144 molecules of ATP to adenosine diphosphate (ADP) (22).

The DNA

Let us now re-examine the structures of each of the organelles of the T-even particles in greater detail. The DNA of each T-even particle contains about 2.2×10^5 base pairs and exists in a single double helix about 7.5×10^5 Å long. Since the DNA is packed into a head having an average dimension of only 750 Å it must be twisted and folded at least 1000 times. Actually, the DNA is packed into the head with some degree of order, for low-angle electron diffraction from individual full heads but not from empty ones produces structured central spots whose orientation parallels that of the particle (11).

If the information contained in this DNA were punched on a standard computer tape, two complementary tapes, each 2000 feet long, would be required to record the entire message! This would be equivalent to a 200-page book. Even so, assuming the viral protein to be one big molecule, this would not provide nearly enough information to determine the position of each of the amino acid residues of the phage particle, to say nothing of specifying the many special enzymes whose construction is directed by the phage DNA. The way out of this infor-

FIG. 7.   T4 bacteriophage, negatively stained with sodium silicotungstate showing the essential identity of the particles.

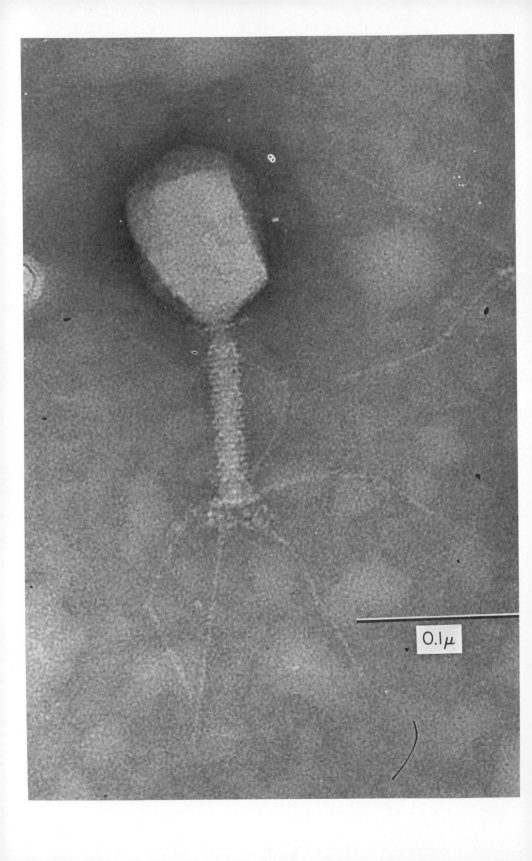

0.1μ

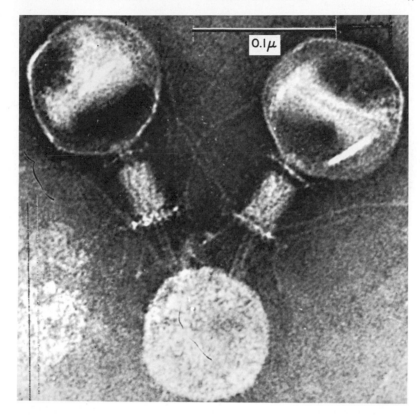

FIG. 9.   Two T6 particles with contracted tail sheaths revealing the presence of a central core or needle.

mational quandary was pointed out by Crick and Watson (13), who noted that if the protein were to be considered as consisting of a number of identical subunits, symmetrically arranged in the particle, only a fraction of the available information would be required to specify them, whereas the remainder could be used to program for other syntheses essential to viral production.

Patterns of Subunits

In the case of a T-even particle we should then expect that each of its organelles would be composed of a number of essentially identical

---

FIG. 8.   One of the T4 particles of Fig. 7 at higher magnification showing the head, neck, collar, tail with 24 cross striations, base plate, and tail fibers.

protein subunits that arrange themselves in a symmetrical pattern. Where one pattern terminates it is designed to fit the adjacent organelle, which in turn is composed of a set of different subunits; and so the structural patterns of various organelles would interlock from the tip of the polyhedral head at one end to the tip of the tail at the other. This, indeed, seems to be the order in which parts are added to the virus particle from a stockpile present in the bacterium during the later stages of infection (19).

In this connection the daughter particles produced by a cell infected with both T2 and T4 phages are most interesting. In the first place a few daughter T2 genomes end up in particles with the properties of T4 phage and vice versa. These genomes are said to be "masked" by their envelopes for they are present under false pretenses. Indeed, a T2 genome in a T4-like envelope can infect a cell like B/2 (on which T2 particles are not adsorbed) and produce viable daughter T2 particles.

However, the greater proportion of daughter particles produced by mixed T2-T4 infection have parts from both parents; they have mixed phenotypes and the phenomenon is termed "phenotypic mixing." These phenomena tell us that the assembly is made from a mixed pool of protein subunits some of which are specified by T2 genes and some by T4 genes. Thus, a phage particle, unlike a free living cell whose DNA necessarily controls the synthesis of every one of its proteins, is capable of utilizing protein specified by a foreign genome. The phenomenon of phenotypic mixing also tells us that T2 parts are so similar to T4 parts that they are structurally compatible on a much finer scale than one could even have guessed from the similarity of T2 and T4 particles as seen in the electron microscope.

From the work of Kellenberger and co-workers it appears that the first stage in the assembly of the virus particles is the aggregation of the viral genome into discrete packets, each packet containing a complete genome. The head membrane then seems to be placed over each packet. When dried by the critical point method, the heads of T-even particles seem to have the shapes of hexagonal prisms capped at each end by a hexagonal pyramid, although some observations suggest that the shape is based instead on the icosahedron (27). Unfortunately, the head membranes of normal T-even particles appear structureless even after the nucleic acid contained within them has been removed to obtain a better view of the possible arrangement of subunits. However, there exist mutant strains of these phages, which under certain conditions of reproduction produce aberrant head membranes which, instead of having the characteristic polyhedral shape, are unable to terminate their

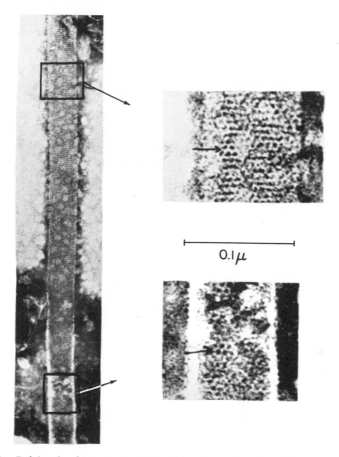

FIG. 10. Polyheads of a mutant of T4 which, when cultured at high temperature, is unable to make a normal polyhedral head, but instead makes long cylindrical structures in which a honeycomb arrangement of subunits can be seen in some areas (14).

structures and so form the long hollow cylinders shown in Fig. 10. In a few areas where the front and back sides of the flattened cylinders coincide one can discern a honeycomb structure, but in most areas of these "polyheads," as they are called, the overlapping of structures is so confusing to the eye that an over-all pattern of structure cannot be seen. Recently, however, Finch, Klug, and Stretton (14) have shown that the diffraction of light from such images as this separates the effects of the front and back layers to produce diffraction patterns like that shown in Fig. 11. Their analysis of this pattern suggests that the polyhead is

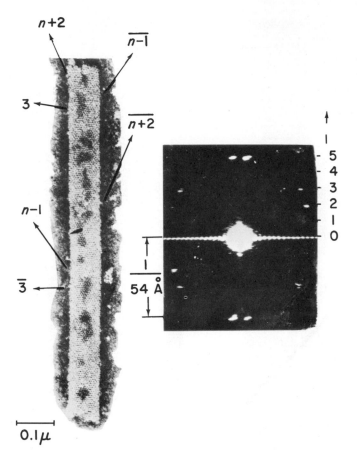

FIG. 11.   A micrograph of a polyhead of the mutant T4 together with a light diffraction pattern made from it by Finch, Klug, and Stretton (14). From their analysis
of the pattern they conclude that the polyhead is a three-start helix in which protein
subunits are arranged on a nearly hexagonal net. The directions of three classes of
rows of subunits are indicated by arrows numbered 3, $n - 1$, and $n + 2$. They give
rise to diffraction spots on the layer lines $1 = 5$, $1 = 3$, and $1 = 2$, respectively. See
Finch, Klug, and Stretton (14) for further details.

made up of essentially identical protein subunits arranged in a three-
start multiple helix, the spaces between helices being 54 Å.

The head membranes of normal particles are made up of similar
subunits for they cross-react serologically with the polyheads. But, in
addition, normal heads contain another antigen not present in the polyheads (20). If the other antigen were to fill up the spaces in the open

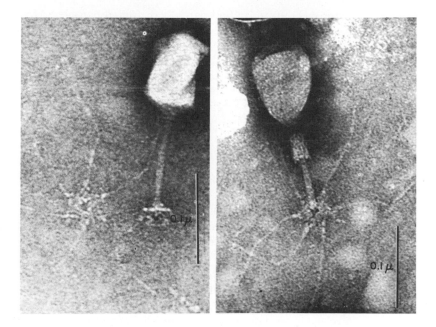

FIG. 12. The partial dissection of T6 bacteriophage in basic solution showing that under these conditons the star-shaped base plate tends to adhere to the tip of the needle (from 7).

structure seen in polyheads, they could well produce a smooth surface in which subunits could not be seen.

The Problem of Termination of Linear Structures

The fact that most of the heads have identical sizes puts us in another informational quandary, for if the structure is, indeed, made up of identical subunits, we are faced with the question as to what decides that particle assembly should terminate after the addition of a specified number of subunits? Can the genes count? Or is there some other principle involved such as the fitting of a second or even a third structure to the assembly?

We are faced with the same problem in attempting to explain how the tails of these phages, made up of identical units as they are, know when to terminate with 24 striations or a total length of some 1000 Å. A possible clue was discovered when the partial dissection of phage particles was observed in dilute basic solution as shown in Fig. 12.

In such solutions it is difficult to find partially disrupted particles. Most particles appear either intact or so badly damaged that it is difficult to recognize the separate parts as belonging to any particular particle. It is as though the various components had stabilized each other in a coherent structure like a Chinese puzzle in which the opening up of one chink causes the structure rapidly to fall apart. Normally, as we have seen in Fig. 9, when the sheath of the tail contracts, the base plate remains attached to the sheath leaving bare the tip of the needle, but in basic solution, when the sheath contracts or is partially dissolved, the base plate remains attached to the tip of the needle. The base plate must, therefore, have an affinity for both the sheath and the tip of the needle.

This observation may be the missing key to the puzzle of how the assembly of a linear structure composed of identical units is terminated after a given number have been added. If the sheath and needle were assembled by polymerization, but were ultimately to be composed of a different number* of units, *n* for one, say, and *m* for the other, such that *n* and *m* had no common denominator, they could both add units until the tip of the assembly was in register, like the lines of a vernier, to fit the elements of the base plate. With appropriate rates of production of the various components, the steric attachment of the base plate could then terminate the linear assembly process at one end, whereas an analogous attachment of the head or collar would terminate the assembly at the other. Such a configuration is drawn schematically in Fig. 13 where the star-shaped base plate is depicted as sterically fitting make up the sheath and 7 discs of another thickness have gone to make the needle. To lend support to this idea we may note that many phages (like P1, P2, and others) have contractile sheaths, and although the lengths of their tails differ from one strain to another, the length within a strain is quite constant. The principles of construction seem quite analogous for all these phages: Needles and relaxed sheaths have the same lengths and in each case the tail structure is terminated by a base plate with an affinity for both the needle and the sheath.

---

* The requirement that $n \neq am$, where a, m, and n are integers and $n \geqslant m$, is not essential to the argument. For if the dimensions of the two kinds of subunits are slightly different, the base plate might fit best when the same number of subunits of both sheath and disc have been added to the linear array. Also, even if the dimensions of the two kinds of subunits were the same, the two concentric helices they formed could have different screw displacements with the base plate fitting best a particular terminal rotational configuration of the two concentric helices.

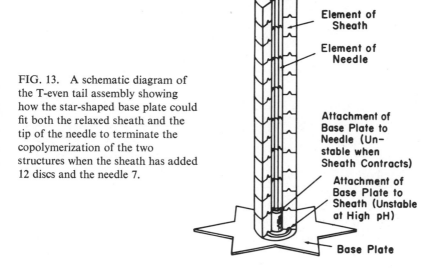

Element of Sheath

Element of Needle

Attachment of Base Plate to Needle (Un-stable when Sheath Contracts)

Attachment of Base Plate to Sheath (Unstable at High pH)

Base Plate

FIG. 13. A schematic diagram of the T-even tail assembly showing how the star-shaped base plate could fit both the relaxed sheath and the tip of the needle to terminate the copolymerization of the two structures when the sheath has added 12 discs and the needle 7.

The Role of Tail Fibers in Adsorption

In Fig. 12 we have a good view of the T6 base plate lying flat on the supporting membrane. Lying flat like this it has the shape of the Star of David with a tail fiber radiating from each of the six points of the star. Many observations indicate that the tail fibers play a prominent role in the adsorption of the phage on its host. As was observed long ago (2), T4 is not adsorbed on its host unless it has been activated by L-tryptophan or some other aromatic L-amino acid. For activation each particle seems to require at least six such cofactor molecules as estimated from the shape of the curve relating the tryptophan concentration and the equilibrium ratio of activated particles to nonactivated particles. That the folic acid molecules in the particle are somehow involved with tryptophan is suggested by the fact that each particle contains six molecules of folic acid and, more directly, that mutants of T4 that do not require tryptophan have an unidentified type of folic acid with an unusual fluorescence spectrum (23,24).

It will be most interesting to know what mechanical roles the tryptophan and folic acid molecules play, for some years ago Jerne, Kellenberger, and Franklin (21) showed that without tryptophan most T4 tail fibers are wrapped around the sheath, but that when tryptophan is added the tail fibers are released from their connection to the sheath.

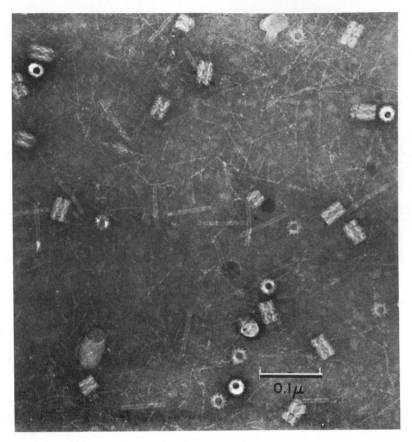

FIG. 14. A preparation of T2 sheaths, needles, and tail fibers made by Dr. N. Franklin using the procedure of Brenner *et al.* (9).

Then, being attached to the base plate at one end, the tail fibers are free to wave about in the medium. This, the first directly observed allosteric effect, seemed to implicate tail fibers in the adsorption mechanism (21). More direct evidence had come from the observation that isolated tail fibers are adsorbed on host bacteria (30). Furthermore, when tail fiber containing preparations such as that shown in Fig. 14 are added to susceptible host bacteria, the bacteria are clumped (29) as shown in Fig. 15. Here the per cent of bacteria clumped is plotted against the log of the tail fiber concentration. We also see that there is an optimal concentration of tail fibers, above which each bacterium is so saturated that there is little chance for tail fibers to form cross bridges between them. This may be considered a prozone phenomenon in analogy to

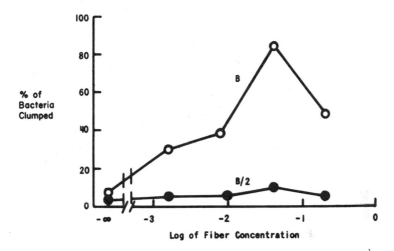

FIG. 15. The clumping of host bacteria *E. coli* B by T2 tail fibers as a function of tail fiber concentration. The percentage of clumped bacteria was determined by observation of the mixture with a dark field microscope. The reaction is specific, for as seen in the lower curve, *E. coli* B/2 on which T2 is not adsorbed is not clumped by T2 tail fibers (from 29).

reactions of antibodies with antigens. It is illustrated schematically by the first reaction shown in Fig. 16 where saturated bacteria do not react with each other. However, saturated bacteria can be clumped either by adding antibodies to tail fibers as illustrated in the second line or by adding unsaturated bacteria as depicted in the third line. That this reaction is specific is shown by the lower curve in Fig. 15 where T2 tail fibers fail to clump a strain of bacteria, B/2 on which T2 is not adsorbed. We conclude that each tail fiber has at least two sites for specific attachment to host cells.

The rates of adsorption of the T-even phages on their hosts are very high and are essentially equal to the calculated rates of collision between particle and bacterium (3). But if adsorption occurred with every collision, how could the reaction be highly specific? For the higher the specificity, the more exquisitely exact the fit would have to be and the more collisions would be required for a collision to lead to steric fitting and adsorption. The presence of adsorption spots in tail fibers offers an ingenious solution to this problem; as the relatively massive phage particle slowly diffuses toward collision with a bacterium, each tiny tail fiber with its high velocity of Brownian motion could engage in many collisions with the bacterial surface and thus enormously increase the chances of finding and fitting one of the receptor spots on the host.

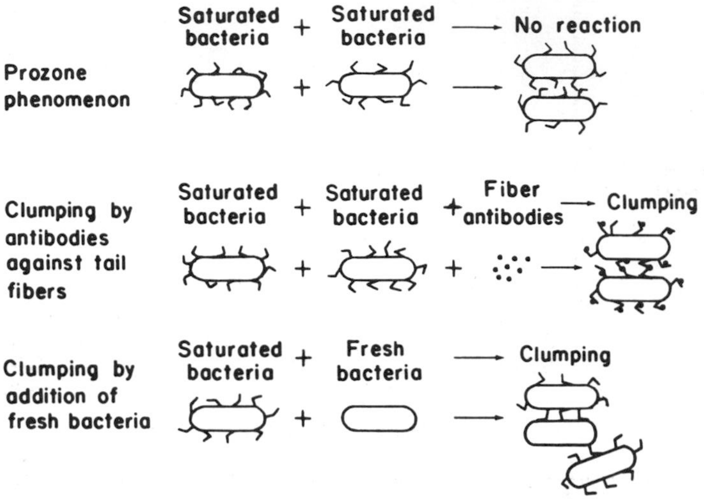

FIG. 16. A schematic drawing illustrating the prozone phenomena between *E. coli* B and T2 tail fibers. In the first line the bacteria are so saturated with tail fibers that they do not clump. However, bacteria in this state can be clumped by antibodies against tail fibers (line 2) or by fresh unsaturated bacteria (line 3) which form bridges between the saturated bacteria (from 29).

The surface of the host is also a complex structure. Figure 17 shows a recent view (8) of the cell wall of *Escherichia coli* strain B through which the phage must inject its DNA if the cell is to act as host. Receptor sites for T2 and T6 are thought to be present in the lipoprotein, the outermost soft layer which seems to be floating off the surface of the wall shown in Fig. 17(a). This lipoprotein layer partially covers a more firmly bound lipopolysaccharide in which the receptor sites for T4 are thought to be contained. A brief treatment of the cell wall of strain B

FIG. 17. Portions of the cell wall of *E. coli* strain B. (a) Cell quick-frozen, cut open at $-30°C$, and floated on a solution of glycerol and ammonium acetate. The cytoplasm was allowed to escape and the specimen negatively stained with silicotungstate. The soft external layer, consisting of lipoprotein, contains receptor spots for T2 and T6 and only partially covers an underlying layer of lipopolysaccharide. The lipopolysaccharide, which is transected by channels, contains receptor spots for T3, T4, and T7. (b) Cell quick-frozen and otherwise treated as in (a), but in addition treated with sodium dodecylsulfate to remove the two external lipoid layers (as well as an internal one) and leaving as residue the rigid mucopolymer seen here which gives the cell its shape. This is the layer that is attacked by the lysozyme contained in the tips of the tails of T-even phages (from 8).

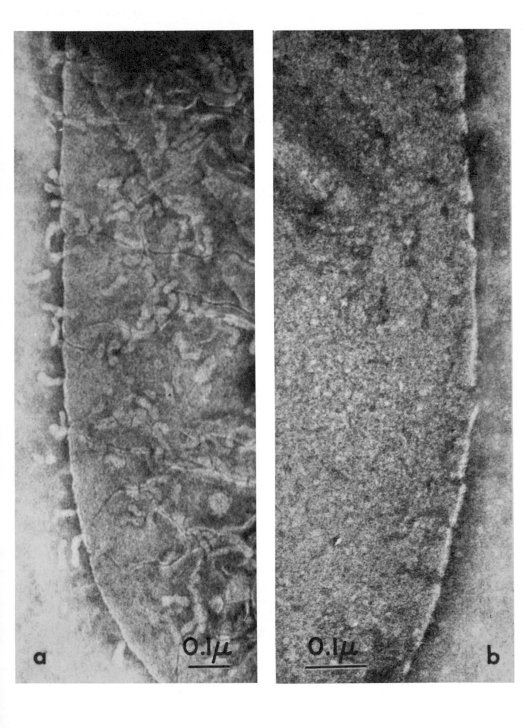

a   0.1μ   0.1μ   b

with sodium dodecylsulfate removes these outermost lipoid layers to expose the thin, inner rigid layer consisting of spherical protein elements attached to a network of mucopolymer bonds, which are susceptible to the action of lysozyme, an enzyme carried by T-even phages (2). In the native cell wall, these mucopolymer chains are protected by the cytoplasmic membrane from the action of lysozyme coming from the inside.

Injection

The involved molecular machinery of the native phage particle is triggered shortly after the tail fibers encounter a susceptible host cell. It is thought that the attachment of the tail fibers to receptor spots on the bacterium leads to the attachment of the base plate and contraction of the tail sheath. This is an interesting transformation. In Fig. 14 one can see contracted sheaths lying on their sides and estimate that there are 12 cross striations corresponding to 12 discs to make up the contracted sheath. In Fig. 18 one can see such sheaths with higher contrast and see that they have the appearance of worm gears. At the high magnification of Fig. 19 one can see a few individual discs lying flat and discern the comma-shaped elements of which they are composed. One might estimate that there are 12 such comma-shaped elements present in each disc, each element measuring about 50 Å across the circle with a 20 Å hole in the center; the tail of the comma is about 30 Å long. Thus, we might guess that the transformation consists of the "relaxed" or extended sheath having 24 discs with 6 elements in each disc being changed into a structure having 12 discs with 12 elements in each disc (6,18). In Fig. 18 one can see that each element of the contracted sheath is oriented so that its tip points obliquely away from the center of the disc in which it lies. With the discs arranged on a screw axis this would give the whole contracted sheath the observed appearance of a worm gear as shown schematically in Fig. 20. It would be interesting to speculate on the positions of the molecules of ATP in the uncontracted sheath and the way in which its conversion to ADP leads to contraction of the sheath. However, at the present time there seem to be too many possibilities to make such speculations worthwhile.

With the base plate attached to the cell wall on one face and to the tail sheath on the other, it is believed that contraction of the sheath might have the effect of pushing the needle against the cell wall. Possibly with appropriate enzymes like lysozyme in the tail structure weakening the cell wall (28, pp. 100–102), the needle would then penetrate through the wall to inject the phage DNA into the bacterium. This view of the

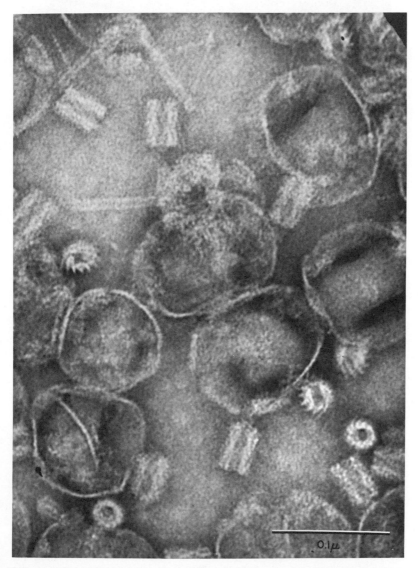

FIG. 18. Contracted T4 sheaths heavily negatively stained to show the worm gear appearance. Empty head membranes, tail fibers, and needles are also visible.

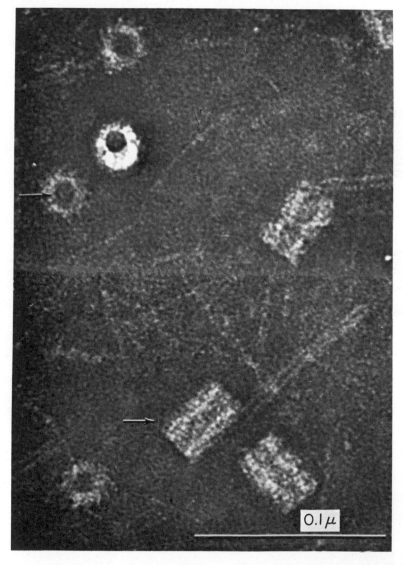

FIG. 19. Partially disintegrated T2 sheaths at high magnification to show the comma-shaped elements (arrows) of which they are composed. A few tail fibers and needles are also visible.

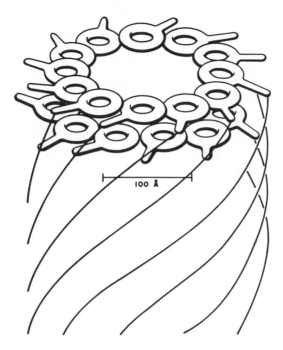

FIG. 20. Schematic drawing showing the postulated helical arrangement of the discs of comma-shaped elements making up the contracted T2 sheath and presenting the external appearance of a worm gear.

injection process, as illustrated in Fig. 21, has not yet been proven experimentally. We do know, however, that an average T4 particle, after it is adsorbed on *E. coli* B in 2*M* glycerol requires about 7 min at 15°C to inject its DNA and form a virus-producing complex that is resistant to osmotic shock (5). At the higher temperature of 37°C, of course, the time for injection is much shorter, being of the order of 1 min. It is still not clear what forces drive (or pull) the DNA into the host cell, but, once a bit of the DNA strand enters, one would expect the rest to follow by diffusion since there are many more degrees of freedom for the DNA in the huge bacterium than in the relatively tiny head of the phage particle.

CONCLUSION

With injection we are brought to the end of the virus particle as such. The protein envelope has done its job of protecting the long, essential

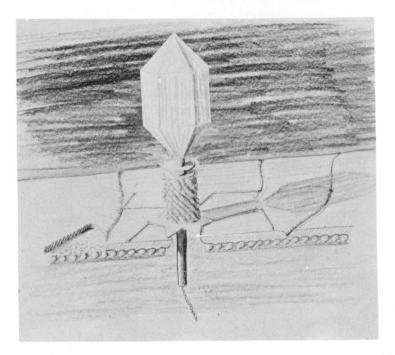

FIG. 21. A schematic drawing showing the adsorption of a T-even phage particle on the cell wall of its host and the postulated injection of its nucleic acid through the various wall structures into the cytoplasm.

strand of DNA. The tail fibers have successfully found a susceptible host cell and triggered the complex tail mechanism to inject the DNA into the cell. Though the virus particle itself has now "had it," the virus principle lives on in the form of the DNA and its activities within the host. Many of these activities we know are concerned with the synthesis of proteins and we now know which amino acids most of the three-letter words of the DNA code stand for.

But knowing the code falls short of satisfying our curiosity about how biological systems work. Like anthropologists who have just learned a few words in the language of a hitherto unknown civilization, our curiosity will hasten our probe into the equivalents of its social structure, its economy, its modes of communication and energy utilization, its inventiveness or mutability, and its means of propagating and perpetuating itself. We are already getting a few glimpses into this dynamic civilization at the molecular level which seems to run so automatically.

REFERENCES

1. Anderson, T. F., *The Pennsylvania Gazette 40*, 261 (1942).
2. Anderson, T. F., *J. Cell. Comp. Physiol. 25*, 1 (1945).
3. Anderson, T. F., In *The Nature of the Bacterial Surface*, Ed. A. A. Miles and N. W. Pirie, Blackwell Scientific Publications, Oxford, p. 76 (1949).
4. Anderson, T. F., *Trans. N.Y. Acad. Sci. 13*, 130 (1951).
5. Anderson, T. F., *Cold Spring Harbor Symp. Quant. Biol. 18*, 197 (1953).
6. Anderson, T. F., In *Viruses, Nucleic Acids, and Cancer*, Symposium on Fundamental Cancer Research, 17th, The Williams and Wilkins Co., Baltimore, p. 122 (1963).
7. Anderson, T. F., and Stephens, R., *Virology 23*, 113 (1964).
8. Bayer, M. E., and Anderson, T. F., *Proc. Natl. Acad. Sci. U.S. 54*, 1592 (1965).
9. Brenner, S., and Horne, R. W., *Biochim. Biophys. Acta 34*, 103 (1959).
10. Brenner, S., Streisinger, G., Horne, R. W., Champe, S. P., Barnett, L., Benzer, S., and Rees, M. W., *J. Mol. Biol. 1*, 281 (1959).
11. Coleman, J. W., *The Diffraction of Electrons in Ultramicroscopic Biological Particles of Ordered Structure*, Dissertation, University of Pennsylvania, p. 117 (1963).
12. Crane, H. R., *The Scientific Monthly 70*, 376 (1950).
13. Crick, F. H. C., and Watson, J. D., In *Ciba Foundation Symposium on the Nature of Viruses*, Ed. G. E. W. Wolstenholme and E. C. P. Miller, Little, Brown and Co., Boston, p. 5 (1957).
14. Finch, J. T., Klug, A., and Stretton, A. O. W., *J. Mol. Biol. 10*, 570 (1964).
15. Hayes, W., *The Genetics of Bacteria and Their Viruses*, Blackwell Scientific Publications, Oxford (1964).
16. Herriott, R. M., *J. Bact. 61*, 252 (1951).
17. Hershey, A. D., and Chase, M., *J. Gen. Physiol. 36*, 39 (1952).
18. Kay, D., In *Viruses, Nucleic Acids, and Cancer*, Symposium on Fundamental Cancer Research, 17th, The Williams and Wilkins Co., Baltimore, p. 7 (1963).
19. Kellenberger, E., *Adv. in Virus Research 8*, 1 (1961).
20. Kellenberger, E., In *Ciba Foundation Symposium on Principles of Biomolecular Organization*, Churchill, London, In press (1965).
21. Kellenberger, E., Bolle, A., Boy de la Tour, E., Epstein, R. H., Franklin, N. C., Jerne, N. K., Reale-Scafati, A., Séchaud, J., Bendet, I., Goldstein, D., and Lauffer, M. A., *Virology 26*, 419 (1965).
22. Kozloff, L. M., and Lute, M., *J. Biol. Chem. 234*, 539 (1959).
23. Kozloff, L. M., and Lute, M., *Fed. Proc. 23*, 272 (1964).
24. Kozloff, L. M., and Lute, M., *J. Mol. Biol. 12*, 780 (1965).
25. Luria, S. E., and Anderson, T. F., *Proc. Natl. Acad. Sci. U.S. 28*, 127 (1942).

26. Lwoff, A., Anderson, T. F., and Jacob, F., *Ann. Inst. Pasteur* 97, 281 (1959).
27. Moody, M. F., *Virology 26*, 567 (1965).
28. Stent, G. S., *Molecular Biology of Bacterial Viruses*, W. H. Freeman and Co., San Francisco and London (1963).
29. Wildy, P., and Anderson, T. F., *J. Gen. Microbiol, 34*, 273 (1964).
30. Williams, R. C., and Fraser, D., *Virology 2*, 289 (1956).
31. Wyatt, G. R., and Cohen, S. S., *Biochem. J. 55*, 774 (1953).

4

THE ORGANIZATION OF CELLULAR MEMBRANES

J. David Robertson

I shall begin by reviewing the development of the unit membrane theory using more diagrams than electron micrographs.* I shall then deal with certain aspects of unit membrane contact relationships in a particular synapse. After this I will take up some problems of interpretation with which we are currently concerned. The unit membrane theory has not been challenged very seriously, but some are now advancing a theory involving an arrangement of the lipid molecules that, if valid, would require a revision in one aspect of the original theory. My recent views on this problem will be given.

Figure 1 is a diagram that I like to use to illustrate an interpretative problem that we had to deal with about twelve years ago related to membranes. To the upper left there is a segment of a skeletal muscle fiber as one saw it by light microscopy before electron microscopy was applied to the problem. Of course, there was no great difficulty in light microscopy in defining the term "cell membrane," although there was some discussion about whether one existed or not. However, most people were inclined to think that there was such a structure that had a definite molecular organization of its own—not just an interfacial film. The operational method used in classical light microscopic histology to define the "cell membrane" as a morphological concept was to term it the thinnest dense line that could be seen next to the cytoplasm between the inside and outside of a cell.

When we began to look at these structures by electron microscopy in 1952, we saw in the designated region the detail indicated in (b). Of course, these details appeared in micrographs that we would now consider to be of low resolution. We saw collagen fibrils, interstitial filaments, and so on, in what was obviously the extracellular region.

* Details may be found in references 13,14,16,18,19,22,23,24.

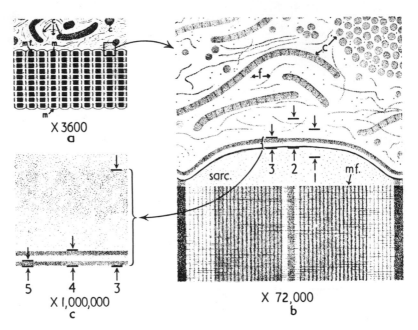

FIG. 1. m, muscle; mf., myofibril; c, collagen unit fibril; f, interstitial connective tissue filament; sarc., sarcoplasm. See text for description.

I've drawn two bars (arrows 1) in (b) that are separated by the resolution limit of the light microscope, that is, ∼0.1 μ. There is a wealth of structure included between the bars. How may we decide what to call the cell membrane? No one had any difficulty in pushing the bottom bar up to the position at arrow 2, or the top one down to arrow 3. But now we were left with a structure about 300 Å thick, which was difficult to define in operational terms. We could not arbitrarily eliminate any part of it with certainty. Most investigators, however, did not bother with this problem. They simply erased the upper arrow and used the operational method of light microscopy calling the thinnest dense line next to cytoplasm the cell membrane.

In 1957 there was an advance in electron microscopic resolution and we saw the structures in the surface indicated in (c). By the same logical processes, the cell membrane would be defined as the bottom thin dense line next to the cytoplasm at the arrows 5. I would like to indicate why this is wrong; the cell membrane actually is rather rigorously definable as the structure seen between the arrows 4. This structure consists of a pair of dense lines each about 20 Å thick separated by a light zone about 35 Å across. This is the structure for which I have used

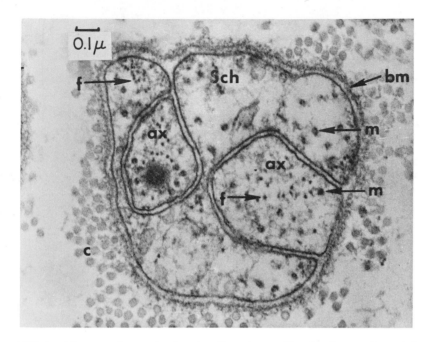

FIG. 2.   Electron micrograph of nonmyelinated nerve fiber showing two axons (ax) surrounded by a Schwann cell (Sch). Note the filaments (f) less than 100 Å in diameter and the microtubules (m) in both the axons and the Schwann cell. The basement membrane (bm) surrounds the Schwann cell; numerous collagen fibrils (c) are seen outside. × 77,000.

the term "unit membrane." This is the fundamental "unit" that is always present, wherever there is a membrane derivative (for instance, a membranous organelle). Now, let me discuss some of the evidence on which I have based this rather broad generalization.

Figure 2 is an electron micrograph from the period before we began to see the unit membrane structure very clearly. It shows a Schwann cell of a peripheral nerve fiber with two axons. Note that the membrane structure does not show up distinctly. All that can be seen clearly in the micrograph are the structures diagramed in Fig. 1(b); that is, a thin dense line next to cytoplasm, a light zone, and another dense layer outside. We now think this outer layer is largely mucoprotein and is definable by the term "basement membrane." There is collagen further out. What is the light zone in between the two dense layers?

There was much discussion about this in the mid-1950's. Whenever two cells were seen in contact with one another, as in Fig. 3(a), one saw

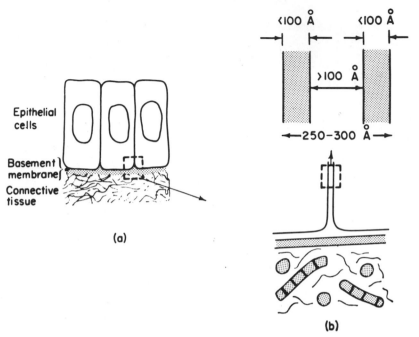

FIG. 3. Hypothetical diagram of a simple columnar epithelium showing the junction between two epithelial cells as seen by light micr oscopy (a) and by low power electron microscopy (b). The dotted rectangular area in (b) is enlarged above to give the approximate dimensions of the structures observed.

in sections the kind of relationships indicated in Fig. 3(b), that is, two dense lines separated by a light interspace. The dense lines were somewhat less than 100 Å thick and the light interspace was approximately 100 Å thick, making the whole structure, the membrane complex, about 250–300 Å across. Some important controversies developed, and there was considerable disagreement about the interpretation of these structures in molecular terms (21,30).

Some believed the paired membrane structure had the kind of molecular constitution indicated in Fig. 4(b). The dense layers were thought to be primarily protein, and the light interspace between the cells was believed filled with organized lipids. I want to show you why I think this is incorrect. Instead, the light gap between the two membranes is a highly hydrated layer as in Fig. 4(c), and the whole membrane structure is included in the dense band next to cytoplasm which, by some techniques, appears as a single dense line of variable thickness and by others shows up as the set of paired dense lines that I define as the unit membrane structure.

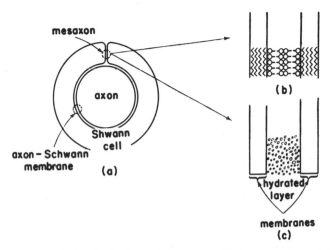

FIG. 4. Diagram indicating in (b) and (c) two possible interpretations of the structure of paired membrane complexes like the mesaxon or axon-Schwann membrane complex in (a).

Figure 5 is an electron micrograph showing the characteristic unit membrane structure at the surface of a human red blood cell. This structure, however, does not always appear. It is only seen after certain fixation methods. In my laboratory we obtain pictures like this most of the time, particularly using $KMnO_4$ fixation methods. However, others find different appearances and have reasoned that the triple-layered appearance might merely be a special case (2). This could, of course, be correct, if taken only at face value. However, there are good reasons to believe that it represents the most meaningful image and that the other images are less real. In fact, the unit membrane pattern can be demonstrated by OsO_4 and by formalin-dichromate fixation, as well as with glutaraldehyde and other methods. However, $KMnO_4$ most consistently and reproducibly demonstrates the pattern. At present, most people see the triple-layered structure with a variety of different methods, and I think most are beginning to agree that it is demonstrable in the best preparations regardless of what techniques are used.

How can one make a rigorous molecular interpretation of the unit membrane structure? The key to this comes out of a consideration of the structure of vertebrate peripheral nerve fibers. Figure 6 illustrates the basic pattern of organization of unmyelinated fibers in the vertebrate peripheral nervous system. It shows a Schwann cell, with several axons that are pushed down into the cell to varying degrees. The deeply embedded ones carry the surface of the Schwann cell with them. The

FIG. 5. Electron micrograph of a portion of a human red blood cell showing the unit membrane structure at its surface. × 280,000.

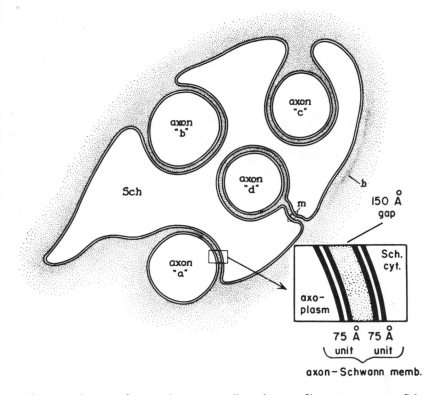

FIG. 6. Diagram of a vertebrate unmyelinated nerve fiber. m, mesaxon; Sch, Schwann cell; b, basement membrane.

unit membranes, side by side, make up one of the membrane complexes that we call a mesaxon after Gasser (7,8). The key to the membrane problem comes out of the development of myelin from nonmyelinated fibers of similar organization.

Geren (9), studying the evolution of the myelin sheath in developing chick nerve, saw nonmyelinated fibers like those in Fig. 7(a). They differed from the usual ones only in having a single axon and a single Schwann cell with a mesaxon leading to the outside. She also observed some of these fibers with a spiral mesaxon as in Fig. 7(b). This led her to postulate that myelin might originate from a spiral mesaxon. About that time, at The University of Kansas Medical School, I made a micrograph that showed an outer and inner mesaxon in adult, fully developed lizard myelin. Although crucial details were still lacking, it became quite clear that myelin probably evolved by a spiral elaboration of the mesaxon as shown in Fig. 7(c), with the two unit membranes coming

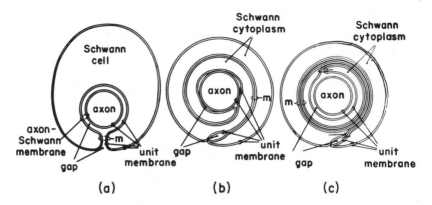

FIG. 7. Diagram showing stages in the evolution of peripheral nerve myelin: (a) protofiber; m, mesaxon; (b) intermediate fiber; (c) myelinated fiber at early stage.

together to make the future intraperiod line by apposition of the two outside surfaces of the Schwann cell membrane. Later on, the cytoplasm is excluded between the mesaxon loops, and the membranes come together to make the major dense lines.

However, I am getting ahead of the story. In 1955, we could not say all this. Vital information had to be obtained and the unit membrane pattern shown in the diagrams in Fig. 7 still had to be seen and related to myelin. The demonstration of the spiral nature of the lamellae did not alone mean much, because it did not prove that myelin contained only membrane material. Additional nonmembranous material might have been laid down between the mesaxon membranes. It was not until 1957 that we had enough evidence to draw the complete diagram.

Let me now illustrate the development of peripheral nerve myelin. In Fig. 8, showing developing mouse sciatic nerve, at "1" you see a Schwann cell and one axon, closely related. At "2" there is a short mesaxon. At "3" one sees a Schwann cell, sectioned through its nucleus, with an early spiral mesaxon. At "4" one sees a mesaxon that goes around in several loops. At higher magnification in Fig. 9 one can see in these fibers the unit membrane details such as the beginning of the intraperiod line. This particular micrograph dates from 1957, when we first began to see these structures clearly. At this stage of development, an intermediate fiber in three dimensions would appear as illustrated by Fig. 10, with the axon in the middle and the Schwann cell wrapping around it. There is a fantastic increase in surface membrane as myelination proceeds. Later, one sees, as in Fig. 11, the formation of compact myelin, with the major dense line originating by apposition of the

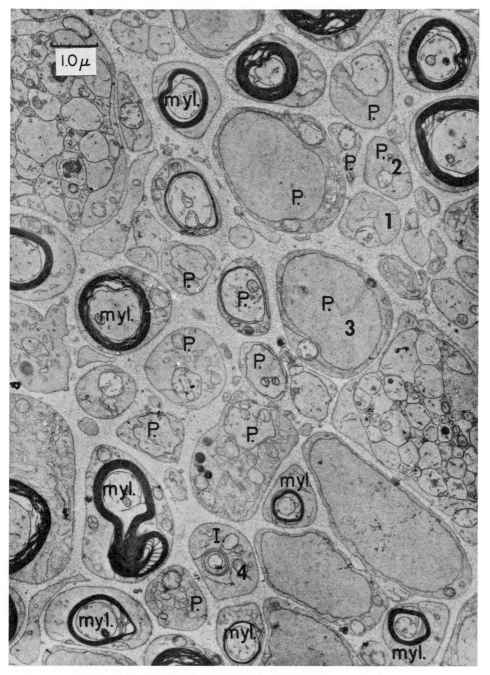

FIG. 8.   Developing mouse sciatic nerve showing various stages in the formation of myelin. **P.**, protofibers; **I.**, intermediate fibers; **myl.**, myelinated fibers. See text for numbers. × 12,500.

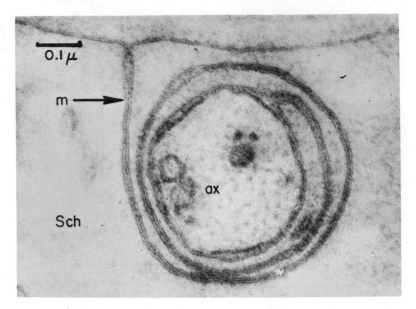

FIG. 9. Portion of an intermediate myelinating fiber showing the two unit membranes extending from the surface of the Schwann cell (Sch) to make up the mesaxon (m). Where they come together along their outside surfaces one sees the beginning of the intraperiod line. ax, axon. × 120,000.

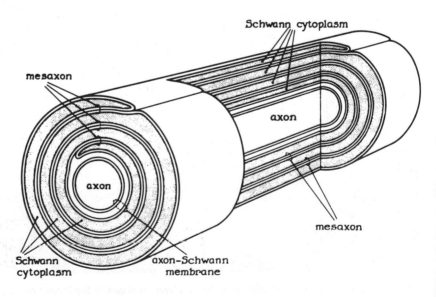

FIG. 10. Diagram of intermediate myelinating fiber.

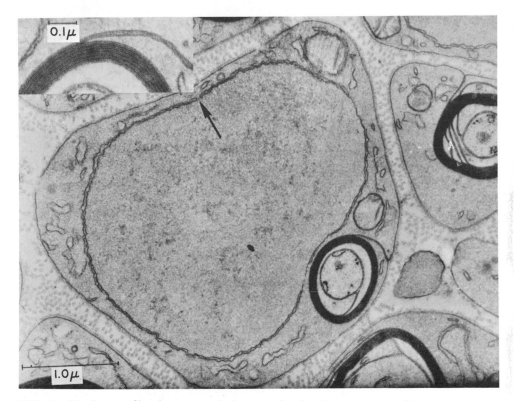

FIG. 11. Myelinating fiber in mouse sciatic nerve showing the compact myelin structure. The Schwann cell contains a nucleus in which a nuclear pore is visible (arrow). The inset enlargement shows the junction of the mesaxon with the compact myelin. Note the origin of the major dense line by apposition of the cytoplasmic surfaces of the mesaxon loops. × 30,000; inset × 90,000.

cytoplasmic surfaces of the membranes. One sees here how the intraperiod line arises by apposition of the outside surfaces of the unit membranes of the mesaxon, and the major dense line by apposition of the cytoplasmic surfaces.

Now I want to dwell on differences between the various fixation methods which we use. Figure 12 shows myelin fixed with OsO_4. It displays a very regular major dense line (m), but you may see how irregular and vague the intraperiod line (i) is. This is, in fact, the key to much of the confusion. The free surface of the Schwann cell, with osmic fixation, often appears as a single dense line, which is mainly representative of the major dense line component, that is, the cytoplasmic half of

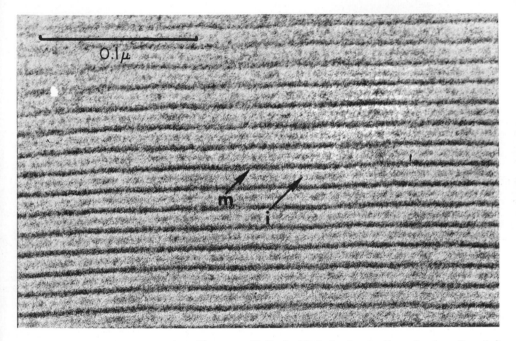

FIG. 12.   Portion of intact myelin fixed with OsO₄ showing the major dense lines (m) and intraperiod lines (i). × 480,000.

the membrane. Figure 13 shows a comparison between the outer end of a mesaxon in a developing fiber fixed with KMnO₄ (a) and one fixed with OsO₄ (b). The unit membrane pattern is seen only in (a). At the outermost extremity of the mesaxon the two membranes are stuck together and show a single line down the middle, which is analogous to the intraperiod line. This line is formed by the contact of two outside membrane surfaces. The over-all mesaxon structure here is about 150 Å across. In (b) is seen an analogous region after OsO₄ fixation. The triple-layered unit membrane structure is not visible, but where the two membranes come together at the outer extremity of the mesaxon, they form a structure that is again about 150 Å across. I believe this is because the outer half of the membrane is not fixed well by OsO₄ and one does not see it at free surfaces in such cases. However, its presence is manifested by the width of the paired membrane complex wherever two membranes are in close contact and in compact myelin some visible residues are retained.

If we compare the junction of the mesaxon with compact myelin after KMnO₄ fixation, as in Fig. 14(a) (arrow), we see very clearly that

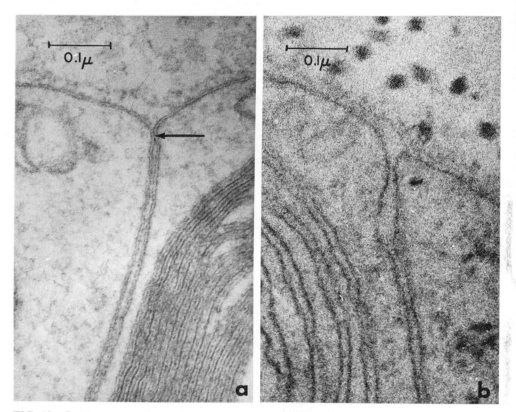

FIG. 13. In (a) a mesaxon is shown after $KMnO_4$ fixation; in (b) a similar region is shown in an intermediate myelinating fiber after OsO_4 fixation. Note the formation of the intraperiod line (arrow) by apposition of the outside surfaces of the two unit membranes of the mesaxon. (a) × 160,000; (b) × 250,000.

the major dense line originates from the contact of the cytoplasmic halves of the two membranes. In (b), after OsO_4 fixation, we hardly see the intraperiod line, and we do not see it at all where the mesaxon comes off the compact myelin (arrow). Nevertheless, where the major dense line is formed, we see exactly the same relationships that were seen in (a). The over-all period is approximately the same in either case. A consideration of these facts leads one to the conclusion (with the exception of compact myelin) that the whole membrane structure is revealed in the case of $KMnO_4$ fixation, and only a part of it by OsO_4 fixation. Furthermore, one concludes that myelin contains nothing but closely apposed Schwann cell membranes. There is not room for anything else except small molecules under 15 Å in diameter.

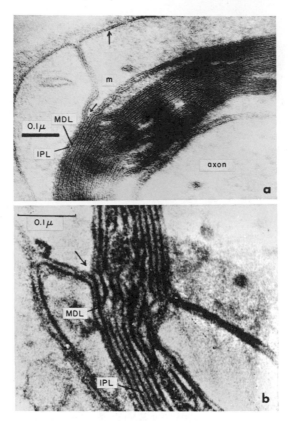

FIG. 14.   (a) A portion of a myelinated fiber with the outer mesaxon after $KMnO_4$ fixation; (b) the same after OsO_4 fixation. Note the formation of the major dense line (MDL) by apposition of the mesaxon with the compact myelin and the intraperiod line (IPL) by apposition of the outside surfaces of the two unit membranes of the mesaxon. (a) $\times 160,000$; (b) $\times 250,000$.

What does all this mean? Something was known about nerve myelin before we had electron microscopes. In the mid-1930's, we knew from the work of W. J. Schmidt (28) something about the molecular arrangements in the myelin sheath. We knew, chemically, that it contained lipids and protein. From the optical properties and X-ray diffraction analyses done on fresh, unfixed, myelinated nerve fibers, W. J. Schmidt deduced that there was a lamellar structure present before we saw it by electron microscopy. He also deduced that the lipid molecules were radially arranged and the protein molecules tangentially disposed in each lamellar sheet. It was known from the X-ray diffraction studies of Schmitt et al. (27) that the lamellae repeated at a period of about

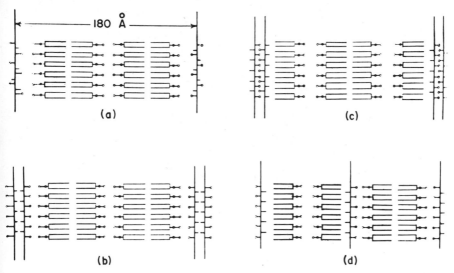

FIG. 15. Myelin sheath structures (radial direction). Diagram taken from Schmitt, Bear, and Palmer (29).

180 Å in the radial direction. Schmitt, Bear, and Palmer (29), taking into consideration their own data and that of W. J. Schmidt (28), realized that all one could fit into this repeating structure, in view of the sizes of the molecules that were concerned, was two bimolecular leaflets of lipid, and some monomolecular films of protein, or nonlipid material. However, they did not know exactly where to put these molecules, or how to relate them. They knew only how many could be fitted into the repeating unit and that the lipid molecules must be radially arranged and the nonlipid interspersed tangentially. They drew several alternative models, which would satisfy the biophysical data (Fig. 15).

More recently, Finean (4) repeated and extended the older work. Taking advantage of some of the electron microscopic data, he concluded that the most probable arrangement of the molecules in the repeating unit in the radial direction is that shown in Fig. 16. He postulated two bimolecular layers of lipid, with the polar groups directed outward and covered by monomolecular films of nonlipid. He proposed two of these units per repeating period. Since the units are symmetrical, a "difference factor" was inserted between the nonlipid layers so that two units could be included in the repeat period.

We were able at this point to take this biophysical evidence from living, fresh, unfixed nerve fibers, derived by completely different

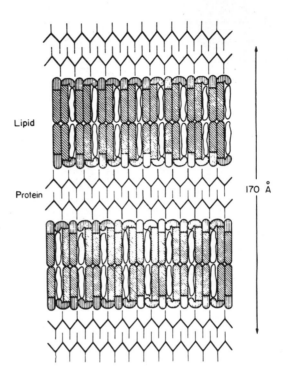

FIG. 16.   Diagram taken from Finean (4), showing his conception of arrangement of
lipid and protein molecules in the radial repeating unit of myelin.

methods, put it together with electron microscopy, extrapolate to the
surface of the Schwann cell, and conclude something about the molecular
organization of the unit membrane (1,14,16). We made the assumption
that the repeating period by electron microscopy was, indeed, the same
as that detected by X-ray diffraction. There is good evidence for this on
symmetry grounds alone. The repeating structure in myelin is the
mesaxon. On such considerations, as in Fig. 17, we may put the molecular diagram from the X-ray diffraction and polarized light evidence
beside the electron microscopic diagram and extrapolate to the surface
membrane. This leads us to a molecular pattern for the unit membrane
structure. There is a core of lipid covered on the inside and outside by
monomolecular films of nonlipid. Figure 18 is a highly schematic
diagram of the general pattern of organization that we are dealing with
in the unit membrane.

    This diagram illustrates one other thing that perhaps is not clear—
that the inside surface of the membrane is chemically different from the

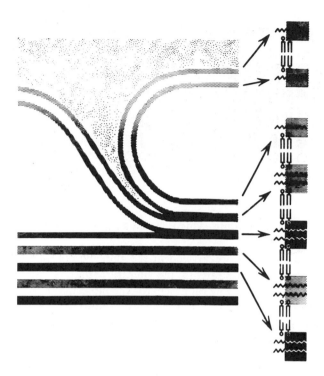

FIG. 17. Diagram superimposing evidence about the molecular organization of the nerve myelin from X-ray diffraction and polarized light on the right and the arrangement of the myelin sheath at the junction with the molecular as seen by electron microscopy. By extrapolation the molecular pattern of the Schwann cell membrane is deduced.

outside surface. It is a chemically asymmetric structure. There are two reasons for this assumption. First, the major dense lines and the intraperiod lines that represent, respectively, these two layers, are obviously chemically different because they react differently to fixatives. Second, if the layers were not chemically different, the X-ray repeat would be half of the observed value, thus the need for Finean's difference factor. The unit membrane is an asymmetric structure. The diagram demonstrates, further, that in the cell membrane structure the lipid is in the smectic state; that is, the lipid molecules are in a close-packed bilayer arrangement with the polar groups directed outward, and covered by monomolecular films of nonlipid. It shows further, that there are only two layers of lipid molecules in the thickness of the membrane, with two other molecular layers on the outside. Thus, a limit is placed on the

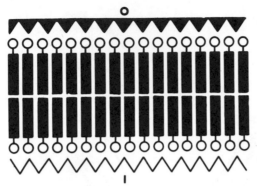

FIG. 18. Highly schematic drawing of the pattern of arrangement of molecules in the unit membrane structure. Circles represent the polar heads of lipid molecules; the dense bars, the nonpolar carbon chains; the zig-zag lines, monomolecular films of nonlipid. The outer (O) mono-layer is filled in to indicate that it is chemically different from the inner (I).

thickness of the membrane, which depends on the particular molecular species involved.

There was, before we arrived at the unit membrane concept, an idea of membrane structure in the literature that is rather similar. This was proposed as a general model for the molecular organization of cell membranes by Danielli and Davson (1) on entirely different grounds. They deduced their model on indirect evidence from certain features of cells and from permeability studies. The Danielli-Davson model is illustrated in Fig. 19. We started out with this model before the electron

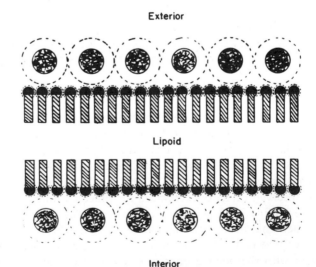

FIG. 19. Hypothetical molecular diagram of membrane structure published in 1935 by Danielli and Davson (1). Note the symmetrical nature of this membrane and the indefinite numbers of lipoid layers.

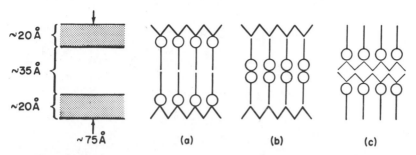

FIG. 20. Diagram illustrating on the left the dense and light strata seen in the unit membrane structure. In (a), (b), and (c), three possible molecular interpretations of the pattern are given.

microscope was available. Have we made any progress? Have we contributed more than the Danielli-Davson model? We can, in fact, say several things that couldn't be said before. First, we can restrict the number of lipid molecules present in the membrane to two, instead of leaving it indefinite, as Danielli and Davson were forced to do. Second, we can place a limit on the thickness of the nonlipid monolayers. These probably are not over 20 Å thick, suggesting that the protein monolayers may be fully spread. In any case, they cannot be more than a few polypeptide chains thick. Third, we can say that the membrane structure is chemically asymmetric. Thus, we have made a step forward in understanding membrane structure.

Now, let us consider this analysis further. What is the significance of the evidence from X-ray and polarized light analysis? Neither is yet unique, though significant progess has been made toward a solution of the X-ray analysis (11,15), and it seems almost certain that the general pattern we chose is correct. However, the evidence at the time we reached our conclusions could have been interpreted in different ways. We could have drawn the molecular diagrams of myelin so as to give any one of the three patterns illustrated in Fig. 20. As far as the X-ray evidence or polarized light evidence was concerned, we couldn't have chosen between them. Why did we choose the one in Fig. 20(a)? This choice was, in the beginning, partly guesswork; however, in the late 1950's, by studying sections of fixed systems of lipids, we obtained evidence that this guess was correct. We knew that if we fixed a protein crystal, embedded and sectioned it in the same way that we did a tissue, we observed a uniform density with the electron microscope (Fig. 21). If we fixed a purified lipid we did not observe a uniform density. Instead, we saw a system of dense and light lines that repeated periodically (Fig. 22). We now had every reason to believe that the molecular

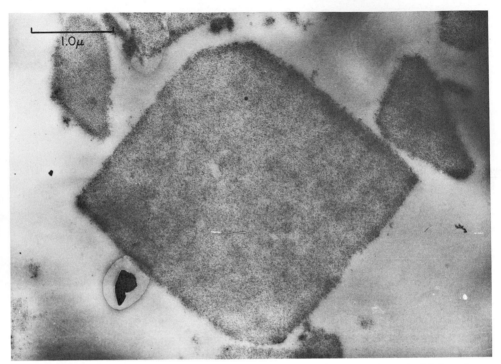

FIG. 21. Crystal of chymotrypsinogen fixed with $KMnO_4$, embedded, and sectioned. Note the preservation of the crystal faces and the relatively uniform density over the crystal substance. × 28,000.

arrangement in egg kephalin when it was fixed was as shown in Fig. 23(a). If we take into consideration the sizes of the molecules involved, the dense lines we saw must have represented either the polar ends of the lipid molecules or the nonpolar carbon chains. It was crucial to decide which of these interpretations to adopt. By classical histological reasoning, we would have assumed that the nonpolar carbon chains produced the density as depicted in Fig. 23(c). However, we concluded that the pattern seen in Fig. 23(b) was the correct one. Here the polar ends of the lipid molecules produce the dense strata. This conclusion was reached in the following way. If a smectic lipid system is hydrated, water enters along the polar surfaces of the lipid layers and separates them into individual bilayers (Fig. 24). This was demonstrated through X-ray diffraction analysis by Schmitt, Bear, and Palmer (29). It was clear, if such a system was fixed, and for each bimolecular leaflet of lipid a pair of dense lines was observed, that it was the polar ends of the

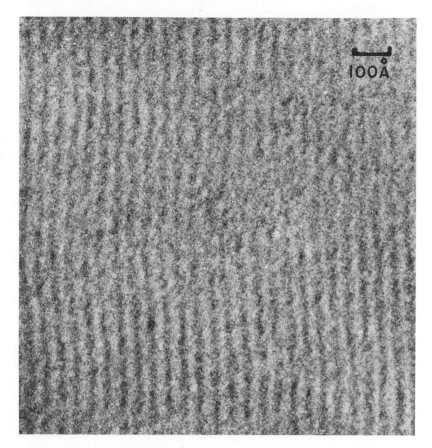

FIG. 22.   Section of egg kephalin fixed with OsO_4, embedded, and sectioned. Dense and light strata repeat at a period of about 40 Å. × 1,000,000.

lipid molecules which produced this density. If we were to see a single dense line for each bilayer of lipid, then the converse would be true; that is, the nonpolar carbon chains would produce the density. Figure 25 shows such a system, and a pair of dense lines is seen for each bimolecular leaflet of lipid. The polar ends of the lipid molecules produced this density and the model we chose was correct. Stoeckenius (32) more recently has provided elegant proof that this is so by electron microscopic studies coordinated with X-ray diffraction studies by Luzzati and Husson (10).

There is a further point I must make concerning the unit membrane. The unit membrane pattern is not peculiar to the surface of Schwann

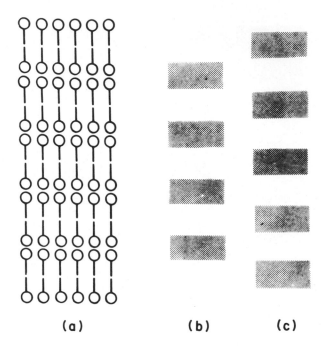

FIG. 23. (a) Diagram showing the most probable molecular configuration of the system shown in Fig. 22; (b) and (c) two possible molecular interpretations of the observed pattern.

cells, but is generally present in all cells. A survey of various organs and tissues from a number of animals demonstrated the ubiquity of unit membrane patterns (16). It is characteristic of membranous organelles such as the endoplasmic reticulum, Golgi apparatus, and mitochondria (20,22,23). It is a general structural pattern seen in all membranes. This is not to say, however, that all membranes are identical. I have said nothing about the particular molecular species making up the membrane. I have dealt only with the general classes of compounds concerned and how they are put together. The details of organization within this pattern are yet to be worked out. That there are important chemical differences in terms of molecular species is made clear, for instance, by the fact that membranes vary considerably in thickness and in the clarity or ease with which the triple-layered pattern is displayed. I believe, however, that all these differences are accounted for by variations in the molecular species involved and not by the differences in the basic pattern of organization. A narrow gauge railroad track is still a railroad track, to use a crude analogy.

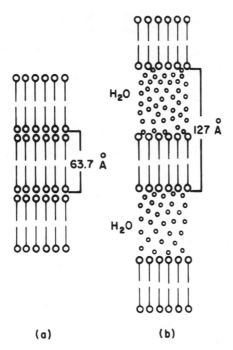

FIG. 24. Diagram from Schmitt, Bear, and Palmer (29), showing the mechanism of hydration of a phospholipid separating out individual bimolecular leaflets. (a) Smectic system; (b) hydrated system.

I think it is fair to say that the unit membrane structure is of general significance; that this pattern of organization is a property of all cells. It is, in this sense, a fundamental biological constant, the characteristics of which could only be guessed at before the electron microscope was applied to the problem.

There is one other point I wish to make about the arrangement of membranes in cells. It is a corollary of the unit membrane concept. Invaginations of the surface membrane sometimes extend rather deeply into cells and become tubular membrane-limited structures. These appear to pinch off and form vesicular structures within the cell, the so-called pinocytotic vesicles. Further, the membranes of membrane-limited structures, for example secretion granules in the pancreas, become continuous with the surface membrane when the vesicular contents are extruded from the cell. Some years ago, from observations on muscle and nerve tissues, I was led to postulate that mitochondria might originate in the way indicated in Fig. 26 (17,21). This is still speculative, but not by any means excluded by the evidence. This

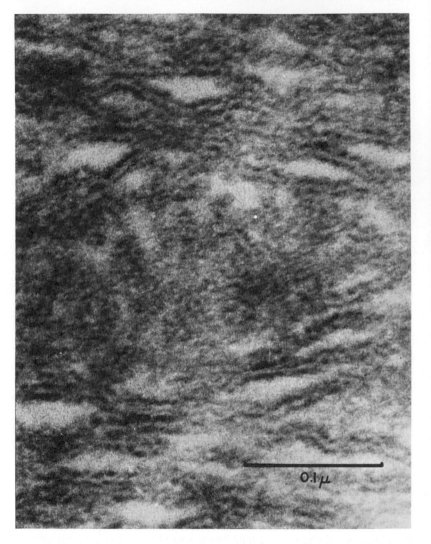

FIG. 25. Egg cephalin fixed with $KMnO_4$, embedded, and sectioned. The system was partially hydrated to separate the individual bimolecular leaflets. $\times$ 360,000.

related mitochondria to the endoplasmic reticulum. The endoplasmic reticulum is related to the other membranous organelles and the surface membrane of cells.

The unitary theory of cell structure to which I adhere is shown in simplified form by Fig. 27. It suggests that a cell is a three-phase system consisting of the following: first, a nucleo-cytoplasmic matrix

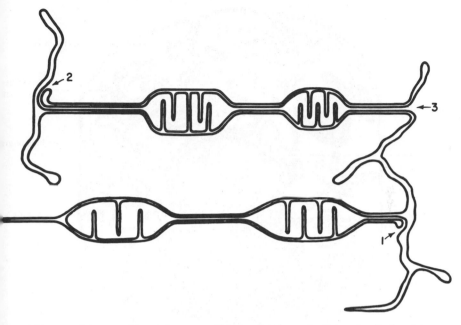

FIG. 26. Diagram illustrating a possible mechanism of origin of mitochondria from endoplasmic reticulum. It is postulated that a circumscribed region of growth develops in an endoplasmic reticulum membrane. The new membrane invaginates into the cisternal cavity, and with further growth and differentiation we have a core of cytoplasmic matrix into which the cristae extend by extension of the inner membrane by intrinsic membrane growth. 1, 2, and 3 indicate places of invagination of the kind postulated. In the mitochondria above between invaginations 2 and 3, invagination 2 meets the one originating at 3, to produce a crista extending entirely across the mitochondrial matrix. This form is frequently encountered in liver cells.

phase that is continuous via the nuclear pores with the whole of the "unstructured" part of the cell; second, a membrane phase, continuous from the nuclear membrane to the outside surface membrane through the endoplasmic reticulum; and third, an outside phase, brought into the cell by invagination. This is a useful concept. It says that the membrane always maintains its asymmetric polarity. It always has the same surface directed toward the cytoplasmic matrix. In phagocytosis, material can be taken in and dealt with by the same membrane surface, though the material may be translocated to another cellular region. In secretion, the reverse might occur. This is, I think, a useful way to think of cells, but whether it is strictly correct is a matter for further investigation. I should point out that the unitary concept does not require that continuity between parts be maintained. It requires only that the polarity

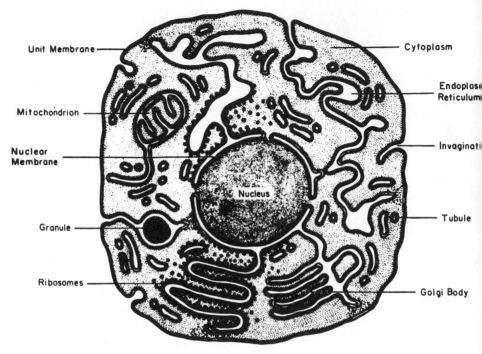

FIG. 27.   General cell diagram discussed in the text.

of the membrane with respect to cytoplasm be constant. Thus, membranes bounded on both sides by cytoplasmic matrix material are excluded.

I now wish to discuss a controversial issue. Is the continuous bilayer concept of membrane structure perhaps wrong in some of its particulars? The problem may be illustrated by micrographs of the club endings on the lateral dendrite of the Mauthner cell. Figure 28 shows one of these by light microscopy; Fig. 29 shows such an ending by electron microscopy; and Fig. 30 shows a higher power view of the synaptic membrane complex. Here is seen a peculiar kind of synaptic relationship. There are regions in which the gap between the membranes is widened, and these alternate with button-like regions in which the gap is closed. Figure 31 illustrates one of the latter at still

FIG. 28.   Light micrograph of cross section through a lateral dendrite of a Mauthner cell in goldfish medulla. Note the club endings at the arrows. × 1,350.

FIG. 29.   Low power electron micrograph of a club ending. × 1,350.

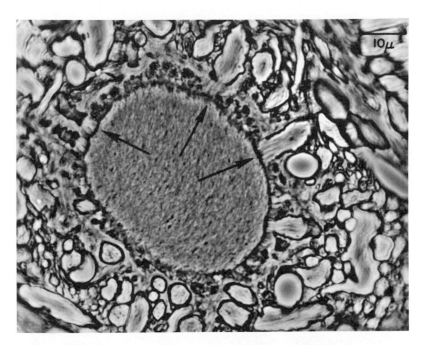

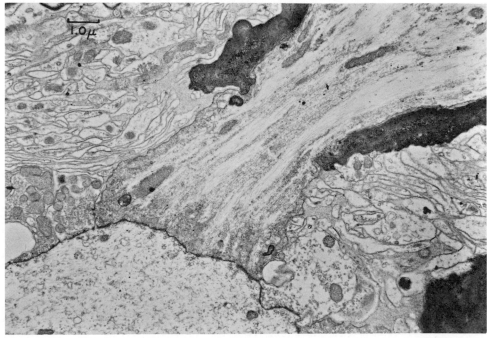

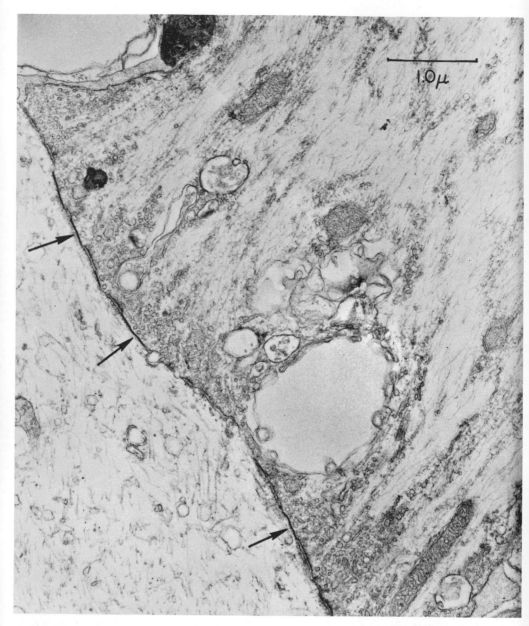

FIG. 30. High power electron micrograph of a club ending of a lateral dendrite showing accumulations of vesicles near the presynaptic membrane and neurofilaments and microtubules of the terminal axons. Note the collar of extracellular matrix material surrounding the axon at the termination of the sheath. The synaptic discs are indicated by the arrows. ×27,000.

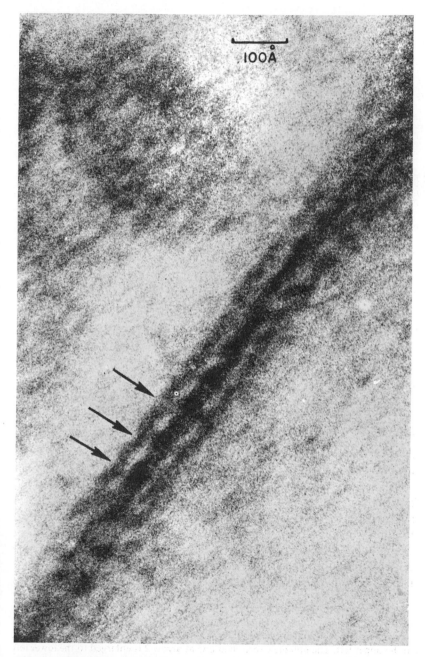

FIG. 31. High power view of synaptic disc like those indicated in Fig. 30 but in material fixed with $KMnO_4$. Arrows indicate scalloping of cytoplasmic surface. $\times 1,360,000$.

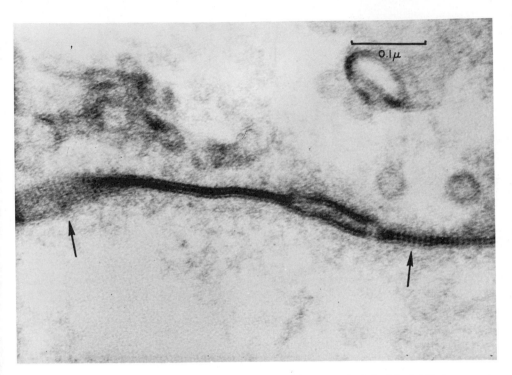

FIG. 32.   Two synaptic discs are shown. The one to the left of the field is transversely sectioned but to the extreme left is obliquely cut. The one to the right is obliquely cut. Note the striations (arrows) in the obliquely sectioned regions. × 264,000.

higher power. This is a "synaptic disc." Here, two unit membranes have fused along their outside surfaces to form an "external-compound membrane." This is a structure about 125–150 Å thick, which is a constant feature of the club ending and is, I think, related to electrical transmission. There are, however, other details of membrane structure appearing in this picture that deserve mention. First, there is the central beading where the two outside membrane surfaces are stuck together; second, the scalloping of the cytoplasmic surfaces indicated by the arrows; third, the vague transverse density, which runs across the membranes from bead to bead. In Fig. 32 are shown some synaptic discs

FIG. 33.   Portion of a club ending in which the synaptic membrane complex is sectioned very obliquely and in one case (arrow 1) frontally. This latter region is enlarged to the upper left. The obliquely sectioned one at arrow 2 is enlarged to the lower left and some of the synaptic vesicles at arrow 3 are enlarged to the middle left. × 51,000; upper inset × 150,000; middle inset × 110,000; lower inset × 130,000.

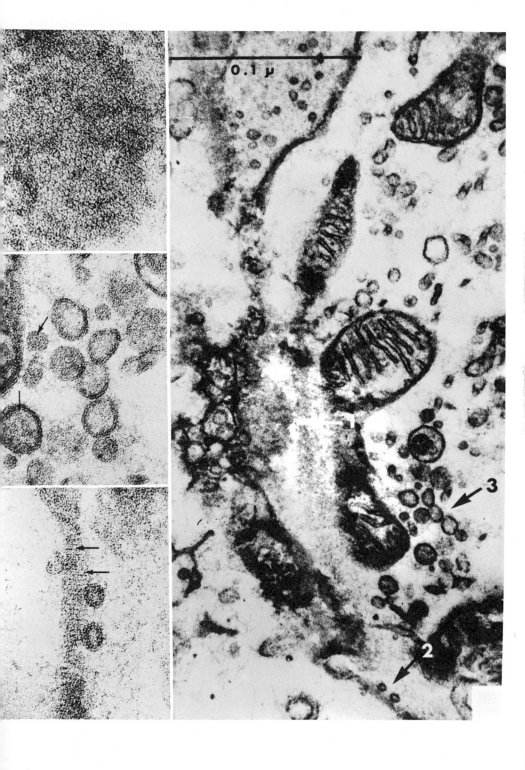

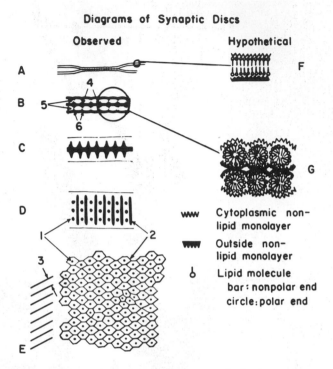

FIG. 34. Diagram illustrating appearance of a synaptic disc in transverse section in (A) at relatively low power. In (B) the central portion is enlarged to show the central beads. Arrows 4 point to the central beads; arrows 5 point to vague transverse densities running across the light central zones; arrows 6 indicate the scalloping of the cytoplasmic surfaces. (C) shows the disc slightly tilted; (D) shows it very obliquely sectioned; and (E) shows it in frontal view. The unit membrane molecular pattern is given in (F). In (G) there is shown a hypothetical molecular interpretation of the pattern in (B) of the general kind favored by Sjöstrand to explain the transverse densities observed by him in other membranes.

tilted on their sides. These discs display a system of lines or striations. As the disc is tilted further, the lines emerge more clearly and (Fig. 33, lower inset) a row of dots (arrows) appears between the lines. When the disc is tipped completely and observed in frontal view, a very regular hexagonal lattice of facets about 100 Å across (upper inset in Fig. 33) is seen. These findings are summarized diagrammatically in Fig. 34. The hexagonal lattice (E) consists of a ring and dot arrangement with the rings made up of dense lines about 20 Å in diameter. The facets repeat at a period of 90 Å. Each facet has a dot in the middle about 25 Å in diameter. The succession of changes as the synaptic disc is progressively tilted is illustrated by (C) thru (E). I believe the beads seen in the middle of the transverse sections are produced by overlap of the borders of the facets. These beads repeat at about the same period as the hexagonal lattice. The central dots seen in each facet in the frontal view are obscured in the transverse sections. What produces the vague transverse densities and the scalloping seen on the outside surface? One possible molecular interpretation of these features is that the lipid core is not arranged in the smectic bilayer manner postulated for the unit membrane [Fig. 34(f)], but that it is arranged as aggregates of closely packed microspheres [Fig. 34(a)]. We shall return to this point and I shall state why I believe that the smectic arrangement holds here as well. I should mention now, however, that Sjöstrand (31) independently made some similar observations on the membranes of mitochondria and endoplasmic reticulum. He concluded that the smectic arrangement of the lipid did not apply and that the lipid was in a microspherical state. He further postulated the existence of protein molecules running across the membranes between each lipid microsphere thus forming a cubic lattice system. I now have reasons for believing that this interpretation is not correct. The transverse densities are due to an overlap effect produced by slightly oblique sectioning (see below).

I took a different tack in the interpretation of these appearances in the synaptic discs when we first saw them. I chose to think of two kinds of substructure: first, a granulo-fibrillar substructure confined to the combined outer surfaces of the two membranes, and second, a globular fine structure represented by the transverse densities and the scalloping of the cytoplasmic surfaces of the membranes. A sharp distinction was drawn between these two types of substructure. The granulo-fibrillar component was thought to be representative of a lattice of structural protein or mucoprotein molecules.

We have found some evidence of both kinds of substructure in synaptic vesicles (Fig. 33, arrow 3, inset), mitochondria, endoplasmic reticulum, and so forth. It is particularly evident in retinal rod outer segment membranes. For instance, isolated retinal rods, fixed with permanganate and disrupted ultrasonically, exhibit a kind of mosaic pattern in the surface, which is reminiscent of the synaptic disc (Fig. 35). It is, however, not so regular and the individual facets are smaller ($\sim$50–60 Å in diameter). Human red blood cell membranes treated in the same way also display a vague mosaic pattern (Fig. 36). Possibly, we are observing a structural protein derivative confined to one or both outer dense strata of the unit membrane and analogous to the granulo-fibrillar substructure of the synaptic disc. If so, we may be observing a principle of membrane organization previously undetected. There is, however, no evidence beyond that of the electron micrographs. Evidence

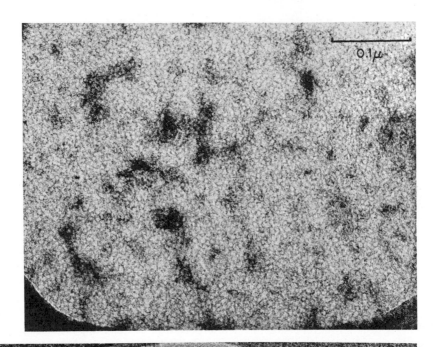

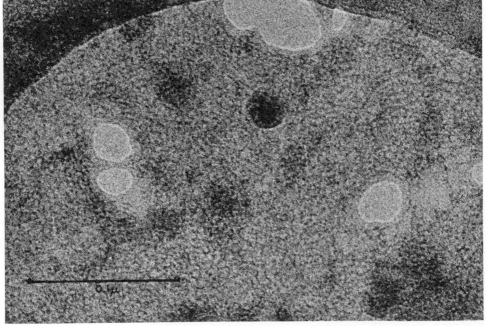

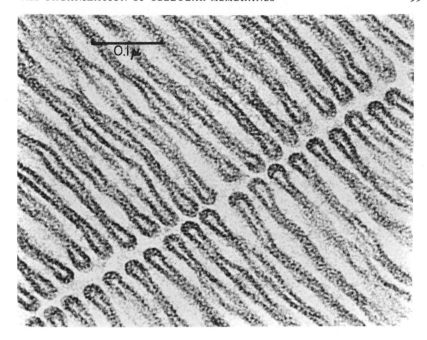

FIG. 37. Portion of frog ROS showing the lamellae with evidence of globular substructure. Fixation with glutaraldehyde followed by OsO_4 and lead staining. $\times 220,000$.

from an independent method is necessary before more can be said. The same applies to the globular substructure involving lipid. In this case, however, there is negative evidence that is probably significant.

The globular substructure under discussion is very prominent in the retinal rod outer segment (ROS) (3,12). The appearance of this globular substructure in the unit membranes of some ROS lamellae of the frog is illustrated by Fig. 37. The fact that the ROS lamellae showed this kind of substructure interested us a great deal because it offered an opportunity to determine if this pattern of organization is meaningful. The technical limitations to an interpretation of molecular

FIG. 35. Fragment of single lamella from a retinal rod photographed over a hole in a carbon film. The discs were prepared from frog retinal rods fixed with $KMnO_4$, disrupted ultrasonically, and deposited on the grid. $\times 228,000$.

FIG. 36. Fragment of a human red blood cell membrane fixed with $KMnO_4$ and disrupted ultrasonically. The fragment, which itself contains several small holes, lies over a hole in a carbon film. The micrograph is deliberately underfocused to accentuate the mosaic pattern. $\times 525,000$.

structure are so great that I do not believe one should depend on electron micrographs alone. Correlative evidence from some such source as X-ray diffraction or polarized light studies is needed to give independent information about the arrangement of molecules in structures if valid conclusions are to be drawn. The ROS is an obvious source for such correlations because polarized light studies and X-ray diffraction analysis may be done *in situ*. X-ray patterns were first obtained from fixed material embedded in methacrylate by Finean, Sjöstrand, and Steinman (6). The lamellar repeat in perch rods was 330 Å and corresponded to the repeat period detected in sections by electron microscopy. If there is any such microspherical arrangement in the lipid layers, we should be able to detect it by similar X-ray methods applied to fresh material.

I should like to demonstrate how we succeeded in obtaining X-ray patterns from fresh ROS's *in situ* (23). The diagram in Fig. 38 illustrates the method. If retinal rods are oriented as in the figure and a finely columnated X-ray beam is passed through them, reflections from the lamellae at small angles will produce spots on a photographic film along the direction of the rod axis. From the specimen-to-film distance one is able to extrapolate back and calculate the lamellar repeat. These spots or arcs will always be on the meridian in the arrangement shown. If there is a pattern of organization in the lamellae of the type shown in Fig. 34(g) (especially if there is protein between the lipid microspheres) a separate set of reflections in the equatorial direction will be obtained. The lamellar repeat should be in the range of 300–400 Å and would be rather difficult to detect. This lamellar repeat period is defined by Bragg's law, in which the periodic spacing, d, is given by the equation $d = n\lambda/2 \sin \theta$. Here n is any integer, λ is the wavelength of the X-rays, and θ is the angle between the diffracted and the undiffracted rays. The larger the spacing, the smaller the angle, and the smaller the angle, the more difficult it is to detect. This is due to the fact that it is difficult to separate the diffracted rays from the main beam if the photographic film is placed close to the specimen. If this difficulty is overcome by using a large specimen-to-film distance, the diffracted rays become very weak and prohibitively long exposure times must be used.

The spacing that would be produced by the lipid globular substructure under consideration is < 100 Å. The reflections, thus, would be further off axis and easier to detect than the lamellar repeat of ~300 Å. If the lamellar repeat in the meridianal direction can be detected, then reflections in the opposite direction, produced by

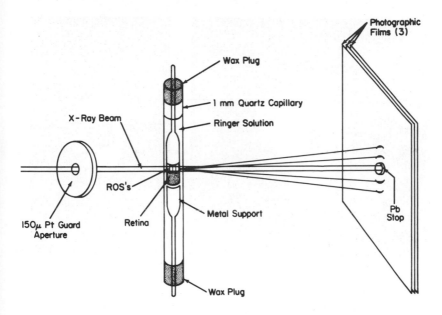

FIG. 38.   Diagram illustrating the method used to record X-ray diffraction patterns from retinal rods. The eyeball is transected under Ringer solution on a paraffin surface with a sharp razor blade, and a small piece of retina is removed. The pigment layer usually detachs spontaneously or is easily stripped off. A small piece of retina is then cut out with the tip of a broken razor blade edge. This is attached gently to the flat surface of a tapered metal rod (preferably platinum). The rod is slipped into a 1 mm quartz capillary tube filled with Ringer solution. Another tapered rod is slipped into the other end of the tube until it just contacts the ends of the rod outer segments (ROS). The tapered ends are sealed with dental wax (Kerrs' sticky wax). The X-ray beam comes from a Franks optically focusing X-ray camera and originates in a Jarrell-Ash (Hilger) microfocus X-ray generator. The beam is <100 μ in diameter. The ROS layer is ~ 40 μ thick for *Rana pipiens* and <80 μ thick for *Rana catesbeiana*. Hence, very little but the ROS layer interacts with the beam. The lead stop is supported by a thin mylar film and removes most of the central undiffracted beam. Three photographic films are used to obtain three exposures of decreasing intensity. This permits diffractions obscured by the central beam on the first film to be detected on the second or third film, as in Fig. 39(b).

globular substructure in the plane of the membranes, should appear on the equator. We have made such studies using a microfocus X-ray unit and a Franks focusing X-ray camera and have produced X-ray photographs showing the lamellar repeat not only in fixed material but also in fresh material. Figure 39 illustrates a pattern from a $KMnO_4$ fixed preparation, in acetone, in which the lamellar repeat

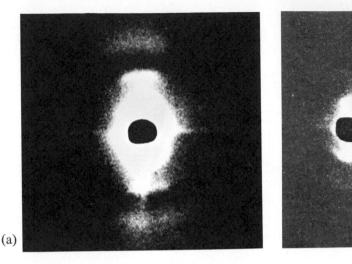

(a)   (b)

FIG. 39.   X-ray diffraction patterns from retina after $KMnO_4$ fixation and immer-
sion in acetone. (a) was recorded on the first film next to the specimen and is over-
exposed around the central beam. It shows the second and third orders of the
lamellar repeat. (b) was recorded on the next film and here the diffracted and parasitic
central rays have been sufficiently attenuated to allow the first-order diffraction spots
to be visible. × 17.5.

is clearly shown. There are three orders of the fundamental spacing of
~270 Å. There are no clear diffractions evident in the meridianal
direction.

The important objective was to obtain patterns from fresh rods *in
situ*. Figure 40(a) illustrates a pattern from such a preparation. This
was obtained after 13 hr of exposure at room temperature in Ringer
solution. Two orders of the lamellar repeat of 320 Å may be seen in
Fig. 40(a), although the second order is only faintly visible. It shows
clearly, however, in the microdensitometer tracing in Fig. 40(b).
We have obtained patterns from a number of other preparations of
retinal rods treated in the ways summarized in Table I. Some of the
results are presented graphically in Fig. 41. There is no indication of
regular ordered structure in the equatorial direction in any fresh
specimen and no indication of sufficient order to be compatible with
a micellar globular substructure of the lipid layers. This provides
strong support for our belief that the globular substructure represents
artifact (26). We now have evidence (25) that the apparent transverse
densities are due to overlap effects produced by slightly tangential
sectioning of the membrane. In the case of the granulo-fibrillar

TABLE I. *Preliminary Results of Small-Angle X-ray Diffraction Studies of Frog Retinal Rods*

	No.	Meridianal (Å)				Equatorial (Å)
Fresh ROS *in situ* (Ringer)	X58	320	155.5		40 (diffuse)	8.3 (diffuse weak spots)
	X72	556			32 (diffuse)	
	(specimen damaged)					
Fresh ROS-detached (Ringer)	X48	319	166			85 (diffuse weak ring)
KMnO$_4$ fixed ROS-detached (Ringer)	X53	284				
	X54	284				
		300				
KMnO$_4$ fixed *in situ* (H$_2$O)	X97	377				
	X42	380				
	X98	338				
	X43	350				
KMnO$_4$ fixed *in situ*, Pb and U stained (25% acetone)	X79	257	135			
KMnO$_4$ fixed *in situ*, Pb and U stained (75% acetone)	X82	268				
	X83	271				
KMnO$_4$ fixed *in situ* (100% acetone)	X65	302	155	95		81 (diffuse weak spots)
KMnO$_4$ fixed *in situ*, Pb and U stained (air dried from 100% acetone)	X102		104			
	X104		104	56		
	X106	205	108	70		62 (diffuse weak spots)
KMnO$_4$ fixed *in situ* (Araldite embedded)	X163	352	176			
Glutaraldehyde fixed[a] *in situ* (Ringer)	X137	374	183			
Acrolein-glutaraldehyde-OsO$_4$ fixed (Araldite embedded)	X153	274	246	137		

[a] *Rana catesbeiana.* All the other specimens are *Rana pipiens.*

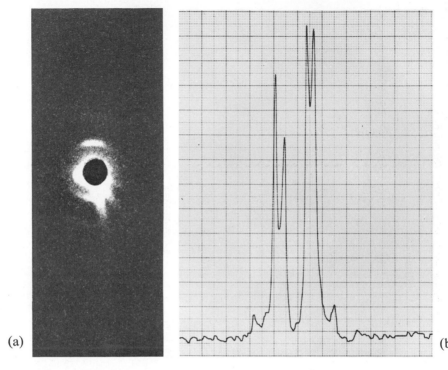

(a)   (b)

FIG. 40.   (a) Diffraction pattern from fresh retinal rods in Ringer solution *in situ*. The first order of the lamellar repeat is visible although it is partly obscured below by parasitic scatter around the central beam. The second-order diffraction is very faintly visible. × 17.5. (b) Microdensitometer tracing across the diffractions in (a). The first and second orders show up clearly.

substructure, we are less certain that artifact is involved since diffractions due to this kind of order would be much more difficult to detect.

In conclusion, I may state that we have good evidence supporting the concept of the smectic bilayer arrangement of the lipid core of the unit membrane. There is no need, at present, to revise the theory to allow for the kind of microspherical globular subunits discussed above. The granulo-fibrillar substructure seen by electron microscopy may be a derivative of real structure. However, here too there is no definite evidence. All that can be said with reasonable certainty is that the original unit membrane concept appears to remain valid as more tests are applied.

Lamellar Spacing in ROS Under Varying Conditions

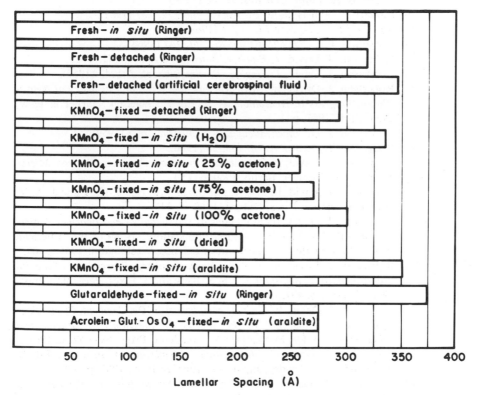

FIG. 41. Graphical representation of the first-order lamellar meridianal spacings after various treatments of rods *in situ*.

REFERENCES

1. Danielli, J. F., and Davson, H. A., *J. Cell Comp. Physiol.* 5, 495 (1935).
2. Elbers, P. F., *Recent Progress in Surface Science*, Ed. J. F. Danielli, K. G. A. Parkhurst, and A. C. Riddiford, Academic Press, New York, 1964, Vol. 2, p. 443.
3. Fernandez-Moran, H., *The Structure of the Eye*, Academic Press, New York, 1961.
4. Finean, J. B., *Biochemical Problems of Lipids*, Butterworths, London, 1956, p. 127.
5. Finean, J. B., and Burge, R. E., *J. Mol. Biol.* 7, 672 (1963).
6. Finean, J. B., Sjöstrand, F. S., and Steinman, E., *Exptl. Cell Res.* 5, 557 (1953).

7. Gasser, H. S., *J. Gen. Physiol. 38*, 709 (1955).
8. Gasser, H. S., *J. Gen. Physiol. 39*, 473 (1956).
9. Geren, B. B., *Exptl. Cell Res. 7*, 558 (1954).
10. Luzzati, V., and Husson, F., *J. Cell. Biol. 12*, 207 (1962).
11. Moody, M. F., *Science 142*, 1173 (1963).
12. Nilsson, S. E. G., *J. Ultrastruc. Res. 11*, 147 (1964).
13. Robertson, J. David, *J. Biophys. Biochem. Cytol. 1*, 271 (1955).
14. Robertson, J. David, *J. Biophys. Biochem. Cytol. 3*, 1043 (1957).
15. Robertson, J. David, In *Ultrastructure and Cellular Chemistry of Neural Tissue, Progress in Neurobiology, II*, Ed. H. Waelsch, Harper & Row, New York, 1957, p. 1.
16. Robertson, J. D., *Biochemical Soc. Symposia. 16*, 3 (1959).
17. Robertson, J. D., *J. Physiol. 153*, 58 (1960).
18. Robertson, J. David, In *Proc. Fourth Internat. Conf. on Electron Microscopy, 1958*, Springer, Berlin, 1960, p. 159.
19. Robertson, J. David, In *Progress in Biophysics*, Ed. B. Katz and J. A. V. Butler, Pergamon Press, Oxford, 1960, p. 343.
20. Robertson, J. David, In *Biophysics of Physiological and Pharmacological Action*, Ed. Abraham M. Shanes, Publication No. 69 of the American Association for the Advancement of Science, Washington, 1961, p. 63.
21. Robertson, J. David, In *Regional Neurochemistry, Proceedings of the 4th Neurochemical Symposium*, Ed. S. S. Kety and J. Elkes, Pergamon Press, Oxford, 1961, p. 497.
22. Robertson, J. David, In *Cellular Membranes in Development, Proceedings of the XXII Symposium of the Society for the Study of Development and Growth*, Ed. Dr. Michael Locke, Academic Press, New York, 1963.
23. Robertson, J. David, In *Intracellular Membraneous Structure*, Ed. S. Seno and E. V. Cowdry, Japan Soc. for Cell Biol., 1965, p. 379.
24. Robertson, J. David, *Ciba Foundation Symposium on Principles of Biomolecular Organization*, 1965, in press.
25. Robertson, J. David, In *Ciba Foundation Symposium on Principles of Biomolecular Organization*, 1965, in press.
26. Robertson, J. David, In *Nerve as a Tissue*, Ed. Kaare Rodahl, in press.
27. Schmitt, F. O., Bear, R. S., and Clark, G. L., *Radiology 25*, 131 (1935).
28. Schmidt, W. J., *Z. Zellforsch u. Mikr. Anat. 23*, 657 (1963b).
29. Schmitt, F. O., Bear, R. S., and Palmer, L. J., *J. Cell. Comp. Physiol. 18*, 31 (1941).
30. Sjöstrand, F. S., *Modern Scientific Aspects of Neurology*, Ed. J. N. Cumings, Edward Arnold, London, 1960, p. 188.
31. Sjöstrand, F. S., *J. Ultrastruc. Rec. Res. 9*, 340 (1963).
32. Stoeckenius, W., *J. Cell Biol. 12*, 221 (1962).

5

MOLECULAR BASIS OF MITOCHONDRIAL STRUCTURE AND FUNCTION

Albert L. Lehninger

For some years it has been known that the mitochondria are the site of the organized enzyme systems responsible for the Krebs tricarboxylic acid cycle and electron transport, and in particular, those energy-transforming reactions involved in oxidative phosphorylation. The designation of the mitochondria as the "power plant" of the aerobic cell is now familiar to all biologists. However, the horizons of research on the mitochondrion are now becoming much broader. The energy of foodstuff molecules is converted by the respiratory chain enzymes in the mitochondria not only into the chemical energy of adenosine triphosphate (ATP), but also into the osmotic energy required for active transport of certain ions, and into the mechanical energy which is involved in the structural changes in mitochondria during swelling and contraction phenomena. Moreover, very recent work shows that mitochondria rapidly replicate their complex structure in dividing cells and that they apparently have their own genetic apparatus. It is therefore clear that in the molecular and enzymatic organization of the mitochondrion we may have important clues to a number of the most important and intriguing problems in contemporary molecular biology.

DISTRIBUTION AND STRUCTURE

Mitochondria are found in all aerobic cells in the animal and plant worlds, except in the simpler bacteria, in which the protoplast membrane serves the same biochemical functions as the mitochondrial membrane. The numbers of mitochondria per cell vary enormously (25,32). In simple fungi such as yeasts, there are relatively few, as is also the case in sperm cells, some of which contain but 24 mitochondria. At the

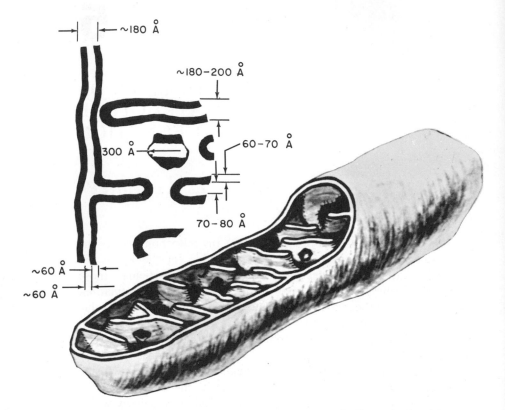

FIG. 1.   Schematic representation of the structure of a liver mitochondrion.

other extreme, the amoeba *Chaos chaos* has about 500,000 mitochondria. A rat liver cell has about 1,000 and a renal tubule cell perhaps 300. There is increasing evidence that each cell type normally contains a specific number of mitochondria, which is preserved by division of the mitochondria after the host cell divides. The recent work of Luck indicates that such division of the mitochrondria is nearly exact in *Neurospora crassa* (27).

Figure 1 shows the major elements of mitochondrial structure as revealed by electron microscopy. Although the outer and inner membranes appear to be identical after fixation with osmium tetroxide, and thus have been presumed to consist of "unit membranes," they do not appear so when examined with negative staining methods. Actually, there is some evidence that they are biochemically different; in all probability the inner membrane contains most if not all of the electron transport enzymes and phosphorylating enzymes (that is, the "respiratory assemblies"). Normally, the outer membrane is smooth, whereas the inner membrane undergoes puckering or invagination to form the internal membranous structures called *cristae mitochondriales*, which occur in widely different conformations in different cell types. Presumably the space between the outer and inner membranes contains organized protein layers, since the distance between the two dense osmium lines is remarkably constant in all types of mitochondria.

The intramitochondrial compartment contains the *matrix*. Liver mitochondria contain relatively few cristae, but a relatively large amount of matrix, as is seen in Fig. 1. On the other hand, muscle mitochondria contain many cristae, which fill the lumen nearly completely, but relatively little matrix. All mitochondria appear to contain so-called "dense granules" (Fig. 1). As will be seen later, they may be related to the capacity of mitchondria to accumulate various ions, particularly Ca^{++}, from the surrounding medium. Very recently, still another type of internal structure has been reported, namely fine filaments arranged in a helical structure in the matrix (29); they have been suggested to contain deoxyribonucleic acid (DNA).

Mitochondria vary widely in shape (25,32). In liver and kidney cells they are cylindrical in general form, but in muscle they may be slab-like. In fibroblasts, in which mitochondria are relatively free-swimming, they assume many different conformations, presumably by means of respiration-linked swelling-contraction activities. The mitochondrion can sometimes assume very complex configurations. For example, in the midpiece of some spermatozoa, the mitochondria are ribbon-like, and are wrapped helically around the motile fiber system of the tail, to yield a strategic juxtaposition of the ATP-forming mitochondrion with the ATP-utilizing contractile system of the tail.

LOCATION AND PROPORTIONS OF OXIDATIVE ENZYMES
IN THE MITOCHONDRIA

Some generalizations may be made concerning the internal location of the characteristic enzymes and enzyme systems of mitochondria. These have been deduced from analysis of the soluble and insoluble fractions that result when mitochondria are disrupted with detergents such as cholate or digitonin, or by physical methods such as sonic radiation. No matter how mitochondria are disrupted, the cytochromes and flavoproteins of the respiratory chains are exclusively found in the insoluble particles, which presumably derive from the membranes. In

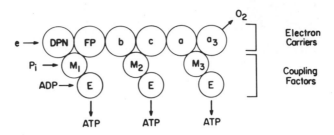

FIG. 2. Schematic representation of a respiratory assembly. It shows the electron carriers of the DPN-linked chain (including Coenzyme Q and cytochrome *c*, which are not indicated), as well as the coupling factors. The complete assembly also contains succinic dehydrogenase, as well as other membrane-linked enzymes associated with electron transport, such as the flavoprotein glycerophosphate dehydrogenase and possibly β-hydroxybutyrate dehydrogenase.

fact, such membrane fragments usually contain a complete complement of the enzymes necessary for electron transport. If they are carefully prepared under relatively mild circumstances, they also retain the capacity to couple phosphorylation of adenosine diphosphate (ADP) to electron transport.

On the other hand, most of the dehydrogenases and other enzymes of the Krebs tricarboxylic acid cycle are found in the soluble fraction, and for this reason are generally held to be present in the internal matrix of the mitochondrion, or possibly in the intermembrane space. However, it is most probable that many of the Krebs cycle enzymes are organized into complexes located near or on the cristae, but in such a manner that they are very easily detached when the mitochondria are disrupted. In fact, the enzymes required in the oxidation of pyruvate to acetyl-Coenzyme A are already known to exist in a well-defined supramolecular complex, the structure of which has been very nicely shown in recent work by Fernández-Morán and Reed (11).

There is another important line of evidence supporting a considerable degree of regularity in the molecular organization of the repiratory chain enzymes, as well as the Krebs cycle enzymes. Chance and Williams deduced from examination of the difference spectra of mitochondria that the flavoproteins and cytochromes exist in simple molar ratios to each other (5). Evidently the respiratory chains consist of a specific number of each type of cytochrome and flavoprotein, presumably juxtaposed in a specific sequence, in a so-called "respiratory assembly," which is schematized in Fig. 2. The proportions of the cytochromes to each other appear to be constant in mitochondria of many

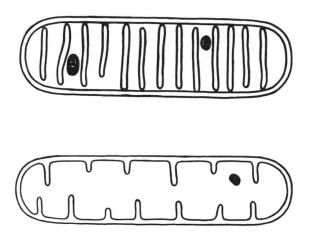

FIG. 3.   Conformation of cristae in mitochondria of rat liver (above) and kidney (below).

different cell types (45). In addition, Pette and Bücher have shown that certain enzymes of the Krebs cycle, as well as diphosphopyridine nucleo- tide (DPN) itself, also appear to occur in constant molar proportions to each other and to the cytochromes; these ratios are also constant in mitochondria from many types of cells (37). These important findings from Bücher's laboratory clearly suggest that the biosynthesis of mitochondrial enzymes is under operon control.

THE CRISTAE: VARIATIONS IN CONFORMATIONS AND SURFACE AREA

Since the cristae are made up of infoldings of the inner mitochon- drial membrane, which in turn contains the functionally active respiratory assemblies which are presumably disposed at regular intervals, it is instructive to consider the many variations in conformation and area of the cristae observed in mitochondria from different cell types (25,32). Liver mitochondria (Fig. 3), which respire relatively slowly, have a relatively small number of cristae compared to mitochondria of other cells, and the infoldings form an accordion-like pleated structure. On the other hand, kidney mitochondria, which respire more rapidly, contain a large number of disc-like cristae arranged like a stack of coins. Kidney mitochondria have cristal membranes, which only rarely appear to be continuous with the inner mitochondrial membrane. From

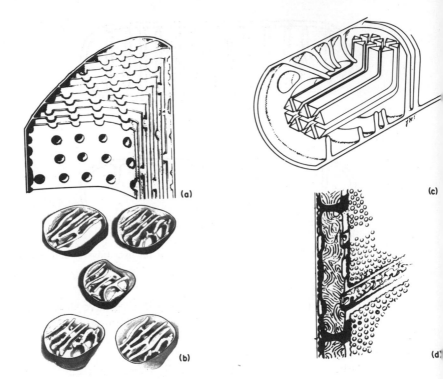

FIG. 4.   Conformation of cristae in mitochondria from different cells. (a) The mitochondria in flight muscle of blow-fly have sheet-like cristae with regular fenestrations. (b) Serial sections through mitochondrion of anterior horn cell show the tube-like cristae, with anastomoses. (c) The mitochondria of the cricothyroid muscle of bat have angular, prismatic conformation. (d) The mitochondria of flight muscle of dragonfly are slab-like and regularly packed among the myofibrils; the cristae are viliform. See text.

serial sections, however, it has been deduced that the cristae and the inner membrane are, in fact, continuous, but only through a rather narrow neck. In mitochondria of certain neurons, the cristae are tube-like, and frequently anastomose to form an irregular network, as shown in Fig. 4; in other types of neurons the cristae are longitudinal. Smith has shown that in mitochondria of the flight muscle of the dragonfly the inner membrane is invaginated to form thousands of microvilli, which vastly increase the surface of the inner membrane (46). On the other hand, he showed that in blow-fly mitochondria, the lumen is completely filled with regularly arranged, sheet-like cristae, each of which is perforated at regular intervals, so that the perforations are exactly aligned in the structure (47). These fenestrations may be adaptations to permit easy diffusion of oxygen, substrates, ATP, and phosphate throughout these rather large mitochondria. One can imagine that the diffusion process could be aided by swelling and shrinking cycles. Another peculiar arrangement of cristae has been observed by Fawcett and his colleagues (39) in mitochondria of the cricothyroid muscle; the cristae are folded in an extremely regular, prismatic arrangement, giving an almost crystalline appearance (Fig. 4).

The surface area of the cristae of mitochondria from different cell types appears to be related directly to intensity of respiratory activity. For example, the mitochondria of flight muscle of insects, which have extremely profuse and densely packed cristae, are capable of 20 times the rate of respiration of liver mitochondria, which have relatively few cristae. It is possible to make some first-order approximations of the relationships between the surface area of the cristae and the number of respiratory assemblies. In a single liver mitochondrion, the calculated surface area of the outer membrane is approximately 13 μ^2. The inner membrane of liver mitochondria has approximately three times this area, or about 39 μ^2. In a single liver mitochondrion, there are approximately 17,000 respiratory assemblies, as deduced from the cytochrome content. Thus, there are about 650 respiratory assemblies in each square micron of membrane surface; each respiratory assembly then is set in a patch of a little over 400 × 400 Å. Presumably the inner mitochondrial membrane has a standard pattern of construction, so that the respiratory assemblies and the basic molecular units of the membrane in which each assembly is organized have fixed dimensions. In fact, Bücher and his colleagues have shown that, in the embryological development of the mitochondria of locust flight muscle, an increase in the number of respiratory assemblies is accompanied by a corresponding increase in the area of the inner membrane (3).

OXIDATIVE PHOSPHORYLATION

The mechanism of oxidative phosphorylation, and its reconstruction from purified, well-defined enzymes, are the prime targets of the most fundamental work in mitochondrial biochemistry today. Solution of these problems will undoubtedly also solve the mechanism of active ion transport by mitochondria and the mechanochemical changes that accompany swelling-contraction cycles. Conversely, however, the latter activities can also be expected to illuminate approaches to the mechanism of oxidative phosphorylation, since all three modalities of energy

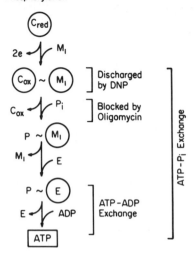

Interaction of Energized Carrier
and Coupling Factors in Oxidative
Phosphorylation

FIG. 5. A hypothesis for the reaction pattern of oxidative phosphorylation. This is the representation of Wadkins and Lehninger (cf. 25). The enzymes M and E are coupling factors. Enzyme E alone can catalyze the ATP-ADP exchange. The probable sites of action of dinitrophenol (DNP) and oligomycin are also shown.

coupling in electron transport appear to be brought about by the same set of enzyme molecules.

Nearly all workers agree (cf. 5,24,25) that the first step in respiratory energy conservation is the formation of high-energy complexes of three specific respiratory carriers in the chain, as a pair of electrons passes through each of these carriers (Figs. 2 and 5). These complexes are formed with so-called "coupling factors," designated as M in Fig. 5. These high-energy complexes (carrier $\sim$ M) are then believed to undergo an interaction with inorganic phosphate so that a high-energy phosphate derivative is formed with the coupling factor. In the final step, this phosphate group is believed to be transferred to ADP to bring about formation of ATP. It is probable that all the steps involved are reversible. There is now strong evidence that the first high-energy intermediate, now designated Carrier $\sim$ M, is discharged by the uncoupling agent 2,4-*dinitrophenol*, with the regeneration of the free components. On the other hand, the antibiotic *oligomycin* acts at a lower point; it blocks the covalent interaction of phosphate with the higher-energy intermediate. The action of these inhibitors are important landmarks (5,24,25).

Currently there is much work on the isolation, specificity, and molecular nature of the coupling factors. Green and his colleagues favor the concept that each of the three energy-conserving sites of the chain has one and only one specific coupling factor, which they designate Coupling Factors I, II, and III (54). On the other hand, other workers, including Racker (38), and our own group (24,25,52,53), feel that the matter is a little more complex than this. It appears more likely that the complete energy-coupling mechanism at each of the three sites consists of two or more coupling enzymes (such as M and E in Fig. 2), which presumably act in sequence. It is possible that one of these components, possibly the terminal phosphate-transferring enzyme E, that is responsible for making ATP, may be common to all three sites; the other factors, such as M_1, M_2, and M_3 in Figs. 2 and 5, may be specific for each of the three sites. These factors may also exist as molecular complexes, such as M_1E, M_2E, and M_3E; possibly they can be isolated as such and thus behave as single molecular entities.

The terminal step in oxidative phosphorylation, namely the transfer of phosphate to ADP (Fig. 5), appears to be brought about by an enzyme that catalyzes an ATP-ADP exchange reaction; considerable evidence for this step has been developed over the past six years by Wadkins and Lehninger (13,24,52,53). They have isolated this enzyme, purified it 300-fold to essential homogeneity, and found that it can restore phosphorylation at Site III in depleted mitochondria. Although the purified exchange enzyme is not inherently sensitive to dinitrophenol or oligomycin, it can be converted into an oligomycin- and dinitrophenol-sensitive form by adding it to suspensions of digitonin fragments of mitochondrial membranes (52). Evidently the exchange enzyme can recombine to form a specific complex, presumably with a preceding enzyme of the energy-coupling sequence.

The possibility that the ATP-ADP exchange enzyme catalyzes the terminal step of oxidative phosphorylation and is common to all three sites is confirmed by Green and his colleagues (54), who have found that their coupling factor for Site III contains ATP-ADP exchange activity, which is apparently inherent in the molecule. In addition, they have indicated that such exchange activity also exists in coupling factors I and II. Conceivably the ATP-ADP exchange reaction is a reflection of the terminal step common to all three sites, but that differences among the various coupling factors lie in the manner in which this enzyme is associated with the preceding protein component(s) acting in the complete energy-coupling chain.

Very recently, Glaze and Wadkins (13) have demonstrated that the highly purified ATP-ADP exchange enzyme of beef liver mitochondria

Complexes of Carriers and Coupling Factors

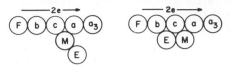

Possible Allosterism in C·E Complex

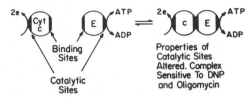

FIG. 6. Interaction of ATP-ADP exchange enzyme and reduced cytochrome c. Presumably the binding involves separate binding sites. At least one other factor, designated M, must participate with exchange enzymes and reduced cytochrome c in the complete coupling mechanism, which may involve a ternary complex.

forms a complex with reduced cytochrome c, which can be detected by kinetic analysis (Fig. 6). Oxidized cytochrome c (or other heme proteins) fails to yield such a complex. The most significant finding is that this complex is sensitive to both dinitrophenol and oligomycin, two of the most characteristic inhibitors of oxidative phosphorylation. These findings indicate that the binding sites for these two "hallmark" inhibitors of oxidative phosphorylation are contained in binary complexes of two highly purified proteins. These experiments also indicate that these two enzymes bind to each other at sites other than their catalytic sites. The binding of the two proteins causes characteristic alterations in the properties of the catalytic sites of each, and it therefore appears that the complex of exchange enzyme and reduced cytochrome c exhibits a type of allosterism, which may be called *structural allosterism*. Presumably a high-energy bond may be formed within such a complex, as work of Pinchot, Webster, and others has suggested (24,25). More recent work in our laboratory and elsewhere (20) suggests that a third factor may participate in the formation of this complex, which stabilizes it in such a manner that it is not readily dissociated (53). As shown in Fig. 6, the coupling factors may be grouped geometrically in a ternary complex with a carrier. Further work along these lines can be expected to reveal not only the mechanism of oxidative phosphorylation, but also the mechanism of mitochondrial ion transport and mechano-chemical energy coupling.

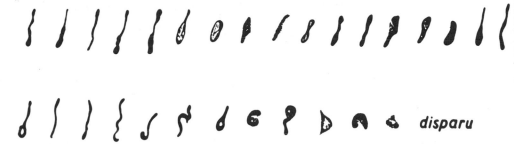

FIG. 7.   Changes in shape at 60-sec intervals in a single mitochondrion of a cultured fibroblast cell (Frederic, J., *Arch. Biol. (Liège) 69*, 167 (1958)).

MECHANOCHEMICAL ACTIVITIES: ACTIVE SWELLING AND CONTRACTION CYCLES IN MITOCHONDRIA

Beginning with the early experiments of Raaflaub in 1953, a large body of evidence has accumulated that high-energy intermediates generated in electron transport control reversible changes in the structure of the mitochondrion, in such a way that a transition between a swollen and shrunken state may be observed on allowing mitochondria to pass from one respiratory state to another (23,25). Phase contrast observation of mitochondria in living cells (25,32) indicates they undergo remarkable changes of shape and volume, which are associated with respiration (Fig. 7). Two major types of swelling-contraction cycles have been observed and are illustrated in Fig. 8. The so-called "low amplitude" cycles, which amount to less than a 1 or 2% change in volume, have been observed in all types of mitochondria tested *in vitro* (34,35). In this type of cycle, swelling of the mitochondria occurs, with a decrease in optical density, when ADP is lacking and the mitochondria are respiring in State 4, that is, at the resting rate. Swelling continues until ADP is added, and the mitochondria then contract, with an increase in optical density; concomitantly there is oxidative phosphorylation of the added ADP. Such low-amplitude cycles are completely reversible, and they may be repeated many times *in vitro* without damage to the mitochondria. These cycles may, however, be blocked or altered by addition of characteristic inhibitors and un-couplers of oxidative phosphorylation (34,35).

The other type of swelling-contraction cycle is the so-called "high-amplitude" cycle, in which the mitochondria may double or even quadruple in volume during the swelling phase and then contract again

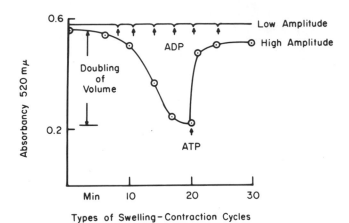

FIG. 8. Changes in optical density during low-amplitude and high-amplitude swelling-contraction cycles.

to approximately the original volume (Fig. 8). Such large volume changes occur under either *in vitro* or *in vivo* conditions. High-amplitude swelling and contraction have been observed in mitochondria of liver, kidney, and the fibroblast. However, mitochondria from heart and skeletal muscles show only limited capacity to undergo such high-amplitude cycles, and mitochondria of the brain show absolutely no ability to undergo high-amplitude cycles, although they can participate in low-amplitude cycles. Presumably the amplitude of the swelling-contraction cycles is in part determined by the physical conformation of the cristae. Liver mitochondria have an accordion-like structure and can easily expand, whereas brain mitochondria apparently have structural constraints which do not permit high-amplitude swelling. It is probable that high-amplitude swelling-contraction cycles are mechanistically similar or related to the low-amplitude cycles (13,25).

It is the high-amplitude cycles that have been most thoroughly studied *in vitro*. After our finding in 1955 that thyroxine is a profound mitochondrial swelling agent, it has been recognized that a number of specific, physiologically occurring substances can accelerate mitochondrial swelling (23,25). These include thyroxine, Ca^{++}, phosphate, certain sulfhydryl compounds such as glutathione and cysteine, certain disulfide compounds such as oxidized glutathione and the disulfide hormones insulin, oxytocin, and vasopressin, and, finally, certain higher fatty acids such as oleate. High-amplitude swelling will not occur anaerobically or in cyanide-poisoned systems; respiration is required in

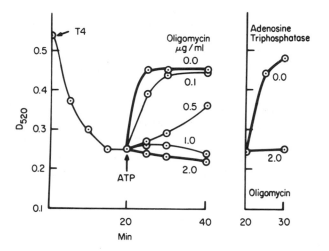

FIG. 9. Parallel inhibition of mitochondrial contraction and mitochondrial adenosine triphosphatase activity by oligomycin.

addition to a swelling agent. The contraction of such swollen mitochondria can be brought about either by reinstituting phosphorylating respiration by addition of ADP and a respiratory substrate, or, more simply, by adding ATP (21). ATP-linked contraction is a function of the activity of the respiratory chain and its coupling factors, since it is completely abolished by oligomycin and other true inhibitors of oxidative phosphorylation. There is a direct parallelism between the inhibition of mitochondrial contraction by oligomycin and the inhibition of the mitochondrial adenosine triphosphatase activity, as is shown in Fig. 9. High-amplitude swelling and contraction appears to be almost entirely a function of the membranes and its components. This deduction has been made from experiments with water-lysed mitochondria, so-called mitochondrial "ghosts." When these are washed free of matrix protein, they will still undergo contraction in the presence of ATP.

There is a remarkable resemblance in the properties of the adenosine triphosphatase activity of the mitochondrial membranes and the adenosine triphosphatase activity of the actomyosin contractile system of skeletal muscle, as shown in Table I. These systems not only engage in mechanochemical coupling, but also share a number of characteristic biochemical properties. Most striking are the common effects of 2,4-dinitrophenol, the bimodal sulfhydryl dependence, and the fact that both systems show a rather specific type of O^{18} exchange reaction between water of the medium and inorganic phosphate, which has not been observed in other phosphate-transferring enzyme systems. For these reasons, we postulated in 1959 (21) that the mitochondrial membrane may contain contractile protein systems analogous to the actomyosin system (23,25). Although this hypothesis appeared somewhat far-fetched at first, more recently some evidence has appeared to support this concept. Two years ago, Ohnishi reported the isolation of a protein similar to actomyosin from mitochondria (33). It showed the solubility, adenosine triphosphatase activity, viscosity changes on ATP addition, as well as the "super-precipitation" phenomenon that are characteristic of myosin from muscle. Some of their observations have been repeated in our laboratory and in Green's, although it is our experience that such contractile protein fractions are still relatively heterogeneous and require much further painstaking biochemical work before their identification can be accepted.

TABLE I.   *Similarities Between Coupling Enzymes of Oxidative Phosphorylation and Actomyosin System*

Mechanochemical properties
Adenosine triphosphatase activity shows "latency"
Adenosine triphosphatase activity stimulated by 2,4-dinitrophenol
Divalent cations required
Dissociable, multicomponent systems
Bimodal-SH dependence: latency and activity
Both show O^{18} exchange ($H_2O^{18} \rightleftharpoons P_i$)

Recently, Vignais and Vignais in our laboratory showed that such contractile protein preparations were active in stimulating the ATP-linked contraction of aged and swollen mitochondria. These experiments appeared to offer the first direct evidence that mitochondrial contractile protein had anything to do with the mechanochemical change during contraction. However, after further investigation, it was the surprising result that the contractile activity was not conferred by the protein part of the mitochondrial contractile protein preparation, but rather by a lipid component, namely phosphatidyl inositol (50,51). This lipid can specifically support the contraction of aged, swollen mitochondria in the presence of ATP. Many other highly purified phospholipids have been tested, but none show this activity; however, phosphatidyl inositol may be replaced by either palmitoyl CoA or palmitoyl carnitine. Fritz (12), Bremer (2), and others have shown that carnitine esters are apparently a transport form of fatty acids in mitochondria. Conceivably these lipids may be functioning as fatty acid acyl group donors in some essential reaction concerned with contraction. These findings do not necessarily exclude a functional role for mitochondrial contractile protein, but they do point up the fact that as yet there is no assay system available for assessing the imputed role of mitochondrial contractile proteins.

In addition to phosphatidyl inositol, two other substances have been identified as "contraction" factors, namely, catalase and gluta-thione peroxidase (30). Mitochondria swollen by reduced glutathione under certain conditions will not contract in the presence of ATP unless these enzymes are added (30).

Swelling-contraction cycles such as observed in mitochondria have also been observed to occur in isolated chloroplasts upon illumination, as shown by Packer and his colleagues (36). Similarly, isolated proto-plasts of certain bacteria have been known for some time to undergo swelling-contraction cycles, geared either to fermentation or to respiration. It appears that such mechanochemical cycles are characteristic of all membrane systems containing ATP-forming enzyme systems (23,25). The most obvious functions for such contractile processes is that they are concerned with water and solute transport in the intact cell, particularly in epithelial cells, in which the mitochondria lie in the axis of active transport mechanisms. But it is also possible that swelling and contraction are elements in cybernetic or feed-back devices for the integration of the rate of respiration with the ATP-ADP ratio in the cytoplasm. There is some presumptive evidence for such a role. It has been found that the permeability of the inner mitochondrial membrane increases greatly toward certain solutes when mitochondria undergo swelling, and decreases when they contract. The extremely high rates of respiration of flight muscle mitochondria are possible only because the membrane is relatively impermeable to Krebs cycle intermediates, which are tightly retained inside the mitochondrial structure. Presumably the ATP-ADP ratio determines the structural state and, thus, the per-meability of the membrane. Swelling-contraction cycles may thus represent a control mechanism operating in an oscillatory steady state (25).

ACTIVE ION TRANSPORT BY ISOLATED MITOCHONDRIA

It has been known since the work of Bartley and Davies in 1953 that isolated mitochondria of liver and kidney are capable of actively re-taining, or even accumulating from the medium, certain cations such as K^+ and Mg^{++}, as well as anions such as phosphate and sulfate, during respiration. However, until very recently, very little was known of the stoichiometric relationship between such ion retention or accumulation mechanisms and electron transport. Furthermore, there appeared to be no generally accepted hypothesis of the function of such active ion movements in mitochondria (23,25,26).

An entirely new approach to the significance of mitochondrial ion transport was made possible by the discovery of Vasington and Murphy in our department in 1961 (49), which was quickly confirmed in other laboratories (26). They showed that isolated kidney mitochondria may accumulate extremely large amounts of Ca^{++} from the suspending medium during respiration, in a process blocked by respiratory inhibitors such as cyanide and by uncoupling agents such as 2,4-dinitrophenol. Whereas the *net* accumulation of K^+ and Na^+ from the medium by respiring mitochondria is relatively limited and bears no simple relationship to the rate of respiration, possibly because of a high rate of back-diffusion, the uptake of Ca^{++} is relatively massive, with little back-diffusion, and is related to the amount of oxygen taken up. In addition, later work showed that phosphate of the medium is also accumulated by mitochondria when Ca^{++} is accumulated. The molar ratio of Ca^{++} and P_i accumulated within the mitochondria during active respiration was found to be about 1.67, which is exactly that of calcium hydroxyapatite (41). The amounts of Ca^{++} and phosphate that can be accumulated by respiring mitochondria are remarkably large, up to 3 μmoles of calcium phosphate per mg of mitochondrial protein, or almost 25% of the dry weight of the mitochondrion. The affinity for Ca^{++} is extremely high, with the result that extremely high ratios of internal to external Ca^{++} can be maintained during respiration (4,7). Sr^{++}, Ba^{++}, and Mn^{++} are also accumulated by mitochondria, presumably by action of the same system. All mitochondria examined to date, whatever the cell type from which they were isolated, possess the same active ion transport capacity (26,41).

Experiments on mitochondria massively loaded with Ca^{++} have revealed that they have a much higher specific gravity than normal unloaded mitochondria, as might be expected. Data in Fig. 10 show that after Ca^{++} loading, mitochondria may be separated from normal mitochondria by isopycnic centrifugation in a density gradient of sucrose or cesium chloride (15). Figure 11 shows an electron micrograph of fully loaded mitochondria after osmium fixation, demonstrating the large electron-dense patches corresponding to granules of calcium phosphate. Such granules are observed not only in osmium-fixed, but also in aldehyde-fixed mitochondria, as well as in mitochondria simply dried in the absence of fixative (15). Although the deposits have the

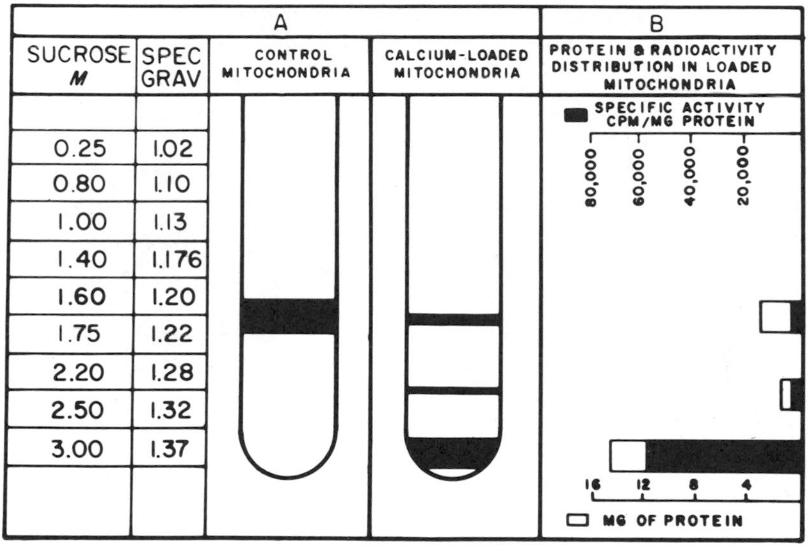

FIG. 10.   Separation of Ca^{++}-loaded rat liver mitochondria from normal mito-chondria in a density gradient of sucrose.

Ca/P ratio of hydroxyapatite, they are not crystalline, as determined by X-ray or electron diffraction methods (15). They therefore resemble the pre-apatite stage which occurs in early stages of calcification of bone and enamel. There is some evidence (26) that these granules arise from the normal "dense granules" of mitochondria (Fig. 1) by accretion of Ca^{++} and phosphate.

Later we showed that there is a direct and exact relationship between the molar amounts of Ca^{++} and phosphate accumulated by mitochondria with the number of electrons passing through each of the three energy-conserving sites of the respiratory chains; this relationship may be as precisely measured as the P:O ratio of oxidative phosphorylation (41). These results are schematized in Fig. 12, which shows that as each pair of electrons passes each of the three energy-conserving sites in the respiratory chain, 1.67 molecules of Ca^{++} and 1.0 molecule of phosphate are removed from the surrounding medium and caused to accumulate in the mitochondrion. Actually, the energy-linked accumulation of Ca^{++} and phosphate by mitochondria is a process that is alternative to oxidative phosphorylation. It has long been known that Ca^{++} is an uncoupling agent and prevents the formation of ATP; quite simply, Ca^{++} replaces ADP somewhere in the normal process of

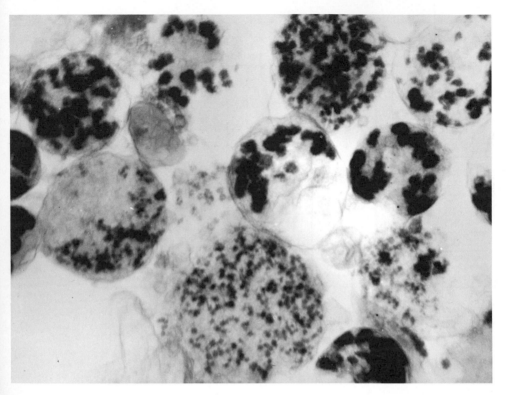

FIG. 11. Electron micrograph of rat liver mitochondria loaded with Ca^{++} and phosphate, showing sites of amorphous granules (fixed in osmium tetroxide).

oxidative phosphorylation and instead of ATP being produced, calcium phosphate is accumulated.

When mitochondria are exposed to much smaller concentrations of Ca^{++} in the suspending medium, some new stoichiometric relations emerge (42). In Fig. 13, it is seen that when mitochondria are slowly respiring in State 4, that is, in the absence of ADP, and if a known amount of Ca^{++} ions is added, there is an immediate stimulation of respiration and then the rate of respiration abruptly returns to the original resting level. On analysis of the Ca^{++} content of the medium, we find that virtually all of the Ca^{++} added to the suspension has been accumulated, exactly at the time when the rate of respiration has declined to the original resting level. Several such cycles may be repeated showing that the accumulation of small amounts of Ca^{++} has not altered or damaged respiratory control in the mitochondria. About 1.7 molecules of Ca^{++}

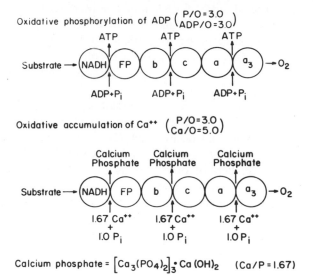

FIG. 12. Diagram showing stoichiometry of oxidative phosphorylation and oxidative accumulation of Ca^{++} and phosphate; these are alternative processes.

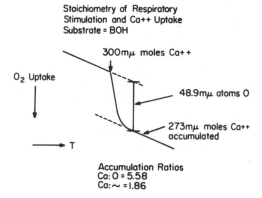

FIG. 13. Stoichiometry of cyclic respiratory stimulation and accumulation of Ca^{++}. After return of the oxygen uptake to the resting rate, the accumulated Ca^{++} is retained by the mitochondria in a dynamic steady state.

are required to activate each energy-conserving site and allow it to transfer electrons so that oxygen uptake may ensue; concomitantly the Ca^{++} is accumulated. After Ca^{++} is accumulated in such a reversible cycle, it exists in a steady state in the mitochondria, in which the internal concentration of Ca^{++} may be several thousand times the external concentration. The affinity of such intact mitochondria for Ca^{++} is extremely high, since no more than approximately $1 \times 10^{-6}M$ Ca^{++} ions remain in the suspending medium in such a steady state. This steady state is characterized by a passive efflux of Ca^{++} from the mitochondria, counterbalanced by an active accumulation coupled to the resting respiration (9).

These recent studies on Ca^{++} accumulation by mitochondria have also shed some light on the active movements of protons and of K^+ and Na^+ ions in mitochondria. For each Ca^{++} ion accumulated by the mitochondria, approximately one H^+ ion is extruded (42,43). We have examined the movements of other anions and cations for clues as to coupling of ion movements. These recent studies suggest that K^+ moves out of mitochondria along with H^+, as Ca^{++} moves in. Such ion movements in mitochondria are not sensitive to ouabain (26).

The question may be raised as to the biological significance of ion movements in mitochondria. Actually, ion movements are an obligatory and normal event in oxidative phosphorylation, since there is a net removal of H^+ ions from the medium as ADP is phosphorylated to ATP (25). It also appears quite possible that mitochondria, during the course of their morphological evolution, have acquired the ability to maintain their own internal ionic composition constant for maximal or optimal function of their enzyme systems, in the face of local fluctuations in the cytoplasmic environment. Mitochondria may also participate in regulating the concentration of ionic Ca^{++} in the cytoplasm, in relationship not only to excitation and relaxation of contractile fibers, but also to calcification and decalcification processes. Recent electron microscopic investigations have shown that the mitochondria of osteoclasts in higher animals may contain dense granules of what appear to be calcium phosphate (14), indicating that in such specialized cells, mitochondria have the ability to store accumulations of calcium and phosphate temporarily.

BIOGENESIS OF MITOCHONDRIA: NUCLEIC ACIDS AND PROTEIN SYNTHESIS

Very recent developments in several laboratories indicate that mitochondria are capable of the biosynthesis of some of their important macromolecular constituents, including proteins, and that they may contain an independent genetic apparatus. Isolated mitochondria are capable of causing the energy-linked incorporation of radioactive amino acids into insoluble membrane proteins (19,40,48). It appears very significant, however, that no incorporation into specific mitochondrial enzymes such as catalase and cytochrome *c* has been observed (40,48). Mitochondrial protein synthesis is inhibited by puromycin and exhibits other features of ribosomal protein synthesis.

Perhaps the most significant recent development has been the finding that amino acid incorporation into mitochondrial protein is dependent on a whole chain of reactions starting from DNA. In brief it has been found that protein synthesis in mitochondria is inhibited under appropriate conditions not only by puromycin, but also by actinomycin D, a specific inhibitor of DNA-dependent synthesis of messenger RNA (mRNA) (18,19). The implication is that mitochondrial DNA directs the synthesis of a mitochondrial form of mRNA, which in turn presumably codes the synthesis of mitochondrial structural proteins. Because of the possibility that mitochondrial preparations are contaminated with nuclear DNA, as well as microsomal RNA, such conclusions must of course be regarded with some skepticism. However, four groups of investigators, headed by Kalf (18), Luck (28), Neubert (31), and Wintersberger (55), have shown that mitochondria do in fact possess an actinomycin-sensitive DNA-dependent RNA-polymerase. Kalf (18) and Luck and Reich (28) have shown that mitochondria possess a distinctive kind of DNA, which can easily be differentiated from nuclear DNA by density gradient centrifugation; such mitochondrial DNA differs in molecular weight and in base composition from the nuclear DNA of the same cell. This type of DNA within the mitochondrial structure is a fairly large molecule capable of coding many proteins. There has been no successful demonstration to date that an artificial mRNA, such as poly U, can direct the incorporation of radioactive amino acids into mitochondrial proteins, but it seems almost a certainty that such a demonstration will soon be forthcoming. Although mitochondria of higher animals and plants do not appear to contain recognizable ribosomes, Luck and Reich have detected what appear to be ribosomes in the mitochondria of *N. Crassa* (28).

These recent findings are of the most fundamental biological importance, since they represent a direct demonstration of a cytoplasmic or satellite genetic system, which may be capable of operating independently of nuclear DNA. Presumably they relate to the division and replication of mitochondria, which may proceed at very high rates; in *Neurospora*, Luck has shown that mitochondrial replication may be complete in much less than an hour (27). These findings may also provide an important key to testing the validity of the old hypothesis that mitochondria originated for microorganisms, which parasitized the host cell and evolved into true symbionts (25).

STRUCTURE OF THE MITOCHONDRIAL MEMBRANE AND THE RESPIRATORY ASSEMBLIES

The earliest hypotheses on the structure of the mitochondrial membranes were proposed by Sjöstrand and by Palade in the light of the "unit membrane" hypothesis elaborated by Robertson. They suggested that each of the mitochondrial membranes consists of a phospholipid bilayer, coated on each side by a monolayer of protein molecules (25). Such a representation is consistent with the dimensions of the electron-dense bands seen after osmium or potassium permanganate fixation, with the known dimensions of phospholipid bilayers, and with the diameters of most globular proteins. The occurrence of a phospholipid bilayer in the mitochondrial membranes is also consistent with the high electrical resistance and capacitance of these structures (25). The recent work of Thompson and his colleagues on the electrical properties of reconstructed phospholipid bilayers, showing they are almost identical with those of natural membranes (17), further substantiates the occurrence of a continuous lipid phase. It appears to be most difficult to dismiss such evidence in favor of hypotheses involving globular lipid micelles in a noncontinuous phase, which would not be expected to have a high electrical resistance.

Green and his colleagues have provided evidence that a large fraction of mitochondrial membrane protein is made up of a recurring, insoluble protein called structural protein, which readily polymerizes and forms complexes with phospholipids and with electron carriers (8). Possibly structural protein molecules coat either side of the phospholipid bilayer, as is suggested in Fig. 14.

There is much interest now in the molecular nature of the respiratory assemblies and how they are attached to the mitochondrial membranes. In 1957, the author postulated a very simple structure for the respiratory assemblies of mitochondria in terms of the unit membrane hypothesis (22). It is given in Fig. 14. In this representation it was assumed that the protein coats of the mitochondrial membrane consisted of recurring protein molecules, perhaps the "structural protein" of Green and his colleagues. At specific intervals, these structural protein molecules were assumed to be replaced by a complete set of respiratory enzyme molecules in the plane of the membrane, as indicated in Fig. 14. In this representation, the respiratory assembly thus is *part* of the membrane structure. Even today this planar arrangement is not without some theoretical support, since it provides the possibility for the asymmetric orientation of the enzyme molecules so as to permit the vectorial or

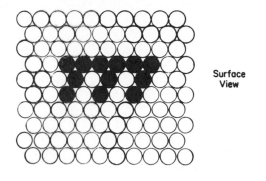

Surface
View

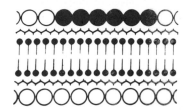

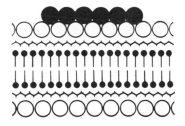

Edge Views

FIG. 14.   Schematic representation of membrane structure and respiratory assemblies in terms of "unit membrane" hypothesis. At lower left, the assembly is pictured as being in, and thus a part of, the membrane. At lower right, it is pictured as being attached laterally to the membrane.

directional action of their respective active sites. That these assemblies are more or less regularly spaced was deduced from early findings that the ratio of electron transport activity to dry weight in membrane fragments was found to be constant, regardless of the size of the fragments.

A variation of this hypothesis was later presented in which the respiratory assembly was not part of the structural protein monolayer, but rather was attached to it in a lateral manner (Fig. 14). This hypothesis has the advantage that a sheet of continuous and uniform membrane structure could be biosynthesized without the necessity of any special templates for assembly of the enzyme components of the respiratory chain. Such assemblies could be put together independently and then added to the finished membrane later, during the course of mitochondrial biosynthesis.

Although there is no specific morphological or biochemical evidence that completely excludes either of the above representations, more recent work has suggested an alternative geometrical organization of respiratory

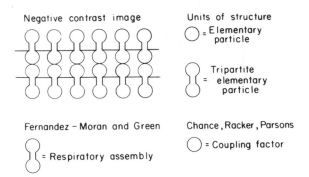

FIG. 15. Schematic representation of negative contrast image of mitochondrial inner membrane, after Fernández-Morán (10) and Smith (47). The elementary particles are attached by a stalk to a second, somewhat smaller particle located in the membrane core. Green and Fernández-Morán postulate the dumbbell structure is a respiratory assembly, whereas Racker, Chance, and Parsons postulate the elementary particles are coupling factors.

assemblies in the mitochondrial membrane. Fernández-Morán, confirmed by many other investigators since, has shown that negative staining of unfixed mitochondria by phosphotungstate yields images suggesting the occurrence of many globular particles (called "elementary particles") of about 70–90 Å diameter (cf. Fig. 15) attached by a stalk to the membrane (10). This arrangement is seen only in the interior mitochondrial membranes and not in the outer. It was postulated by Green and his colleagues that the "elementary particles" consist of a complete set of respiratory enzymes, on the basis of the fact that respiratory particles of a somewhat similar structure, but larger size, can be isolated from pretreated heart mitochondria (1). Unfortunately, the discrepancy in size between the "native" elementary particle and the isolated particles does not permit an unequivocal demonstration of the identity of these particles. The elementary particles of the intact membrane as visualized in the electron microscope have a calculated particle weight of no more than about 400,000, whereas a complete respiratory assembly requires a particle weight of about 1,400,000 (47). Other investigations by Smith (47) have revealed that the negative contrast image of the mitochondrial membrane contains considerable fine structure, as is shown in Fig. 15. More recently, Green and his colleagues consider that the true "elementary particle" is tripartite, and consists not only of the single particle, but also the corresponding stalk and complementary particle in the core of the membrane. Although this view reconciles in part the discrepancy with regard to the particle weight, there is still no proof of this suggestion. More recently an alternative view as to the nature of these "elementary particles" has been put forward by Chance, Racker, and Parsons (6). They have postulated that the elementary particles are not complete sets of respiratory chain enzymes, but rather clusters of coupling factors required for coupling phosphorylation to respiration. They have brought forth a number of interesting pieces of evidence in support of this view. Nevertheless, despite the rather specific hypotheses proposed for the function of the "elementary particles," there is as yet no complete certainty that the elementary particles are not an artifact of phosphotungstate staining. Furthermore, it is perhaps somewhat embarrassing that such particles have also been seen in other types of membranes not known to contain cytochrome systems. Nevertheless, these hypotheses have heuristic value in evolving a molecular picture of the construction of respiratory assemblies and membranes, and have stimulated much thought and research. Whatever the conformation of the respiratory assembly, it must not only be able to account for the molecular interactions between successive electron carriers and for the formation of ATP, but it must also account for the vectorial or directional aspects of mitochondrial ion transport, as well as of the swelling-contraction cycles, which are evidently also driven by the respiratory assemblies.

Finally, it must be pointed out that the molecular structure of such respiratory assemblies must be considered in the light of recent advances in the biochemistry of the operon and of genetic repression. For this reason, recent investigations on the biogenesis of electron carriers and mitochondrial structure in glucose-repressed yeast or in dividing *Neurospora* cells (16,27,44), may be of the greatest value in elucidating the molecular basis of the morphogenesis of mitochondria.

Thus, we see that the mitochondrion, once considered to be merely a convenient package for the enzymes of respiration and phosphorylation, can now be looked on as a biological microcosm, one which embraces many of the most fundamental problems cell biologists face today. We can therefore expect the mitochondrion to become an even more exciting arena of research in molecular biology in the coming years.

Figures 1, 3, 4(c), and 11 are reproduced from Lehninger, A. L., *The Mitochondrion*, W. A. Benjamin, Inc., New York, 1964. Figure 4(b) is reproduced from Anderssen-Cedergren, E., *J. Ultra Structure Res.*, Supp. 1, 124 (1959). Figure 4(d) is reproduced by permission of The Rockefeller University Press from *The Journal of Biophysical and Biochemical Cytology*, *11*, 119 (1961).

REFERENCES

1. Blair, P. V., Oda, T., Green, D. E., and Fernández-Morán, H., *Biochemistry 2*, 756 (1963).
2. Bremer, Jon, *J. Biol. Chem. 238*, 2774 (1963).
3. Brosemer, R. W., Vogell, W., and Bücher, T., *Biochem. Z. 338*, 854 (1963).
4. Carafoli, E., Weiland, S., and Lehninger, A. L., *Biochim. Biophys. Acta*, In press.
5. Chance, B., and Williams, G. R., *Adv. Enzymolygy 17*, 65 (1956).
6. Chance, Britton, *VIth Int. Congress Biochem.* Abstracts, p. 617 (1964).
7. Chappell, J. B., Cohn, M., and Greville, G. D., In *Energy-linked functions of mitochondria*, Ed. B. Chance, Academic Press, New York, 1963, p. 219.
8. Criddle, Robert S., Bock, Robert M., Green, David E., and Tisdale, Howard, *Biochemistry 1*, 827 (1962).
9. Drahota, Z., Carafoli, E., Rossi, C. S., Gamble, R. L., and Lehninger, A. L., *J. Biol. Chem.* In press.
10. Fernández-Morán, H., Oda, T., Blair, P. V., and Green, D. E., *J. Cell. Biol. 22*, 63 (1964).
11. Fernández-Morán, H., Reed, L. J., Koike, M., and Williams, C. R., *Science 145*, 930 (1964).
12. Fritz, Irving, B., Schultz, Suzzanne K., and Srere, Paul A., *J. Biol. Chem. 238*, 2509 (1963).
13. Glaze, Robert P., and Wadkins, Charles L., *Biochem. Biophys. Research Commun. 15*, 194 (1964).
14. Gonzales, Federico, and Karnovsky, Morris J., *J. Biophys. Biochem. Cytol. 9*, 299 (1961).
15. Greenawalt, John W., Rossi, Carlo S., and Lehninger, Albert L., *J. Cell Biol. 23*, 21 (1964).
16. Hall, David O., and Greenawalt, John W., *Biochem. Biophys. Research Commun. 17*, 565 (1964).
17. Huang, C., Wheeldon, L., and Thompson, T. E., *J. Mol. Biol. 8*, 148 (1964).
18. Kalf, George F., *Biochemistry 3*, 1702 (1964).
19. Kroon, A. M., *Biochim. Biophys. Acta 91*, 145 (1964).
20. Laturaze, L., and Vignais, P. V., *Biochim. Biophys. Acta 71*, 124 (1964).
21. Lehninger, Albert L., *J. Biol. Chem. 234*, 2187 (1959).
22. Lehninger, Albert L., *Rev. Mod. Physics 31*, 136 (1959).
23. Lehninger, Albert L., *Physiol. Rev. 42*, 467 (1962).
24. Lehninger, Albert L., and Wadkins, Charles L., *Ann. Rev. Biochem. 31*, 47 (1962).
25. Lehninger, Albert L., *The mitochondrion: Molecular basis of structure and function*, W. A. Benjamin, Inc., New York, 1964.
26. Lehninger, A. L., Carafoli, E., and Rossi, C. S., *Biological Reviews*, Camb. Philosoph. Soc. To be submitted.

27. Luck, David J. L., *J. Cell Biol. 16*, 483 (1963).
28. Luck, David J. L., and Reich, E., *Proc. Natl. Acad. Sci. U.S. 52*, 931 (1964).
29. Nass, Margaret M. K., and Nass, Sylvan, *J. Cell Biol. 19*, 593 (1963).
30. Neubert, Diether, Wojtczak, Anna B., and Lehninger, Albert L., *Proc. Natl. Acad. Sci. U.S. 48*, 1651 (1962).
31. Neubert, Diether, and Helge, Hans, *Biochem. Biophys. Research Commun.* In press.
32. Novikoff, Alex B., In *The Cell*, Ed. J. Brachet and A. E. Mirsky, Academic Press, New York, Vol. 2, 1961, p. 299.
33. Ohnishi, T., and Ohnishi, T., *J. Biochem. (Tokyo) 51*, 380 (1962).
34. Packer, Lester, *J. Biol. Chem. 235*, 242 (1960).
35. Packer, Lester, *J. Biol. Chem. 236*, 214 (1961).
36. Packer, Lester, and Marchant, Reginald H., *J. Biol. Chem. 239*, 2061 (1964).
37. Pette, D., and Bücher, T., *Z. Physiol. Chem. 331*, 180 (1963).
38. Racker, Efraim, and Conover, Thomas E., *Fed. Proc. 22*, 1088 (1963).
39. Revel, Jean P., Fawcett, Donald W., and Philpott, C. W., *J. Cell Biol. 16*, 187 (1963).
40. Roodyn, D. B., Reis, P. J., and Work, T. S., *Biochem. J. 80*, 9 (1961).
41. Rossi, Carlo Stefano, and Lehninger, Albert L., *Biochem. Z. 338*, 698 (1963).
42. Rossi, Carlo S., and Lehninger, Albert L., *J. Biol. Chem. 239*, 3971 (1964).
43. Saris, Nils-Erik, *Soc. Scient. Fenn. 28*, 1 (1963).
44. Schatz, Gottfried, *Biochem. Biophys. Research Commun. 12*, 448 (1963).
45. Schollmeyer, Peter, and Klingenberg, Martin, *Biochem Z. 335*, 426 (1962).
46. Smith, David S., *J. Biophys. Biochem. Cytol. 11*, 119 (1961).
47. Smith, David S., *J. Cell Biol. 19*, 115 (1963).
48. Truman, D. E. S., and Korner, A., *Biochem. J. 83*, 588 (1962).
49. Vasington, Frank D., and Murphy, Jerome V., *J. Biol. Chem. 237*, 2670 (1962).
50. Vignais, Paulette M., Vignais, Pierre V., and Lehninger, Albert L., *J. Biol. Chem. 239*, 2011 (1964).
51. Vignais, Pierre V., Vignais, Paulette M., and Lehninger, Albert L., *J. Biol. Chem. 239*, 2002 (1964).
52. Wadkins, Charles L., and Lehninger, Albert L., *Fed. Proc. 22*, 1092 (1963).
53. Wadkins, Charles L., and Glaze, Robert P., *Canadian J. Biochem.* In press.
54. Webster, George, and Green, David E., *Proc. Natl. Acad. Sci. U.S. 52*, 1170 (1964).
55. Wintersberger, E., *Z. Physiol. Chem. 336*, 285 (1964).

6

THE ORGANIZATION AND DEVELOPMENT OF CHLOROPLASTS

Lawrence Bogorad

The maize chloroplast of which a cross section is shown in Fig. 1 carried on photosynthesis. Before the leaf cell it occupied was prepared for examination with the electron microscope, this plastid produced carbohydrates and oxygen from light, carbon dioxide, and water. The principal objective of the following discussion is to determine how far current evidence permits us to associate certain segments of the photochemistry and biochemistry of photosynthesis with specific parts of the chloroplast. This obviously involves examining some current experimental approaches to this problem.

Another function of immature plastids is to grow up—current knowledge of the course and control of development of plastids in higher plants is described not only because of the intrinsic interest of the metabolism of subcellular organelles, but also for whatever insight such a discussion may provide about the nature of the photosynthetic apparatus.

It has been clear since the work of Ingen-Housz in the 18th century that photosynthetic activity is associated with the green parts of plants. Chlorophylls, the green compounds, are localized in chloroplasts in all photosynthetic organisms except blue-green algae and photoautotrophic bacteria.

Some photosynthetically active chloroplasts contain chlorophyll, but may not be green. Brown or yellow plastids occur in algal groups in which certain carotenoids are present in concentrations high enough to mask the chlorophyll. In chloroplasts of red algae large amounts of the bile pigment-protein phycoerythrin conceal chlorophyll *a*. In addition to these and other nongreen but photosynthetically active

The author is Research Career Awardee of the National Institute of General Medical Sciences, U.S.P.H.S.

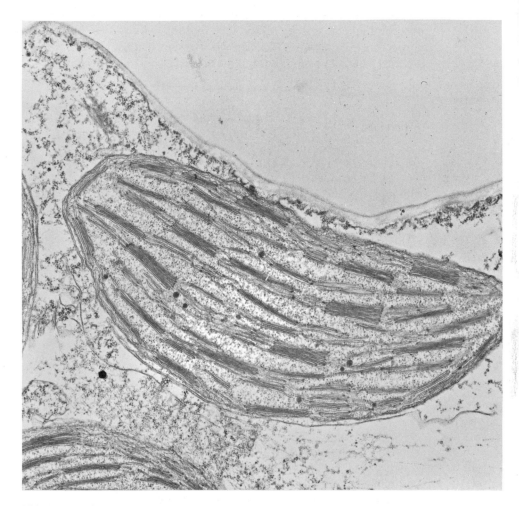

FIG. 1.   An electron micrograph of a section through a mature chloroplast in a maize leaf. Sack-like structures (thylakoids) occur in layered groups (grana), but some thylakoids extend between grana. (Reproduced through the courtesy of Dr. Ann Jacobson.)

chloroplasts, some plants or plant parts contain colored plastids, which do not carry on photosynthesis. Chromoplasts in ripe tomato fruits and in carrot roots lack chlorophyll, but contain carotenoids. Leucoplasts are colorless plastids frequently specialized for starch or oil storage. These various types of plastids within a single species or a single organism are probably genetically and metabolically related; there are instances, such as the ripening of a tomato fruit, in which one can observe the conversion of a green chloroplast into a red-orange chromoplast from which chlorophyll is absent. Such interrelationships are extremely interesting, but will not be explored further here.

THE GROSS ANATOMY OF CHLOROPLAST STRUCTURE AND FUNCTION

Some algal cells contain a single plastid. The cup-shaped chloroplast of *Chlamydomonas* is almost as large as the entire cell; the familiar ribbon-shaped plastid of *Spirogyra* twists from end to end of each cell. At the other extreme in numbers are the 40 or so disc-shaped chloroplasts found in each palisade cell in the leaves of some species of higher plants; each of these plastids is the size of some entire algal cells, that is, 5–10 μ in diameter by 2–3 μ in thickness.

The observation that the greenness of leaf cells is "particulate" tells us that chloroplasts have outer limits, but additional details are discernible with the light microscope. Some plastids are not homogeneous, but appear to contain granules dispersed throughout a matrix or *stroma*. These granules were termed *grana* by Meyer who first observed them in 1883.

Intact chloroplasts can be obtained by grinding leaves in buffered isotonic sucrose (about 0.5 M); enrichment of plastids can be achieved by differential centrifugation of the homogenate (38,62). Relatively low centrifugal fields, about 500 to 1000g, are required to sediment intact chloroplasts of higher plants. Plastids isolated in sucrose are easily broken by treatment with distilled water, thus clearly demonstrating that the outside membrane of a chloroplast is osmotically active and not infinitely elastic.

Once it became possible to isolate chloroplasts, analyses of their components were undertaken. It would seem that the establishment of a precise empirical formula for chloroplasts, in terms of fats, proteins, and so on, could easily be achieved, but, in fact, values obtained by different investigators studying a single species sometimes show great variation. The differences are attributable, at least in part, to contamination of chloroplast preparations by other cell constituents or to loss of materials from plastids during isolation. There are gradations between whole chloroplasts and broken ones—they leak. The amounts and kinds of materials which leave the plastids because of leakage depend upon the isolation and purification procedures used. Despite these difficulties, Arnon and his collaborators (6) and many others after them have isolated chloroplasts in good enough condition to do photosynthesis.

Menke and Menke (65) found that chloroplasts of spinach and several other plants contain about 70–80 % water. Some assays for other components of spinach chloroplasts by Chibnall (23) and by Menke (62) are shown in Table I. The differences in composition of the chloroplast

TABLE I.   *The Composition of Spinach Chloroplasts and Cytoplasm*

	Chibnall (1939)		Menke (1938)	
	Chloroplasts	Cytoplasm	Chloroplasts	Cytoplasm
Protein (%)	39.6	96.5	48.0	85.0
Lipoids[a] (%)	25.1	1.9	37.0	0.7
Residue (%)	16.9	1.6	7.0	11.0
Ash (%)	18.4	—	8.0	3.0

[a] All compounds soluble in ether or ether-alcohol.

preparations obtained in these two laboratories illustrate the difficulties of isolating plastids without losing any of their components. On the other hand, much more striking than the variations in the values for the composition of the two chloroplast fractions are the differences, shown clearly in both cases, between the compositions of chloroplasts and cytoplasm. The ratio of protein to lipid is almost 3:2 in chloroplasts, but about 50:1 to 90:1 in the cytoplasm.

The distribution of some substances within the chloroplast can be demonstrated in a very simple way. If green plastids obtained by centrifuging a cell-free homogenate at about 1000g are treated with distilled water, green particles can be obtained only after centrifugation in very much higher fields, that is, 5000g or higher. This simple experiment indicates that the greenness of the chloroplast is associated with particulate material smaller than plastids themselves, but still comparatively large in size. This green sediment, which will be discussed in greater detail later, contains about equal amounts of protein and lipoidal materials.

When isolated plastids are spread on an electron microscope grid, dried, and shadowed with a heavy metal, as was done by Granick and Porter in 1947 (41), grana appear as layers of discs. In 1952 Steinmann published electron micrographs of *Aspidistra* grana isolated in distilled water. Each granum consisted of about 30 discs; each disc (after vacuum drying) was about 70 Å thick by about 600 Å in diameter. Thus, the green chlorophyll containing material, which can be sedimented after breakage of chloroplasts with distilled water, consists of these discs, frequently still associated with one another in grana.

With the availability of the techniques of plastic embedding, heavy metal staining, and thin sectioning for electron microscopy, the stacked discs of the grana could be seen in profile as lamellae and visualized as cross sections of closed sacs or thylakoids (from the Greek "sack-like"). Electron-opaque regions within grana-containing chloroplasts stained with permanganate, for example, are thought to consist of the outer edges of two appressed thylakoids. The electron-lucid region between them would thus be visualized as the central region of each sac. The dimensions of the dense and light bands vary with the species and the methods of preparation employed. For example, when viewed in thin section, the grana of *Aspidistra* consist of dark bands approximately 65 Å thick alternating with electron-lucid zones of about equal thickness. Thus, if grana are visualized as stacks of thylakoids with appressed electron-dense outer edges, the dimensions of the profile of each thylakoid within a granum would be: an approximately 30–35 Å thick electron-dense region; a 60 Å electron-lucid area; and the other edge— another 30–35 Å thick electron-dense region. As described above, when grana of *Aspidistra* are isolated in distilled water, spread on an electron microscope grid, and vacuum dried, the total thickness of each thylakoid is approximately 70 Å—somewhat thinner than the 120 Å estimate made for a cross section of the disc from thin sections of embedded material from the same plant.

The electron micrograph of a cross section of a chloroplast such as the one shown in Fig. 1 demonstrates another common feature of higher plant chloroplasts. Lamellae are present not only in grana, but also between grana. The frequency of these stroma lamellae, or intergrana lamellae, varies among chloroplasts of the same plant and to an even greater extent when chloroplasts of different plants are compared. The problem of how the grana lamellae and those between grana are related geometrically has received considerable attention and appears to be fairly complicated. One interpretation of these geometric interrelationships is shown in Fig. 2, which illustrates Weier's interpretation of the system as a fretwork (96) based on studies of tobacco and bean chloroplasts. Wehrmeyer (95) has compared surface and profile views of lamellar systems of spinach and arrived at a somewhat different conclusion as to the possible arrangement of chloroplast lamellar systems.

Chloroplasts of algae and some other plants frequently lack grana, or alternatively each plastid can be considered a single granum. There

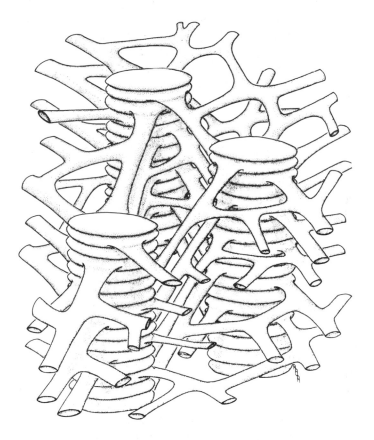

FIG. 2.   An interpretation by Prof. T. E. Weier of the relationships among photosynthetic membranes of a tobacco chloroplast. (Reproduced through the courtesy of Prof. T. E. Weier, The University of California, Davis.)

are no localized regions of stacks of lamellae, but instead sets of lamellae appear to traverse the entire chloroplast. In three dimensions this means that the thylakoids are of uniform length—each about as long as the plastid—and that several thylakoids may be closely associated (attached) throughout their length. Gibbs (35) has examined the situation extensively and has found some differences in the number of lamellae in the trans-plastidic bands among different algal groups. The electron micrograph of the chloroplast of *Cyanidium caldarium* in Fig. 3 is shown as an example of a granaless chloroplast of an alga. Systems of alternating electron-dense and lucid layers are also present in blue-green algae in which the photosynthetic apparatus is not separated

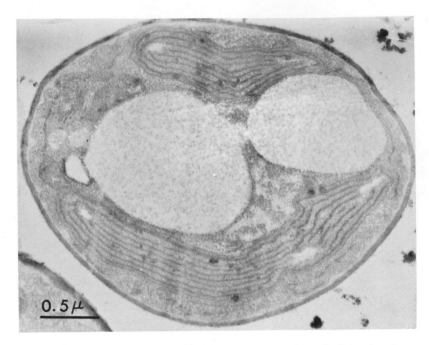

0.5 μ

FIG. 3. An electron micrograph of a cross-section through a cell of the alga *Cyanidium caldarium*. The chloroplast is surrounded by a limiting membrane, as in maize, but grana are lacking (66). × 40,000.

from the cytoplasm by a membrane. Figure 4, which is an electron micrograph of *Anacystis*, illustrates this point.

Before we go deeper into the question of plastid organization, it is worth examining chloroplast function briefly. From the view of the whole plant the principal function of the chloroplast is photosynthesis. Even a brief and somewhat arbitrary look at photosynthesis may help us in an attempt to understand the relation between the chloroplast's structure and its function as the organelle of photosynthesis.

Van Niel's analysis of photosynthesis as a group of closely integrated but more or less independent processes plus knowledge acquired subsequently encourages an attempt to determine where within the plastid each of the following processes or group of processes might be localized: (a) light absorption and the transport of electrons from the potential of the oxygen electrode (that is, H_2O) energetically up to approximately the level of the hydrogen electrode; (b) the photolysis of water and the release of oxygen; and (c) the reduction of carbon from the level of this element in carbon dioxide to that in a carbohydrate

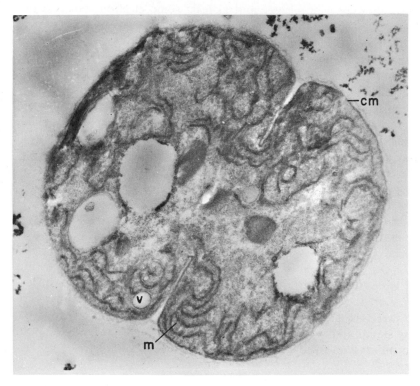

FIG. 4. As is typical of blue-green algae, the photosynthetic lamellae of *Anacystis nidulans* are not separated from the remainder of the cell by a membrane (66).

molecule. The discovery of the photoproduction of adenosine triphosphate (ATP) (photosynthetic phosphorylation) and the reduction of nicotinamide adenine dinucleotide phosphate (NADP) revealed the link between electron transport and carbon reduction in photosynthesis.

As described, the chloroplast can be broken when treated with distilled water and the greenness can be centrifuged out. Obviously light absorption will be done by the green part of the plastid, but early in the investigation of photosynthesis carried out by isolated plastids, it was found that if the supernatant fluid from centrifuged, osmotically broken chloroplasts and the green sediment were mixed together, the ability of the broken chloroplasts to fix CO_2 was partially restored (3). Thus, even after osmotic breakage of the plastids, the chlorophyll associated with the insoluble particulate matter, the thylakoids, is photosynthetically active; the photochemistry of photosynthesis is done by these fragments. In fact, the Hill reaction, which consists of light absorption, oxygen release, and at least some electron transport (an electron is conveyed from water to an artificial acceptor such as ferric ion or an oxidized dye molecule), can be done by insoluble green chloroplast fragments smaller than those obtained merely by breaking plastids osmotically. Photosynthetic phosphorylation can also be performed by less than intact chloroplasts. The enzymes of carbon chemistry, on the other hand, are contained in the soluble fraction of broken chloroplasts. This carbon chemistry is not much different from that which the cytoplasm may be capable of except that chloroplasts contain an extraordinarily large amount of ribulose diphosphate carboxylase, the enzyme that catalyzes the reaction:

$$\text{ribulose-1, 5-diphosphate} + CO_2 \rightarrow 2 \text{ phosphoglyceric acid}$$

Approximately 25% of the total protein of the tobacco chloroplast is that of fraction I—a complex which includes ribulose diphosphate carboxylase.

Our concern with organization for photosynthetic function thus brings us to consider primarily the insoluble portion of the chloroplast. How are the components of the lamellae arranged? In order to begin to answer this question it is necessary to know the composition of the thylakoids and to look more intensively at the components and mechanisms of photosynthesis.

ORGANIZATION AND FUNCTION AT THE MOLECULAR LEVEL

Chemical analysis of lamellar material, which may be obtained by breaking chloroplasts and centrifuging out the thylakoids, seems a simple matter; however, in organic chemistry, and especially in organic biochemistry, the easiest compounds to find are those known or strongly suspected to be present. Information about what should be sought has come from a number of different kinds of studies of photosynthesis. For example, when plastids of higher plants are extracted with acetone, two chlorophylls, a and b, are recovered in a ratio of about 3a:1b, but other sorts of experiments indicate that in vivo the situation is more complex—functionally there are several kinds of "chlorophyll a."

The Photosynthetic Unit; Multiple Forms of Chlorophyll a in vivo

The flashing light experiments of Emerson and Arnold (30) suggested that not all chlorophyll molecules do the same thing in photosynthesis. In experiments of this kind, the rate of oxygen release (that is, photosynthesis) is compared with the number of quanta of light supplied during a very short flash, for example, to a suspension of algae. If all chlorophyll molecules were functionally equivalent, light saturation of photosynthesis would be expected to occur when one quantum of light is absorbed per chlorophyll molecule. It has been found, however, that saturation is achieved at much lower levels—when one quantum of light is supplied for every 400–600 (or in some experiments about 2000–3000) chlorophyll molecules. The level of saturation varies with the species and age of the plant.

Interpretations of such data led to the concept of the photosynthetic unit. One implication of this concept is that the energy of a quantum absorbed by one chlorophyll molecule can be transferred to another, then another, and so on. The second implication is that somewhere in this statistical or physical unit of, let us say, 400 chlorophyll molecules is an energy sink, a reaction center at which the energy of the quantum absorbed is converted into the potential energy of an electron or into chemical energy.

Supporting evidence for functional differences among molecules of chlorophyll *in vivo* comes from several types of experiments of which the following is an example.

When chlorophyll dissolved in an organic solvent such as acetone is illuminated a great deal of the energy absorbed by the pigment is re-emitted as red fluorescence. The wavelength of greatest fluorescence intensity is characteristic for each type of chlorophyll, and it is possible to distinguish chlorophyll *a* from chlorophyll *b*, for example, by its fluorescence maximum. This is true for chlorophylls *in vivo* as well as *in vitro*. Duysens (26) compared the intensity of the fluorescence emitted by chlorophyll *a* when green algae or other plants were illuminated with light of a wavelength absorbed mostly by chorophyll *a* or mostly by other pigments; for example, chlorophyll *b*. His observation that chlorophyll *a* fluoresced regardless of which of the plastid pigments was the principal absorber of the light clearly indicated that energy could be transferred among the pigments of the chloroplast and that chlorophyll *a* could serve as a terminal acceptor. However, there appear to be several types of chlorophyll *a in vivo*.

The existence *in vivo* of types of chlorophyll *a*, which differ from one another in absorption spectrum, has been demonstrated primarily by French and his co-workers (89), who designed a spectrophotometer which can be used to study the absorption of pigments in whole cells and to compute and present the first derivative of the absorption spectrum. By this means, more precise absorption maxima can be obtained, and, in addition, pigments present in small amounts can be detected more readily. Most plants examined in this way have been found to contain at least two or three varieties of chlorophyll *a*, each with a different absorption maximum in the red region of the spectrum: chlorophyll a_{670}, a_{683}, a_{695}. Thus, although chemically there is only one chlorophyll *a*, there appear to be a number of different associations in which chlorophyll *a* molecules can exist *in vivo*; each of these associations has a unique absorption maximum.

Now that the problem was compounded by the realization that several types of chlorophyll *a* coexist in the plastid, more refined techniques were required to determine which one (or ones) is a terminal acceptor of absorbed energy. Butler (19,20) studied the absorption and fluorescence excitation spectra of leaves at 77°K and detected an absorption band at 705 mμ. When this band was excited, fluorescence emission with a maximum at 720 mμ was detected. This provided further evidence for a species of chlorophyll *a* which absorbs at very long wavelengths. This particular absorbing form, which perhaps is at or close to the energy sink, has been studied extensively by Kok (51), who detected a reduction in the amount of light absorbed at about 700 mμ by green tissues when they were illuminated.

Kok (51) has also partially purified from spinach leaves a pigment complex which exhibits light-induced absorption changes at about 700 mμ. It is estimated that this chlorophyll$_{700}$ (or P 700, as Kok has designated it) constitutes about 2–5 % of the total plastid chlorophyll.

Evidence for the existence of some forms of chlorophyll with special orientation and with absorption maxima in the neighborhood of 700 mμ also comes from studies of the dichroic ratios of plastid lamellae and of individual algae. Sauer and Calvin (80) found that the major chlorophyll *a* absorption band in spinach lamellae is at 678 mμ, but that a peak in the dichroic ratio spectrum occurs at 695 mμ. They interpret this to mean that a small fraction, about 5 %, of the total chlorophyll *a* is strongly oriented. Olson (69) found dichroic maxima at around 705 mμ in *Mougeotia*, *Euglena*, *Spirogyra*, and some other algae, as well as in chloroplasts of spinach and other higher plants. Additional evidence for some chlorophyll *a* molecules being oriented and having an absorption maximum at about 695–705 mμ, and a fluorescence emission maximum at about 720 mμ, comes from the extremely interesting bifluorescence studies on *Euglena* and *Mougeotia* by Olson (69). In these experiments, immobilized cells are illuminated with light polarized in various planes, and the plane of polarization of the light emitted as fluorescence is determined. Regardless of the plane of polarization of the light absorbed, the emitted (fluorescent) light is always polarized and in the same plane, that is, independent of the plane of polarization of the incident radiation! This indicates, first, that the energy of the light absorbed by variously oriented chlorophyll molecules is all transferred to a specific type of pigment, and, second, that this particular species, which has a fluorescence emission maximum at 720 mμ, consists of oriented molecules of chlorophyll a.

To summarize: It appears from a number of kinds of evidence that (a) chlorophyll molecules in the plastid do not act entirely independently, but appear to be associated in some sort of physical or statistical functional unit; (b) there are various types of chlorophyll a in $vivo$ and spectral differences probably reflect the association of chlorophyll a with other chlorophyll molecules, proteins, or other compounds; (c) of the various spectral types of chlorophyll a, the variety absorbing at $about$ 700 mμ, a small fraction of all the chlorophyll a molecules of the plastid, appears to be oriented within the chloroplast structure, whereas the bulk of the chlorophyll is not arranged in a regular manner; and (d) the pigment complex absorbing at 700 mμ is a terminal receiver of the energy absorbed initially by other kinds of pigments. The general proposition then is that the bulk of the pigment molecules in the plastid act as light gatherers, whereas relatively few others are at an active center at which light energy is converted into potential or chemical bond energy.

Another component of the photosynthetic machinery, and one which may be close to the oriented chlorophyll molecules with an absorption maximum at about 700 mμ, is cytochrome f. When green leaves are illuminated, the absorption of reduced cytochrome f (at 553 mμ) is seen to drop—that is, more of the cytochrome becomes oxidized. The argument that this cytochrome is close to the active center comes from the observation that, at very low temperatures, conditions under which electron transport over long distances and through many compounds would not be very likely, cytochrome f is still seen to become oxidized (22), and, at the same time, chlorophyll a_{700} displays spectral changes—it bleaches. These are the currently available pieces of evidence which argue most strongly in favor of an association of chlorophyll a_{700} (or P 700) with cytochrome f at one kind of active center in plastids.

Without going into the mass of data to support the proposition, it should be pointed out that there are probably two kinds of active centers, or two functionally distinct segments of the active center, each populated by a "different" kind of chlorophyll a. This conclusion is based on a large number of studies now being made of "photosynthetic enhancement." Current usage assigns the P 700, or long wavelength, center the name "System I"; the second type of center is generally termed "the short wavelength system" or "System II." The latter appears to be driven by light absorbed by chlorophyll *b* and other "accessory pigments"; oxygen release appears to be associated with this segment of green plant photosynthesis.

It is not the purpose of this discussion to treat photosynthesis exhaustively, nor is there enough space to chronicle the evidence for all of the other compounds now implicated in photosynthesis. Instead, Table II lists, with their oxidation-reduction potentials, most of the

TABLE II.   *The Oxidation-Reduction Potentials of Some Chloroplast Components*

	E_0'
Plastocyanin	+0.37
Cytochrome *f*	+0.37
Chlorophyll a_{700} (=P 700)	+0.43
Plastoquinone	0.0
Cytochrome b_6	−0.07
NADP	−0.34
Chloroplast ferrodoxin	−0.43

components that are now commonly thought to participate in photosynthesis. Just as one reconstructs a biosynthetic chain by studying the organo-chemical plausibility of arranging intermediates in a sequence, so the course of electron flow in photosynthesis has been reconstructed from this list with the help of additional biochemical evidence.

Figure 5 presents an over-all scheme for photosynthesis in a form not too greatly at variance with many of the data currently available. This does not pretend to be an accurate picture as it exists in plants, but rather as it exists at present in the minds of some students of photosynthesis.

One item not included in the oxidation-reduction list but shown in Fig. 5 is manganese. This metal is thought to be involved in the oxygen release segment of photosynthesis. Some analysts of plastids have assumed that each active center contains one or two manganese atoms and have used manganese content in trying to arrive at an empirical formula for the photosynthetic unit.

By now the questions that must be answered to understand the relationships between structure and function are quite clear. What is the organization of chloroplast thylakoid at the molecular level? Can spectral varieties of chlorophyll *a* be isolated? What are the details of the structure of the active centers, if they indeed exist? Present knowledge provides only a few bits of information along these lines. The

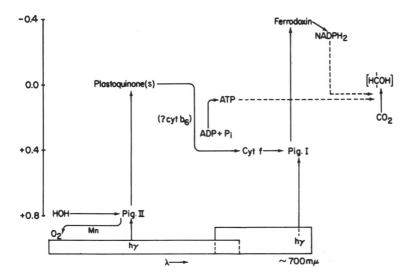

FIG. 5.   Summary scheme of the possible path of electrons in photosynthesis. The rectangles at the bottom of the figure are intended to represent the radiant energy collecting pigment molecules. The overlapping of the rectangles indicates the probability that energy absorbed by pigments which are excited by light of shorter wavelengths can transfer their energy to System II (that is, Pig. I) or System I (that is, Pig. II). The horizontal displacement of participating compounds is roughly in accord with their oxidation-reduction potential. The dashed lines show the connection of electron flow and photophosphorylation with carbon metabolism.

following discussion describes some of the ways in which fuller answers are being sought. Many attempts have been made to dissect lamellae functionally.

Experimental Fragmentation of Photosynthetic Lamellae

It has been known for a long time that fragments of plastids disrupted by ultrasonic treatment or by other means are capable of carrying on the Hill reaction. Holt and French in 1949 summarized such studies by them, by R. Hill, and also by O. Warburg and W. Lutgens (44). In the past few years new attempts have been made to establish which partial reactions of photosynthesis can be performed by various sizes of fragments of plastid lamellae. The recent investigations have taken advantage of newly acquired information about photosynthesis, which has permitted the measurement of several photosynthetic parameters, for example photosynthetic phosphorylation as well as Hill reaction activity, and newly developed or at least more commonly available experimental tools such as preparative and analytical ultracentrifuges, and the electron microscope.

Park and Pon (71) have found lamellar fragments 800 Å in diameter to be as active in carbon dioxide fixation, that is, complete photosynthesis, as the largest pieces tested by them. In order to attain full activity, supernatant fluid from the centrifugation of leaf homogenates at 145,000 g has to be added to the precipitate, which contained the 800 Å particles. The supernatant fraction, which itself contained particles about 200 Å in diameter, was incapable of carrying on light-stimulated carbon dioxide fixation. Thus, according to these experiments, the limit for particles with potentially full photosynthetic activity lies between about 200 and 800 Å.

At lower levels of both particle size and activity, Gross et al. (42) were able to demonstrate Hill reaction activity in particles with a sedimentation constant of 38 S, that is, probably of the order of 300 Å in diameter, obtained from sonically disrupted spinach chloroplasts. In similar sorts of experiments, Thomas et al. (92) found a sudden decline in Hill reaction activity of particles when the average volume of fragments in the fraction declined below about 15×10^5 Å^3; this group estimated that particles with fewer than 40–120 chlorophyll molecules were inactive.

When whole photosynthetic organisms such as algae or isolated chloroplasts are studied with the electron spin resonance (ESR) spectrometer, two signals arise upon illumination: a rapidly rising and decaying narrow signal and a more slowly rising and even more slowly decaying broad signal. ESR signals reflect the presence of free radicals or free electrons. Blois and Weaver (9) have summarized the evidence for the rapid (R) signal being attributable to chlorophyll a, and perhaps specifically P 700, and the slow (S) signal being associated with System II of photosynthesis (see Fig. 5) or one of its components. Beinert and Kok (51) have found that the number of induced spins of the R type ranges from one to four per molecule of P 700, thus further associating the R signal with System I. Obviously ESR analyses are useful for studying how much of the photosynthetic system is intact in broken chloroplast lamellae.

Androes et al. (5) compared the ESR signals of whole chloroplasts and broken segments. The chloroplast fractions studied were comparable to those whose photosynthetic activity had been examined by Park and Pon. The R signal was detectable in even the supernatant fraction of a 45,000 g (20 min) centrifugation—this is the fraction in which Park and Pon could not demonstrate light-driven carbon dioxide fixation; it contains particles 100×200 Å in size as well as some larger fragments. On the other hand, even large fragments, of the order of 800 Å in diameter, fail to exhibit the S signal. In general, the capacity to generate the R signal is retained by the smallest particles obtained upon disruption of plastids and also by 72% acetone-treated photosynthetic material (7); the S signal is associated with a much more easily lost property or component of the plastid. Androes et al. (5) feel that they have provided evidence that the S signal is associated with some kind(s) of protein of the chloroplast because when the fraction containing 800 Å diameter lamellar segments is examined before washing a (quantitatively) small S signal is detectable; also, leached chloroplasts give a much smaller S signal than whole, freshly prepared plastids.

It seems from some experiments of M. B. Allen and her co-workers (1,2) that the R signal generating system, which is one of the most persistent properties of thylakoids, can be divided into two parts. They have isolated green particles of molecular weight of about 10^6 from *Chlorella pyrenoidosa* by freezing cells, then grinding them, subjecting the supernatant fluid of a low-speed centrifugation to ultrasonic treatment, and then centrifugation in a density gradient of glycerol. This lamellar fragment has an absorption maximum at 672 mμ and a ratio of chlorophyll *a* to *b* which is close to 1 (instead of about 3 as in whole cells). It also differs somewhat from the bulk of the chloroplast material in the nature of its carotenoids. This type of fragment is capable of carrying on the Hill reaction when incubated with dichlorophenol indophenol and illuminated. Like the spinach particles studied by Androes et al. (5), this Chlorella P 672 lipo-protein-chlorophyll complex exhibits an R type ESR signal. However, although it has many characteristics normally associated with the R signal, this signal differs from that displayed by the spinach particles in that it persists, that is, fails to decline rapidly, after illumination is terminated. Subsequent addition of supernatant fluid from the preparation of this particle, of 2,6-dichlorophenol indophenol, or of potassium ferrocyanide brings about a rapid decay of the signal. The suggestion is that these particles, ranging in size from 70 to 75 Å up to 300 Å, contain some of the photochemical machinery, but lack a source of electrons required to reduce the photoinduced chlorophyll radical (assuming that such a radical is the source of the R signal they observe).

Attempts have also been made to disassemble thylakoids by the use of detergents. Rabinowitch (74) has summarized experiments dating from 1912 by Herlitzka to obtain green aqueous extracts of leaves and studies by Lubimenko and by Noack in the 1920's directed toward obtaining optically clear green preparations from leaves. In 1938 Stoll and Wiedemann continued studies along these lines, but it became clear through the work of E. L. Smith and his co-workers in 1940 and 1941 that all the previous preparations, that is, "chloroplast solutions," made by grinding leaves with distilled water were suspensions of variously sized particles, all of them comparatively large; these "solutions" produced no sharp sedimentation boundary in the ultracentrifuge and the particles were usually large enough to cause turbidity. The turbid chlorophyll-protein suspensions could, however, be clarified by the addition of various detergents. According to Smith and Pickels (86,87), digitonin and sodium desoxycholate split the chlorophyll from the protein with which it is associated *in vivo* and the pigments sediment in digitonin micelles whereas the protein, free of pigment, forms a separate boundary in the ultracentrifuge. The molecular weight of the protein was estimated to be approximately 265,000. Smith and Pickels reported that, on the other hand, sodium dodecylsulfate does not disrupt the pigment-protein association, but brings about the splitting of this complex into smaller units.

Wolken (for example, 101) extracted a pigment-protein complex from *Euglena* in a 1–2% digitonin solution. According to Wolken, the digitonin preparations contained sufficient nitrogen to suggest that protein was associated with this complex, contrary to the conclusions reached by Smith and Pickels (86,87). Also, the published sedimentation patterns of Wolken did not display the 265,000 molecular weight protein observed by Smith and Pickels. Eversole and Wolken (32) reported that their digitonin preparations from *Euglena* were capable of catalyzing (a) the photoreduction of 2,6-dichlorophenol indophenol, (b) the photolysis of water—or at least oxygen evolution, and (c) the conversion of inorganic phosphate into an acid-labile form. These observations have not been extended.

More recently, Wessels (97) has prepared green fragments by treating spinach chloroplasts with 0.27% digitonin, and Boardman and Anderson (12) have separated a variety of sizes of fragments from spinach chloroplast preparations treated with 0.5% digitonin.

In Wessels' experiments fragments sedimenting between 5,000 and 50,000 g were shown to be capable of performing cyclic photophosphorylation (when provided with phenazine methosulfate) and of NADP photoreduction when a suitable electron donor was included in the reaction mixture. Boardman and Anderson (12) performed experiments similar to those of Wessels except that the digitonin preparation was fractionated by differential centrifugation and more properties of the fragments were studied—the ratio of chlorophyll *a* to *b*, the reduction of chlorophenol-2,6-dichloroindophenol (TCIP), the reduction of NADP, and the reduction of NADP with ascorbate and TCIP as an electron-donating couple. The ratio of chlorophyll *a* to *b* in the whole chloroplast suspension was 3.0, but in the fraction sedimenting at 144,000 *g* the ratio was 6.2; the supernatant fluid of their centrifugation showed a ratio of chlorophyll *a* to *b* of 5.4. Among the fractions obtained by centrifugation, the particles precipitating at between 1,000 and 10,000 g showed all three of the photochemical activities tested but particles smaller than this, including the supernatant fraction of the 144,000 g centrifugation, were capable only of NADP reduction when ascorbate and TCIP were provided. This suggests that only the largest particles in Wessels' heterogeneous preparation were performing. The physical and functional relationships between thylakoid segments obtained by sonic disruption and by detergent treatment are not yet clear.

The preceding is an outline and not an exhaustive enumeration of investigations performed along these lines, but it includes representative experiments done in an attempt to understand the photosynthetic apparatus by segmenting it. Interpretation of the success of the segmentation depends upon the level of understanding of photosynthesis and the kinds of partial reactions one can see under various conditions. Obviously, the most complete system does "whole photosynthesis" including carbon dioxide fixation and oxygen release. This sort of activity can be carried out by intact chloroplasts, but also, as pointed out in the work of Park and Pon (71) and others, by soluble plastid components incubated with segments of lamellae as small as 800 Å in diameter and as thick as the thylakoid, that is, about 100 Å.

Below the level of complete photosynthesis it is difficult to say which kind of segment is "more complete" than any other. The interpretations depend very largely on one's view of photosynthesis and the interrelations of phenomena experimentally determined as partial reactions. One general difficulty with the experiments cited in attempts to meaningfully fragment the photosynthetic apparatus is the rarity of reconstitution experiments. Negative evidence—that is, that an activity is lost—tells us only that and not whether an essential part has been broken away. We do not know whether a part of the lamella has been simply hammered into uselessness or has indeed been unscrewed in such a manner that, with proper care, it could be reassembled. Even in experiments in which one has a piece of a lamella of known size—and obviously in many of the experiments cited, particularly the ones using detergents, one has no notion of size—we have no idea how much of the limitation in activity is strictly a function of the reduced size. Further-more, it is quite clear that it is possible to chemically strip away many essential components and obtain preparations with restricted activity probably without dissociating the lamellae at all. For example, in the enrichment of lamellae for P 700, Kok (51) treated chloroplast prepara-tions with 72% acetone; the remaining protein, which may or may not be seriously altered but from which the bulk of the chlorophyll has been removed, is capable of showing a photoinduced cytochrome oxidation and bleaching of P 700, as well as displaying an ESR signal of the R type when illuminated. Another example of chemical treatment that results in a reduction of function, probably without serious effects on lamellar structure, comes from certain experiments in which it was shown that dried plastids extracted with organic solvents at low temperatures failed to carry on the Hill reaction when rehydrated and illuminated. Bishop (8) showed that this could be corrected by supplying plastoquinone. Thus, the chemical removal of plastoquinone, as well as some other components of the chloroplast, but probably without tearing the lamellae into smaller segments, mimics some of the experi-ments in which plastid fragments allegedly failed to do the Hill reaction because too few chlorophyll molecules were associated with one another or because of disruption of the lamellae by detergents. The organic chemist's proof of structure by synthesis is not a bad principle to be followed in trying to understand what has been done in the course of disruption experiments. Some of the pieces that can be broken from lamellae, such as the P 672 particles of Allen, reassociate at high concentrations; the membrane-like reassociated sheets have different absorption spectra than the smaller separate particles, but have not been shown to be capable of carrying on greater segments of photosynthesis than the dissociated P 672 complexes.

Today the game is open to anyone who has a map of photosyn-thesis and data of the sort outlined above from various experiments in which attempts have been made to associate specific segments of photo-synthesis with chloroplast lamellae fragments prepared in a particular way. The game is played by drawing circles and making guesses as to which parts of this photosynthetic scheme, assuming it is all real, might fit with the kinds of pieces of lamellae described. At the present state of knowledge the game is less profitable than it seems promising before play begins. The questions one would like to answer about how chloro-phylls and proteins and other components of the photosynthetic lamel-lae are arranged cannot yet be answered. In fact, it seems that we hardly have the tools to approach the question in a rational and profitable way.

FIG. 6.   A surface view into a spinach thylakoid. Part of the upper lamella appears to be absent. The quantasomes are the regularly arrayed particles which appear to be subunits of lamellae. (Electron micrograph kindly provided by Prof. R. Park, The University of California, Berkeley.)

STRUCTURAL EQUIVALENTS OF THE PHOTOSYNTHETIC UNIT?

Lamellae appear as smooth structures in electron micrographs of plastid cross sections (Fig. 1). Before thin-sectioning techniques were so well developed and widely used, chloroplast lamellae were examined in the electron microscope from surface view after shadowing with heavy metals. In 1952 Steinmann (90) observed that the surfaces of lamellae of *Aspidistra* had a more-or-less regular granular appearance. This was pursued further by Frey-Wyssling and Steinmann (33). These observations were generally disregarded till Park and his collaborators (70,71) named these subunits quantasomes and obtained excellent electron micrographs of these structures in partially open spinach thylakoids (Fig. 6). In the best pictures the quantasomes appear in a two-dimensional crystalline array, each unit being 185 Å long × 155 Å wide × 100 Å thick. In some micrographs, each of these quantasomes appears to contain four or more subunits. The molecular weight of a single quantasome is estimated to be 2×10^6 and, by fitting the organic empirical formula for lamellae to an approximately 2 million molecular weight unit, the composition of each of these quantasomes has been estimated by Park and Biggins (70), and is given in Table III. Such a

TABLE III.   *The Composition of Spinach Chloroplast Lamellae*[a]
(*per approximately* 2×10^6 *molecular weight*)

Lipid Fraction	Molecular Weight	Protein Fraction	Molecular Weight
230 Chlorophylls	206,400	Protein (C,N,H,O,S)	928,000
48 Carotenoids	27,400	2 Manganese	110
48 Quinine compounds	31,800	12 Iron including two	672
116 Phospholipids	90,800	cytochromes	
144 Digalactosyl diglyceride	134,000	6 Copper	218
366 Monoglactosyl diglyceride	268,000		
48 Sulfolipid	41,000		
Sterols	15,000		
Unidentified lipids	175,000		

[a] From Park and Biggins (70).

unit, according to this formula, contains about 230 chlorophyll molecules—not a bad number for the functional photosynthetic unit. But what the relationship of this empirical formula might be to each of the four subdivisions sometimes seen in the electron micrographs of lamellar surfaces is certainly not known. One of the more disturbing aspects of these structures, if they are to be considered essential subunits of lamellae, is that their packing is variable and depends in part on the conditions under which the plants have grown. If they are essential and fundamental units of the lamellae structure, one would expect them to be present in a uniform way, but this problem may be resolved with additional observations. New techniques for preparing samples for electron microscopy may reveal another pattern of lamellar subunits. As noted earlier, lamellar subparticles of about the size of quantasomes, as seen in the electron microscope by Park and his co-workers, are capable of carrying out the Hill reaction, but not complete photosynthesis, even when soluble components of the chloroplast are added.

Menke (63,64) has summarized studies of chloroplast lamellae by low-angle X-ray scattering, performed in his laboratory with Kratky, Kreutz, and others. Lamellar dimensions determined in this way are

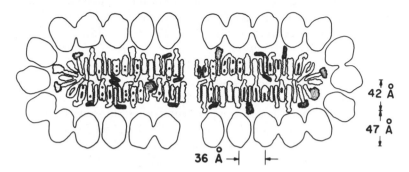

FIG. 7. An interpretation of thylakoid structure based on low-angle X-ray diffraction data. (Drawing reproduced through the courtesy of Prof. W. Menke, The University of Cologne.)

remarkably close to those secured from measurements of sectioned chloroplasts with the electron microscope. Data obtained by studies of lamellae extracted by organic solvents and from unextracted lamellae of *Anthirinum* in the wet state are consistent with the view that each thylakoid consists of layers of different electron density. These are (a) a corpuscular layer consisting of units about 31–36 Å in diameter (across the plane of the lamella) and 47 Å thick, and (b) below this layer, a continuous element approximately 42 Å in thickness. The whole thylakoid, then, would be 178 Å in thickness and, in the view of Menke, would consist of corpuscular units arranged like a flattened chain of beads surrounding the two continuous layers 42 Å thick (Fig. 7). Based on differences in electron density of the outer units and of the inner layers, the continuous layers have been presumed to be lipid.

The corpuscular units, with a dimension of 31 Å in the plane of the lamella, would correspond to about 1/4 of a quantasome as identified in Park's electron micrographs. The X-ray diffraction data provide some idea of possible lamellar substructure, but unfortunately do not help in providing information on the minimum components for formation of chloroplast lamellae, nor about how they are formed. On the latter point, for example, one might visualize that lipoproteins 31 Å by about 89 Å in size might be the units of structure, but the lipid portions when merged with one another would make an apparently continuous layer.

Regardless of whether the interpretations of some recent observations of plastid structure are accurate, these investigations have already provided significant new views about thylakoids. The concept of the plastid photosynthetic lamellae as smooth, that is, nonparticulate, membranes seems dead. However, the electron microscope and X-ray

diffraction analyses do not yet fit with the results of plastid fragmentation experiments. If quantasomes, as observed with the electron
microscope, or the sublamellar elements delimited by low-angle X-ray
scattering, are units of function, why are the 200 Å diameter × 100 Å
thick lamellar fragments capable of only fractions of photosynthesis—
the R-type ESR signal and, in some experiments, activity in the Hill
reaction? The possibility of loss of essential components has already
been mentioned, but, in addition, it seems possible that damage to
lamellae during fragmentation may be greater than imagined; perhaps
some sites for essential components are so badly damaged that they
can no longer accept the kinds of molecules which had been there?

The question of whether or not chlorophyll is necessary for lamellar
formation has been the subject of long discussion. It has sometimes
been suggested that the chlorophyll might be arranged on the outside
of the lamellae or the lamellar subunits, and might somehow serve to
cement lamellae together or perhaps even keep the layers within a
lamella associated. The examination of a series of mutants of *Cyanidium
caldarium* suggests that chlorophyll may be unnecessary for the formation of lamellae or for their association with one another. This
single-celled thermophilic alga normally contains phycocyanin, allophycocyanin, chlorophyll *a*, and carotenoids. Figure 3 is an electron
micrograph of a cell type with the full complement of pigments; Fig.
8(b) is an enlargement of the photosynthetic lamellae of such a cell.
Figures 8(a), 8(c), and 8(d) are electron micrographs of sections of
mutants that lack various pigments. Figure 8(c) is an electron micrograph of the mutant that contains phycocyanin and allophycocyanin,
but lacks chlorophyll. The amount of membranous material present in
each chloroplast is smaller, but those membranes that are present have
the same dimensions and appearance as those in the wild type. The
same is true for mutant GGB-Y, shown in Fig. 8(d), which lacks both
phycobiliproteins and chlorophyll. Figure 8(a) is an electron micrograph
of a section of a mutant type that contains chlorophyll *a* but lacks
phycobiliproteins. The conclusion from observations of this sort is that
chlorophyll is not necessary for lamellar formation. Just where the
phycobiliproteins are located in the chloroplast is not known except
one guesses that they are probably between stacks of lamellae.

THE DEVELOPMENT OF PLASTIDS AND OF PHOTOSYNTHETIC ACTIVITY

Leaves of dark-grown, that is, etiolated, plants contain no chlorophyll, but have protochlorophyllide *a* in concentration from about

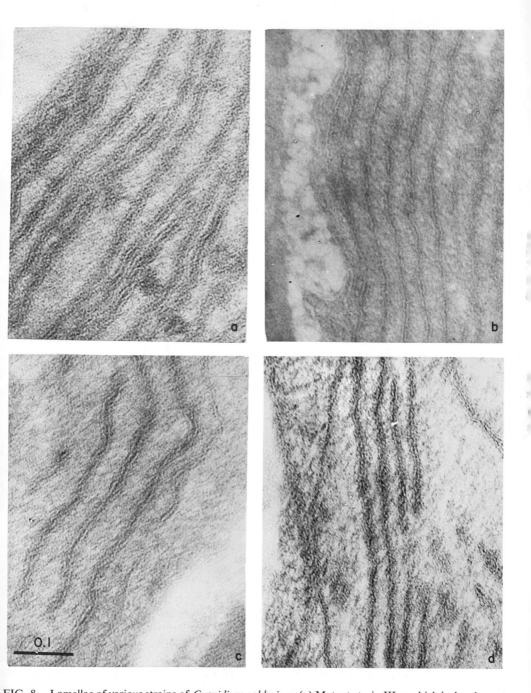

FIG. 8. Lamellae of various strains of *Cyanidium caldarium*. (a) Mutant strain III c, which lacks phyco-cyanin but normally accumulates chlorophyll *a*. (b) Strain III-D-2 (also shown in Fig. 3), which resembles the wild type in that it contains phycobiliproteins and chlorophyll *a*. (c) Strain GGB, which accumulates phycobiliproteins but lacks chlorophyll. (d) Strain GGB-Y, a mutant derived from GGB, which forms neither phycobiliproteins nor chlorophyll (17).

1/100 to about 1/300 of the final level of chlorophyll present in a similar leaf after about 24 hr of illumination. Immediately upon illumination the protochlorophyllide *a* that is present is reduced to chlorophyllide *a*, which is shortly afterward converted to chlorophyll *a* by esterification with phytol. The accumulation of additional chlorophyll may take a complex course depending upon the age and species and little, if any, additional chlorophyll may form for 2 or 3 hr after the initial exposure to light. At the termination of this "lag phase" a period of rapid chlorophyll synthesis occurs. The rapid synthesis then goes on at a constant rate until the final level of chlorophyll is attained. The small amount of light required to convert protochlorophyllide to chlorophyllide is sufficient to initiate the lag phase, but continuous illumination is not required for it to be accomplished. Illumination is necessary, however, to initiate and to maintain pigment formation during the "linear phase" of chlorophyll development (93), which follows the lag period. Some physiological and biochemical aspects of the lag and linear phases of chlorophyll development will be discussed in some detail later.

One of the things that makes the study of chloroplasts most fascinating and makes the answers to problems of assembly and function seem close at hand is that changes can be seen in plastids upon illumination of the leaves. The observations to be described raise many questions, but one hopes that eventually they will all also lead to answers.

In 1954 Leyon (53) and Heitz (43) independently observed that plastids in shoot tips and in leaves of etiolated plants contain a crystal lattice-like structure, which has come to be called the prolamellar body or Heitz-Leyon crystal (Fig. 9). In some species, such as maize, these *proplastids* also contain a few thylakoids or strings of vesicles, which stretch from the prolamellar body to the edge of the plastid. Menke (63,64) has compared electron micrographs of such bodies sectioned in various planes and concluded that they are made up of interconnected, twisted tubules. Von Wettstein and others (28,31,50,68,94,98) have found that when etiolated leaves containing proplastids with crystal lattice-like prolamellar bodies are irradiated with just enough light to transform all the protochlorophyllide to chlorophyllide, the elements of the prolamellar body dissociate as shown in Fig. 10 to make groups of structures which appear in cross section to be vesicles. If the illumination is continued, vesicles, which seem to arise from the fused units of the prolamellar body, are dispersed in rows throughout the plastid. Next, the vesicles fuse to produce a few thylakoids, which stretch almost from one end of the plastid to the other (Fig. 11). Finally, grana formation is initiated as additional small vesicles form at some places along each primary

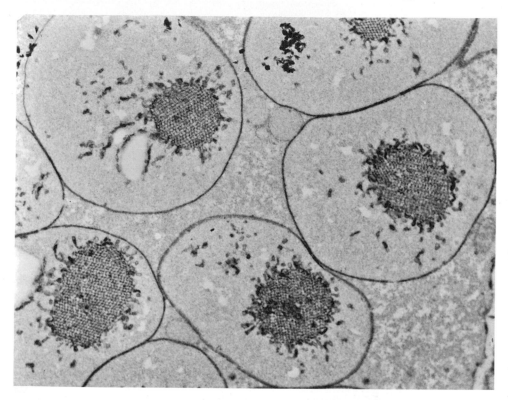

FIG. 9.   An electron micrograph of proplastids in a leaf of a red kidney bean plant grown in darkness for 14 days. The leaf was not exposed to light before being fixed (50). × 14,000.

thylakoid and in contact with it. The time required for these changes depends upon temperature and a number of other conditions, but in general, vesicle dispersal and fusion, as well as active grana formation, occur during the period of linear increase in chlorophyll. If a leaf is returned to darkness after exposure to enough light to transform the protochlorophyllide and cause dissociation of the prolamellar body, additional protochlorophyllide forms and the prolamellar body is reformed (99).

The Photoreduction of Protochlorophyllide

The *action* spectrum for the conversion of protochlorophyllide to chlorophyllide corresponds to the *absorption* spectrum of protochlorophyllide *in vivo*; thus, light absorbed by protochlorophyllide is the

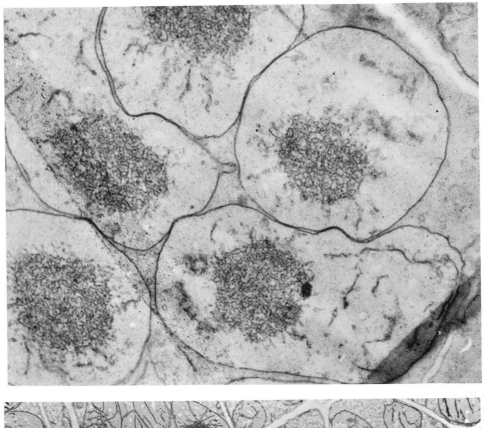
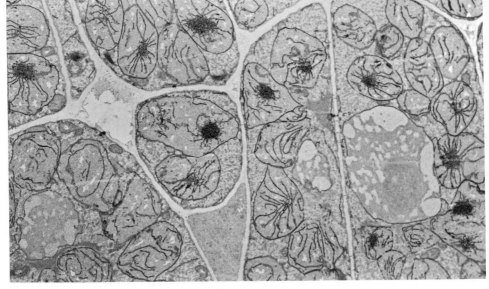

source of energy for its reduction. Protochlorophyllide *a* in ether has an absorption maximum at about 624 mμ, but *in vivo* the absorption maximum in the red region of the spectrum is at about 650 mμ. Shibata (83) observed a series of spectral changes upon illumination of segments of leaf tissue from pole-bean and maize. Immediately upon illumination the absorption maximum at 650 mμ declines, and a new absorption band at 684 mμ develops. This light-dependent transformation appears to be a manifestation of the reduction of protochlorophyllide to chlorophyllide. Within about 10 min, in either light or darkness, the 684 mμ band decreases in intensity, while a new absorption band with a maximum at about 671 to 673 mμ develops and increases in magnitude. After 2 additional hr, also in either light or darkness, a band with a maximum at about 677 mμ replaces the one seen previously at 673 mμ. Additional protochlorophyllide with a maximum at 650 mμ reappears, if the leaves are returned to darkness. The significance of the spectral shifts, which follow the photoreduction of protochlorophyllide, is not known—they may reflect differences in chlorophyll-protein associations or in chlorophyll-chlorophyll interrelationships.

Under certain conditions protochlorophyllide can be photoreduced *in vitro*. With organic solvents such as 80% acetone, protochlorophyllide can be extracted from dark-grown leaves of corns, beans, and other plants. This material in acetone or in ether is as stable in light as most other chlorophylls and porphyrins—it is not converted to chlorophyllide. However, if a leaf of barley or bean, for example, is ground in glycerol in the dark and the glycerol extracts are illuminated, the protochlorophyllide is converted to chlorophyllide. More can be done with glycine buffered extracts of etiolated bean leaves; a protochlorophyllide-protein complex, termed protochlorophyllide holochrome, can be partially purified (10,11,88,89). When a partially purified holochrome preparation is illuminated, the protochlorophyllide is converted to chlorophyllide. Chemically this conversion involves the reduction of ring D of protochlorophyllide by the addition of two hydrogen atoms. The protochlorophyllide holochrome has a molecular weight of the order of 0.5 to 1.0 × 10^6 and a sedimentation coefficient of about 18 S.

The protochlorophyllide holochrome appears to be localized in the prolamellar body—at least the red fluorescence of the porphyrin is

---

FIG. 10.   Plastids in an etiolated bean leaf which was exposed to red light for 10 sec before being fixed. Total light energy provided: 280 ergs/mm^2 (50). × 16,000.

FIG. 11.   Plastids in a leaf of a red kidney bean plant grown in darkness and then exposed to red light for 5 hr. Total light energy provided: 480 kiloergs/mm^2 (50). × 5,000.

confined and not spread throughout the proplastid (13). How the conversion of protochlorophyllide to chlorophyllide results in the dissociation of the elements of the prolamellar body is not clear. It is currently believed that the hydrogen atoms required for the reduction of protochlorophyllide may come from the protein with which it is associated. Changes in the charge on the holochrome or in its conformation *might* result from the reduction of the porphyrin or from the removal of the two hydrogen atoms from the protein; these changes, if they occur, could alter the affinity of the protein molecules for one another and lead to the disarray of the orderly elements of the prolamellar body. Some clues to the cause of the disarrangement of the prolamellar body (that is, "tube transformation") may come with an understanding of why the crystal lattice-like structure is reconstituted when briefly illuminated leaves are returned to darkness (99). Perhaps the structure of the prolamellar body is a consequence of the presence of protochlorophyllide.

As discussed in an earlier section, many compounds besides pigments are associated with the protein in the lamellae of mature plastids. It is not known whether the holochrome acts as an enzyme for the conversion of protochlorophyllide, losing the chlorophyllide after it is formed and picking up another molecule of protochlorophyllide to be converted, or whether the units of assembly of lamellae are protochlorophyllide holochrome molecules augmented by the rolling snowball principle—picking up additional chlorophyll molecules and other compounds closely associated in the chloroplast lamellae until the protein is "ready" for incorporation into the lamellae. It is not known whether the vesicles that form after dissociation of the prolamellar body are composed of the same protein molecules as the crystal lattice-like structure. Answers to this sort of question might tell us about the units of synthesis of chloroplast lamellae and, perhaps, about the structure and composition of the active centers.

The Lag Phase

The lag phase when it occurs—and its occurrence is quite variable, depending upon the age and kind of plant—is initiated by red light and is controlled by the red:far-red photoreversible phytochrome system (67,73).

After a flash of light that is adequate to convert protochlorophyllide into chlorophyllide, and a period of darkness equivalent in length to the duration of expected lag phase, the linear phase of chlorophyll formation begins without delay upon illumination of the leaf. The events of the lag phase are initiated by light, but can be completed in darkness (100). On the other hand, the effect of light in starting the lag phase processes can be reversed. If the initial illumination is followed within a short time by irradiation of the tissue with far-red light (about 730 mμ), the linear phase of chlorophyll synthesis does not begin immediately upon subsequent illumination. Time for the completion of the lag phase is still required (67,73).

Mego and Jagendorf (61) have observed that some enlargement of plastids and augmented protein synthesis occurs during the lag phase. Relatively little pigment is formed until after the termination of the lag phase—whatever limits pigment formation is not relieved for some time after initial irradiation of the plants. If chloramphenicol is administered to etiolated bean leaves before illumination, they produce little pigment (58). This suggests that protein synthesis is required for greening to occur (59).

One of the things that limits pigment development is the availability of δ-aminolevulinic acid (ALA), a compound early in the biosynthetic chain of chlorophyll and other porphyrins. If ALA is supplied, etiolated tissues maintained in darkness form about ten times more protochlorophyllide than they have normally (40). The utilization of exogenous ALA at a rapid rate shows that all the enzymes required for protochlorophyllide synthesis are present and potentially active in etiolated leaves, but that the capacity for ALA synthesis is very limited. (This limitation could be in the activity of ALA-synthesizing enzymes or the availability of ALA precursors.) However, no additional holochrome protein is known to form and the newly produced protochlorophyllide is not converted to chlorophyllide upon illumination.

The Linear Phase of Greening

ALA production in greening leaves is sustained at a high level only during continuous illumination, but it seems probable that some aspect of the potential for rapid synthesis of ALA develops during the lag phase.

If bean leaves which are forming chlorophyll rapidly—that is, during the linear phase—are returned to darkness, the rate of pigment formation falls off rapidly and ceases completely within 1 or 2 hr. Pigment formation in the light at this stage can be stopped also by the administration of chloramphenicol or puromycin, both inhibitors of protein synthesis, or by thiouracil or actinomycin, inhibitors of RNA synthesis (34). These observations suggest that (a) continuing RNA and protein synthesis is required for rapid greening during the linear phase—when the synthesis of these compounds is arrested chlorophyll accumulation stops; (b) during the linear phase light may be acting to promote protein and RNA synthesis; (c) the system for ALA production is labile and decays very rapidly after protein synthesis ceases. Chlorophyll formation commences without a measurable lag when leaves in the linear phase, which have been placed in darkness for a long period, are returned to light (34).

The Development of Photosynthetic Capacity

Regarding the development of the several "*in vivo* types" of chlorophyll a and the onset of photosynthesis, Butler (21) found that during the first 1.5 hr of illumination of 8 day-old Black Valentine bean leaves the chlorophyll appeared as a single symmetrical absorption band with a maximum at about 670 mμ. After 2 hr of illumination, chlorophyll b was detectable and the chlorophyll a began to differentiate into a_{670}, a_{680}, and a_{705}. Butler (19,20) had previously observed that the capacity for the transfer of energy from carotenoids to chlorophyll developed after about 1–2 hr of illumination of etiolated leaves. He concluded that the beginning of photosynthetic activity appeared to coincide with the end of the lag phase, that is, when vesicle dispersal occurred and rapid chlorophyll accumulation commenced.

Anderson and Boardman (4) followed the development of Hill reaction and NADP-reducing activity during later stages of bean plastid development and came to somewhat different conclusions than Butler regarding the time in light required for photosynthetic capacity to develop. Proplastids from unilluminated leaves were inactive in the Hill reaction, but plastids from leaves illuminated for 6 hr (well into the linear phase) exhibited slight activity. Hill reaction activity reached a maximum in plastids from leaves illuminated for 10 hr (by which time considerable lamellar and grana development had presumably occurred) and, then, in more mature plastids, decreased to reach a steady-state level about equal to that shown by plastids from leaves illuminated for 8–9 hr. The capacity to reduce NADP developed somewhat differently. Plastids from leaves illuminated for 8 hr showed no capacity for NADP reduction, those from leaves illuminated for 16 hr reduced NADP at a rate less than half that of mature chloroplasts (chloroplasts isolated from bean plants grown in continuous light), and finally chloroplasts from leaves illuminated for 24 hr showed about twice as much activity as those illuminated for 16 hr, but were not as active as mature plastids. Measurements of NADP-reducing capacity were performed in the presence of added phosphopyridine nucleotide reductase, thus presumably eliminating as a possible confusing factor variations in the activity of this enzyme as the lamellar system develops.

The discrepancies between the data of Butler and of Anderson and Boardman remain to be resolved. They may arise from differences in sensitivities of techniques, interpretation of data, or in the plant material studied. Experiments of the kind performed by Butler begin to give some notion of the course of assembly of the active center.

THE NUCLEIC ACIDS OF CHLOROPLASTS AND RNA METABOLISM DURING PLASTID DEVELOPMENT

Etiolated maize or bean leaves exposed to actinomycin D, an inhibitor of DNA-dependent RNA synthesis, fail to green normally when illuminated (15). In *Euglena*, greening is prevented by exposure to fluorouracil (85) or actinomycin D (60,72). These observations indicate the involvement of nucleic acid metabolism in plastid maturation and pigmentation.

The body of evidence for at least partial hereditary autonomy of plastids is too extensive to be discussed here, but excellent reviews of some of these data have been presented by Rhoades (77) and by Granick (39).

Chloroplasts contain DNA, RNA, and ribosomes. The evidence now goes beyond affirmative answers from qualitative and quantitative analyses; it includes information from radioautography (45,49,91), electron microscopic cytochemistry (45,49,78), qualitative distinctions between ribosomes of chloroplasts and cytoplasm (14,25,29,56,84), and the establishment of differences between DNAs from chloroplasts and nuclei of the same plant (24,47,49,52,75,79).

Figures 12 and 13 show electron micrographs of maize proplastids fixed with formalin and stained with uranyl acetate after sectioning. The leaf tissue, from which the plastid shown in Fig. 13 was taken, was treated with ribonuclease after fixation but before embedding; the other proplastid is from tissue not exposed to ribonuclease. The densely stained 170 Å particles visible in the control section, but absent from the plastid treated with ribonuclease, are thus shown to contain ribonucleic acid and are presumed to be ribosomes. Slightly larger particles, which are equally susceptible to digestion by ribonuclease, are visible in the cytoplasm of the control section (45).

Lyttleton (55) has demonstrated that extracts of white clover leaves contain two classes of ribosomes with apparent sedimentation coefficients of 55 S and 66 S. Two ribosomal components were also

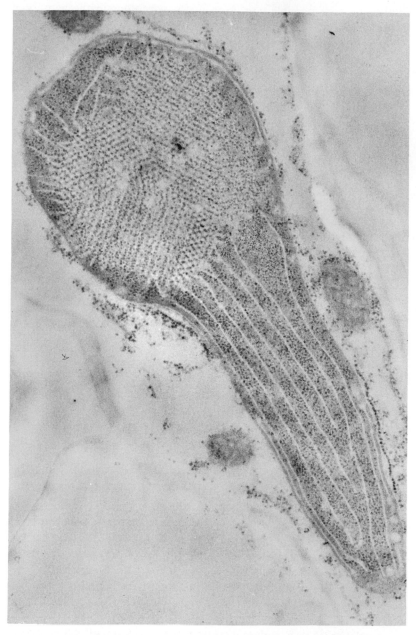

FIG. 12. A proplastid from a leaf of an etiolated maize plant. The fixation and staining techniques increase the contrast of nucleic acids but not that of the prolamellar body and thylakoids. (Electron micrograph by Dr. Ann B. Jacobson.)

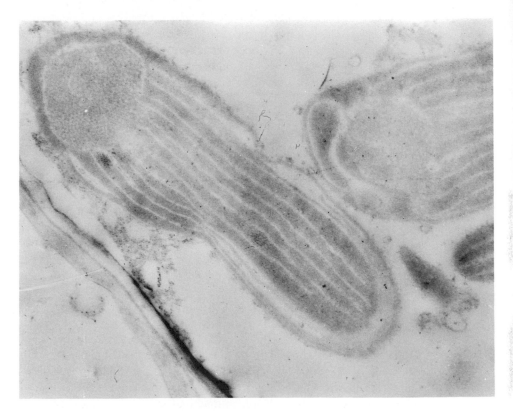

FIG. 13. A maize proplastid similar to that shown in Fig. 12 but treated with ribonuclease after fixation. (Electron micrograph by Dr. Ann B. Jacobson.)

detected in extracts of spinach leaf tissue. The less rapidly sedimenting class ($s_{20,w}$ 66) was isolated from chloroplasts (56). Similarly, Clark et al. (25) have found leaves of *Brassica pekinensis* to contain 83 S and 68 S ribosomes; the latter occur entirely or largely in the chloroplasts. Boardman et al. (14) have found 70 S and 80 S ribosomes in tobacco leaves; the 70 S ones are located in the chloroplasts. Again, Sissakian et al. (84) have shown two classes of ribosomes to be present in pea seedlings; those from the chloroplasts have a sedimentation coefficient ($s_{20,w}$) of 62, whereas the cytoplasmic ribosomes are of the 76 S class. In *Euglena*, Eisenstadt and Brawerman (29) found plastid ribosomes to be about 60 S and cytoplasmic ones to be about 70 S. Thus, there is good evidence for the presence of ribosomes in plastids and also for differences between cytoplasmic and chloroplast ribosomes.

Ribosomes from chloroplasts of *Euglena*, tobacco, and peas have been shown to be active in protein synthesis (14,29,84). Ribosome preparations from tobacco and pea chloroplasts apparently contain template RNA, since they are active in protein synthesis without the addition of RNA from any other source (14,84). Brawerman and Eisenstadt (18) separated RNAs from *Euglena* chloroplasts by sucrose density gradient centrifugation and found amino acid incorporating activity (using *Escherichia coli* as a source of ribosomes) in chloroplast RNAs sedimenting in bands at about 22 S and in the region 11–13 S.

The presence of DNA in chloroplasts is also well established. In 1959 Stocking and Gifford (91), using radioautographic techniques, demonstrated the incorporation of H^3-thymidine into chloroplasts of *Spirogyra*. Radioactivity from H^3-thymidine has been shown to be removable by deoxyribonuclease from chloroplasts of *Nicotiana* (102) and Swiss chard (49). These radioautographic experiments also suggest, but do not prove, that plastid-associated DNA is made in the chloroplasts.

With the electron microscope, Ris and Plaut (78) recognized, in chloroplasts of maize and *Chlamydomonas*, fibrous elements, which resembled strands previously identified as DNA in bacteria prepared for electron microscopy in the same way by Kellenberger *et al.* (46). Filaments of this kind are shown in Fig. 14 in chloroplasts and mitochondria of Swiss chard leaves (49). Strands in clear areas of electron micrographs of chloroplasts and mitochondria of Swiss chard are also seen in material fixed with formalin and stained with uranyl acetate after sectioning (Fig. 15). The strands have been shown to be DNA by the following procedure: After fixation with 10 % aqueous formalin in 0.2 M phosphate buffer (pH 7.4 or 7.6) and partial dehydration and lipid removal with aqueous ethanol, frozen sections about 100 μ thick were prepared with a cryostat microtome. Some sections were treated with deoxyribonuclease, others with ribonuclease, and the control sections were held in an aqueous solution of the same composition as the other sections but lacking the nucleases. At the conclusion of this treatment, all the 100 μ sections were extracted with 5 % trichloracetic acid, washed, dehydrated, embedded, sectioned, and stained with uranyl acetate. Electron micrographs of Swiss chard leaf tissues treated in these ways

FIG. 14. A young plastid in a Swiss chard leaf fixed by the procedure of Kellenberger. DNA strands are shown by the arrow. (a) × 65,000; (b) an enlargement of a portion of the same plastid (49). × 110,000.

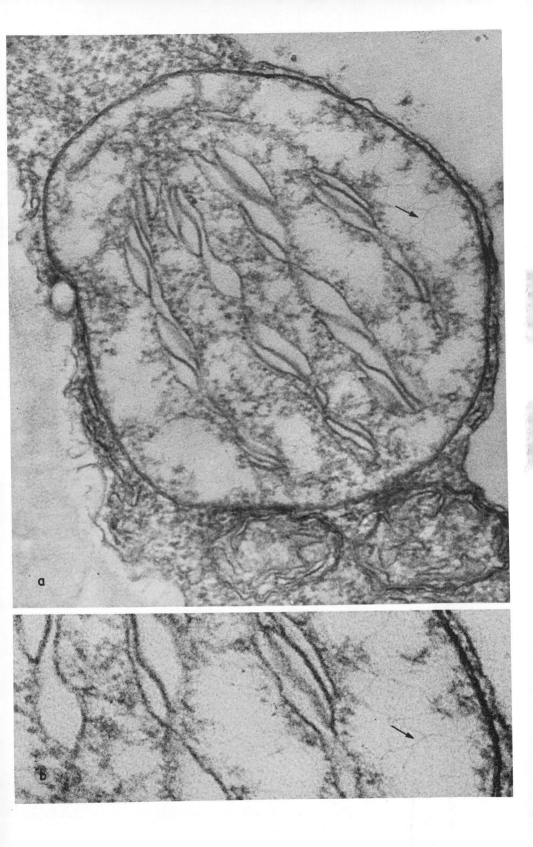

are shown in Figs. 15, 16, and 17 (49). The intensity of staining of the DNA in the nucleus and of the RNA of the nucleolus serves as an internal reference standard for each section examined.

The fibers seen in the micrograph of control tissue are absent from the plastids and mitochondria of sections treated with deoxyribonuclease (Fig. 16). On the other hand, the filaments digested by deoxyribonuclease are apparently not altered by exposure to ribonuclease (Fig. 17); in this material the distribution of the filaments through the interlamellar regions of the chloroplast is more readily followed because of the absence of densely stained ribosomes. These observations demonstrate that plastids and mitochondria contain DNA and that the morphology of the nucleic acid is similar to that of bacteria.

The earliest attempts to determine whether plastids contained DNA were accomplished by isolating chloroplasts by differential centrifugation and performing quantitative analyses for nucleic acids. Chun and his colleagues (24) attacked this and another problem by trying to determine whether nuclear and plastid DNAs might differ sufficiently in composition to be separable by centrifugation in a density gradient of cesium chloride. Crude DNA extracts of a number of plant species were shown to contain a quantitatively major (nuclear) DNA and a minor, or satellite, type. These two kinds of DNA differed from one another in buoyant density (differences in buoyant density reflect differences in base composition, particularly in the ratio of guanosine plus cytosine to adenine plus thymidine). DNA prepared from all the subcellular particles obtained by centrifuging a homogenate of Swiss chard leaves at 37,000 g for 15 min similarly includes a major and a minor type (Fig. 18); the buoyant densities of these two DNAs are 1.689 ± 0.002 and 1.700 ± 0.002 g/ml, respectively. Chloroplasts from a leaf homogenate can be isolated by differential centrifugation and further purified by centrifugation in a density gradient of buffered sucrose. At least 30% of the DNA obtained from Swiss chard chloroplasts purified on a sucrose density gradient appears to be the type with a buoyant density of 1.700 ± 0.002. The enrichment of the DNA preparation for the heavier, formerly minor, type indicates that it is a

---

FIG. 15.   A Swiss chard chloroplast and mitochondrion showing strands of DNA in each (49). × 60,000.

FIG. 16.   Similar to Fig. 15 but treated with deoxyribonuclease. Note the absence of the types of strands seen in Fig. 15 (49). × 48,000.

FIG. 17.   Similar to Fig. 15 but treated with ribonuclease. Note the fibrils as seen in Fig. 15 but the absence of heavily stained small particles (compare Fig. 13) (49). × 52,000.

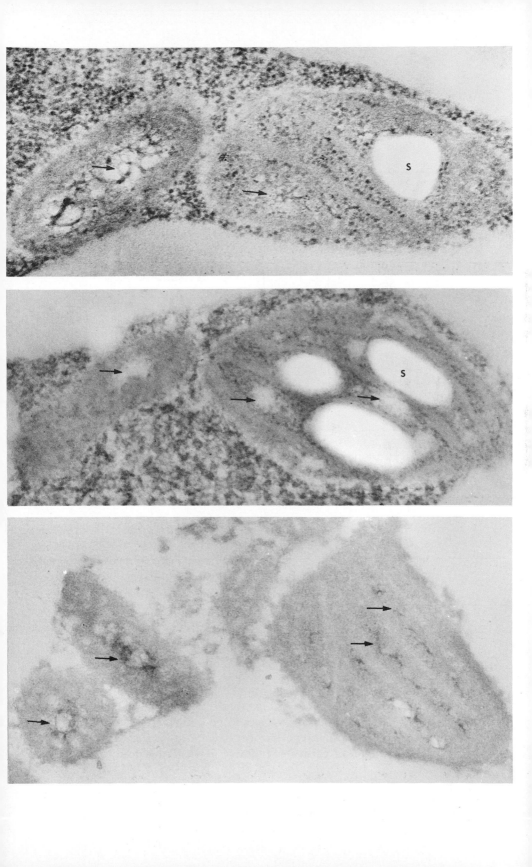

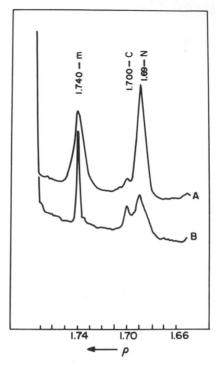

FIG. 18. Distribution of DNA from Swiss chard leaves in a gradient of cesium chloride. A, DNA from centrifuged homogenate; B, DNA from chloroplasts purified by density gradient centrifugation. m, marker DNA; C, chloroplast DNA; N, nuclear DNA (49).

constituent of plastids. Thus, the DNA seen as fibers in the Swiss chard chloroplast has a buoyant density of 1.700 ± 0.002. However, there is no assurance from these experiments that *no* DNA of buoyant density 1.689 ± 0.002 occurs in Swiss chard plastids. The buoyant densities of DNAs from a variety of plants are given in Table IV. In general, plastid DNAs have higher buoyant densities than nuclear ones in higher plants, but the reverse is true of algae. The significance of these differences—even if the generalization proves to be valid—is not clear. Ray and Hanawalt (75) report that nuclear DNA of *Euglena gracilis* ($\rho = 1.707$ g/ml) contains 2.3% 5-methylcytosine, whereas the minor component ($\rho = 1.685$ g/ml), which appears to be associated with the chloroplasts of this alga, has little if any (<0.3%) of this rare base. Chloroplast DNAs appear to be double stranded judging from shifts in buoyant density after heat denaturation. Further evidence for the association of particular types of DNA with chloroplasts has been provided by Edelman *et al.* (27) and Ray and Hanawalt (76). Mutants of *Euglena*, which are incapable of forming chloroplasts, lack the type of DNA judged to be associated with plastids. Finally, along the line of establishing the presence of DNA outside of the nucleus and presumably in the chloroplasts, are the experiments of Gibor and Izawa (37), which demonstrated the presence of DNA in enucleated portions of *Acetabularia*.

TABLE IV. *Buoyant Densities of Various DNAs*

	Nucleus (g/ml)	Chloroplast (g/ml)	References
Euglena gracilis var. bacillaris	1.707	1.686	(27,52,76)
Chlamydomonas rheinhardi	1.721	1.694	(27)
	1.726[a]	1.702[a]	(79)
	1.723	(1.695)[b]	(24)
Chlorella	1.716	(1.695)[b]	(24)
Spinach	1.695	1.719	(24)
Beets	1.695	1.719	(24)
Swiss chard	1.689	1.700	(49)
Broad beans	1.716[a]	1.695[a]	(48)

[a] Calculated from base composition.

[b] Minor band seen during cesium chloride density gradient centrifugation of DNA extracted from whole cells; chloroplasts not isolated.

Aside from the implications to be drawn from genetics, some experiments with *Euglena* are especially noteworthy demonstrations of the involvement of nucleic acid in plastid continuity and development. Two sets of experiments are involved—both of them ingenious. Lyman *et al.* (54) found that at certain low levels of ultraviolet irradiation *Euglena* cells could be "cured" of having chloroplasts. *Euglena* become green when they are illuminated, but not when they are grown in darkness. Lyman *et al.* (54) found that, if dark-grown *Euglena* were irradiated with sublethal doses of ultraviolet light and were then plated out and illuminated, all or most of the resulting colonies failed to become green; the extent of the response was a function of the dosage of radiation. Peaks of effectiveness were found at 260 and 280 mμ (81), and the effect of ultraviolet irradiation could be reversed by visible radiation—that is, greening was a photoreactivable process. Gibor and Granick (36), using an ultraviolet microbeam apparatus, found that, when immobilized dark-grown *Euglena* were irradiated in such a manner that the nucleus was protected, colorless colonies were frequently formed during subsequent growth under illumination. However, cells whose cytoplasm was mostly shielded, while their nuclei (and a small amount of cytoplasm) were exposed, either failed to divide or developed normal looking green offspring.

Further evidence that plastid DNA is functional has been obtained in experiments on RNA synthesis by isolated chloroplasts. Kirk (48) found that chloroplasts isolated from leaves of *Vicia faba* could, without the addition of DNA, incorporate radioactivity from C^{14}-ATP into a material precipitable by 0.2 *M* perchloric acid or by 67% aqueous ethanol. Incorporation failed to occur when the incubation mixture contained deoxyribonuclease or actinomycin D, an inhibitor of DNA-dependent RNA synthesis. Similar results have been obtained with isolated tobacco chloroplasts by Semal *et al.* (82).

As pointed out at the beginning of this section, interference with protein and RNA metabolism appears to block greening of etiolated leaves. This observation has prompted investigations of RNA formation in the leaf cell during early stages of maturation of proplastids into chloroplasts.

Since ribosomes are abundant both in the proplastids and in the cytoplasm of the etiolated leaf (for example, Fig. 12), it would appear possible that the production, or increased production, of some sorts of informational RNA in the nucleus or the proplastids might be sufficient to bring about plastid maturation. Currently available techniques permit not only measurement of gross changes in RNA, but also some limited assessment of the types and location of new RNA formed in response to illumination.

We (16, and Bogorad and Jacobson, unpublished) have supplied leaves of maize grown in darkness for 10 to 12 days with P^{32} as phosphate or with radioactive uridine. Some sets of leaves were exposed to light for from 30 min to about 3 hr, whereas others were kept in darkness for an equivalent period. The RNA was extracted and subjected to sucrose density gradient centrifugation or analysis by chromatography on columns of methylated albumen-coated kieselguhr. In this way the production of new RNA could be determined by establishing differences in the specific activities of various types of RNAs from each source—that is, illuminated or unilluminated leaves.

Figure 19 shows data obtained from such an experiment. The RNA was extracted from leaves 3 hr after P^{32}-phosphate had been administered. One group of leaves was illuminated and another maintained in darkness after the P^{32} had been absorbed (this generally requires 30–45 min under our conditions). The RNA isolated from each group of experimental plants was centrifuged for 6 hr at 36,000 rpm in a 5–20% gradient of sucrose. At the end of the centrifugation fractions

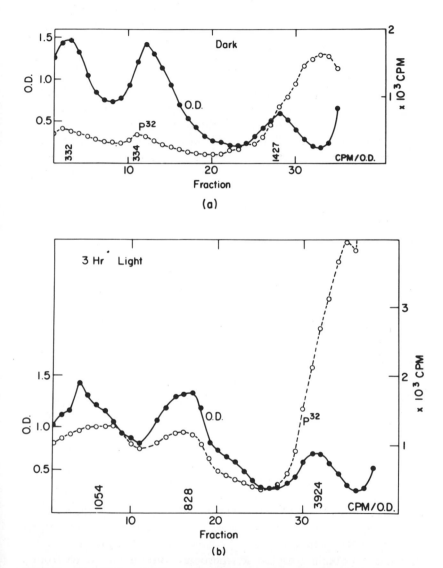

FIG. 19. Distribution of 260 mμ absorbing materials and radioactivity after centrifugation for 6 hr at 36,000 rpm (Spinco Model L centrifuge, SW 39 rotor at about 2°C) in a gradient of sucrose (5 to 20% sucrose in 0.05 M Tris, pH 8.0, 0.1 M KCl) of RNA prepared from maize leaves supplied P^{32} phosphate in darkness. (a) Dark: leaves maintained in darkness for 3 hr after administration of P^{32}; (b) 3 Hr Light: leaves illuminated for 3 hr after administration of P^{32}. Fractions are numbered from bottom of gradient (densest portion) upward.

of equal size were collected. After dilution, a 0.1 ml aliquot of each fraction was used to find the amount of radioactivity present. The amount of RNA in each fraction was determined by measuring the optical density at 260 mμ. The two heaviest RNAs, those in the peaks closest to the bottom of the centrifuge tube, are of the types normally associated with ribosomes; the RNA near the top of the density gradient (highest numbered fractions) is in the size range of transfer RNA. It is clear that the specific activity (cpm/O.D.) of every type of RNA separated by this procedure is three or more times greater in the illuminated than in the unilluminated leaves; thus, exposure of etiolated maize to light apparently stimulates the production of various types of RNA. The effect of light appears to be inductive, at least in the sense that RNA production continues in darkness after the leaves have been exposed to light for a short time. For example, the specific activity of each type of RNA is about the same when comparison is made of nucleic acid isolated from (a) leaves exposed to light for 30 min and then returned to darkness for 90 min and from (b) leaves exposed to light for 120 min. In both cases, the specific activities are higher than those of comparable RNAs from leaves irradiated for only 30 min.

These data from experiments with RNA from whole leaves demonstrate a marked effect of light on RNA metabolism in etiolated leaves, but do not delimit the morphological site or sites of these changes. Does light stimulate RNA production in plastids alone, or outside of the plastid only, or throughout the cell? This question has been explored by isolating plastids and cytoplasmic ribosomes from irradiated and un-irradiated maize leaves supplied with P^{32}-phosphate. The RNAs of these subcellular particles were extracted and then analyzed by sucrose density gradient centrifugation. The radioactivity and 260 mμ absorption profiles are shown in Fig. 20 for plastid fractions. The greatest difference is in the specific activity of the lightest RNA, but the production of every type of RNA in the plastid is strikingly greater after illumination of the leaves. The "cytoplasmic ribosome fraction" is undoubtedly somewhat contaminated with plastid ribosomes—many plastids are broken during homogenization of the tissues—and furthermore the RNA pattern is poor. We have yet to find conditions which permit us to obtain cytoplasmic ribosomes with "good" RNA from a homogenate which yields high quality plastids. However, calculations of the specific activities of the total RNA of the "cytoplasmic ribosome fraction" of illuminated and unilluminated leaves reveal a difference of only about 1.5 times (Fig. 21). It is obvious that plastid RNA metabolism is strikingly and specifically affected by illumination of etiolated leaves; RNA metabolism outside of the plastids is altered slightly, if at

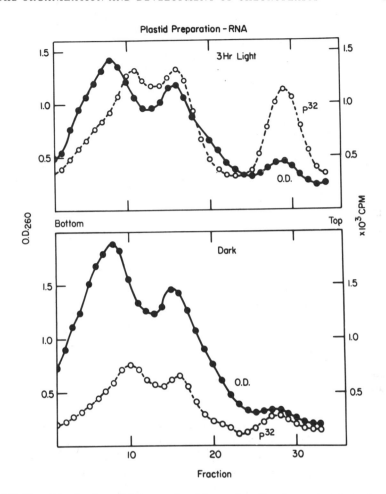

FIG. 20.   Distribution of 260 mμ absorbing and radioactive materials in density gradient of sucrose after centrifugation (see Fig. 19). Upper figure: RNA from plastid fraction prepared from maize leaves illuminated for 3 hr after administration of P³² phosphate. Lower figure: RNA from plastid fraction prepared from maize leaves maintained in darkness for 3 hr after administration of P³² phosphate.

all, by light. The differences observed in the "cytoplasmic ribosome fractions" could be perhaps attributed entirely to contamination by plastid RNA.

Etiolated maize plants of the sort we have used exhibit a lag of about 2 to 3 hr in chlorophyll production. Thus, during the lag period, well before rapid chlorophyll accumulation begins, the plastids appear to form large amounts of new RNA.

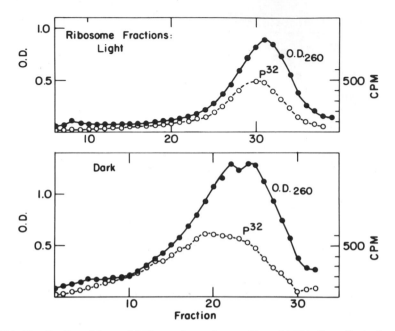

FIG. 21.   Radioactivity and 260 mμ absorption profiles of RNA from "cytoplasmic ribosome fractions" of maize leaves. Each of these fractions was prepared from the corresponding homogenate from which plastids were prepared for determination of the RNA profiles shown in Fig. 20.

The observation of an increase in all kinds of RNA (that is, higher specific activities) we could separate from plants exposed to light led us to examine the possibility of a change in the level of RNA polymerase in proplastids upon illumination of etiolated leaves.

A soluble RNA polymerase has been shown to occur in the supernatant fluid of maize leaf homogenates (57). The activity of this enzyme is not altered by illumination of etiolated plants (Table V). On the other hand, the activity of plastid RNA polymerase is markedly higher in plastids from illuminated leaves than in plastids from unilluminated ones(Table VI). The data are given on the basis of the activity in plastids from equal fresh weights of tissue. Since the number of plastids per cell appears to remain unchanged during the treatment period, the data are also valid for activity per equal number of plastids.

Table VII provides similar data for plastids isolated by differential centrifugation and purified by sucrose density gradient centrifugation. RNA polymerase activity in preparations of this kind are invariably stimulated by the addition of DNA but less thoroughly purified plastid

TABLE V.   *Maize Leaf RNA Polymerase*

Activity of 27,000*g* Supernatant Fractions
Incorporation of C^{14}-ATP[a]

	+CT DNA (cpm)	−CT DNA (cpm)
Unilluminated	652[b]	373
30 min Lt + 90 min Dk	647	318
Protein per 0.80 ml reaction mixture:		
Lt, 1.78 mg; Dk, 1.65 mg		

[a] Reaction mixture = 0.8 ml. Components of reaction mixture: 1.8 μM ea. CTP, GTP, UTP; 1.5 μC ATP (0.14 μM); 0.02 mM Mg Acetate; 0.04 mM mercaptoethanol; 0.04 mM Tris pH 8.0; ±0.2 mg calf thymus DNA (CT DNA) and 0.1 mM NH$_4$Cl, all in 0.4 ml *plus* 0.4 ml protein (enzyme preparation) in 0.5 M sucrose, 0.5 M Tris pH 8.0, 0.001 M MgCl$_2$, 0.01 M mercaptoethanol. Incubation: 10 min, 30°C. Protein per 0.80 ml reaction mixture: from unilluminated leaves 1.68 mg; from leaves illuminated for 30 min and returned to darkness for 90 min before harvest 1.78 mg.

[b] Counts per minute per 0.1 ml reaction mixture.

TABLE VI.   *Maize Leaf Polymerase*

Activity of "Plastid" Fractions
Incorporation of C^{14}-ATP[a]

	−CT DNA (cpm)	+ CT DNA (cpm)
Unilluminated	166[b]	161
30 min Lt + 90 min Dk	419	410
Chlorophyll per 0.80 ml reaction mixture:		
Lt 0.004 mμg; Dk 0.002 mμg		

[a] Reaction mixture = 0.8 ml. Components: 2 μM ea. CTP, UTP, GTP; 1.4 μC ATP (0.14 μM); 0.02 mM Mg Acetate; 0.04 mM mercaptoethanol; 0.04 mM Tris pH 8.0; ±0.2 mg calf thymus DNA (CT DNA) and 0.1 mM NH$_4$Cl, all in 0.4 ml *plus* 0.4 ml of plastid preparation (washed and resuspended 1000 g fraction) in 0.5 M sucrose, 0.05 M Tris, pH 8.0, 0.001 M MgCl$_2$, 0.01 M mercaptoethanol included instead of 27,000 g supernatant solutions. Chlorophyll per 0.80 ml reaction mixture: from unilluminated leaves 2.0 mμg; from leaves illuminated for 30 min and returned to darkness for 90 min before harvest 4.1 mμg. These amounts of plastid suspension are calculated to be derived from almost equal amounts (fresh weight) of tissue, that is, 0.63 mg (fresh weight) unilluminated leaf tissue; 0.60 mg illuminated leaf tissue. (Plastids were prepared from 58 of each type of leaf tissue.) Incubation: 10 min, 30°C.

[b] Counts per minute per 0.1 ml of reaction mixture.

TABLE VII.   *RNA Polymerase Activity*

"Purified" Chloroplast Fractions from Maize Leaves C^{14}-ATP Incorporated[a]		
Exp. 1 (cpm)[b]	Exp. 2 (cpm)	Exp. 3 (cpm)
Dk 10	11	29
Lt 107	43	88
Dk+CT-DNA 25 ·	20	58
Lt+CT-DNA 149	71	103

[a] cpm/0.1 ml. Reaction mixture: 2 μM ea. CTP, GTP, UTP; 1.1 μC ATP (0.14 μM; 0.02 mM Mg Acetate; 0.04 mM mercaptoethanol; 0.04 mM Tris, pH 8.0; $\pm$0.2 mg calf thymus DNA (CT DNA) and 0.1 mM NH$_4$Cl all in 0.4 ml *plus* 0.4 ml plastids in 0.5 M sucrose, 0.05 M sucrose, 0.05 M Tris, pH 8.0, 0.001 M MgCl$_2$, 0.01 M mercaptoethanol. Incubation: 10 min, 30°C. *Within* each experiment the quantities of plastids used in each reaction mixture were determined to be derived from equal amounts (fresh weight) of leaf tissue.
[b] Exp. 1: Lt = 20 min light + 90 min darkness before harvest. Exp. 2 and 3: Lt = 120 min light before harvest.

preparations respond inconsistently to added DNA—probably because of contaminating nuclear DNA.

These experiments reveal that plastid RNA polymerase activity increases during the lag phase and may, at least in part, explain the accelerated production of the various RNAs but the sequence of early events following illumination of etiolated leaves remains to be elucidated. RNA polymerase may be the first enzyme stimulated by light but it is equally possible, if we judge on the basis of available evidence, that RNA polymerase formation is concomitant with the accelerated production of many other plastid proteins during the lag phase. The primary effect of light on lag phase plastid biochemistry remains to be elucidated although it is clear that RNA polymerase activity increases and much new RNA is formed in maize proplastids during the lag period which precedes rapid chlorophyll accumulation and the structural changes characteristic of plastid maturation.

The relationship between plastic and nuclear metabolism in the development of the chloroplast to full photosynthetic activity is just beginning to be explored—very many questions are arising.

SUMMARY AND CONCLUSIONS

It has been inferred from photosynthetic experiments that the bulk of the chlorophyll molecules in a green plant or a photosynthetic bacterium function simply as collectors of radiant energy. This energy is transferred to the small fraction of the pigment molecules associated with compounds involved in photosynthetic electron transport. The light-gathering pigment molecules are probably arranged in a more-or-less random fashion; the chlorophyll molecules at the active, or trapping centers more likely have a specific orientation with regard to one another. The other components of the trapping centers include at least one—and perhaps two—cytochromes. Evidence from experiments on photosynthetic enhancement suggest that there may be two kinds of active centers—or at least two functional parts to a single type. The mechanism for oxygen release in green plant photosynthesis is probably associated with the long wavelength (that is, the System II) center. The photosynthetic unit consists of an active center, or a set of them, and the affiliated light-gathering pigment molecules.

Regarding structure, the presence of membranes or lamellae is a constant feature of the photosynthetic apparatus in organisms ranging in size and complexity from photosynthetic bacteria and blue-green algae to angiosperms. In bacteria the membranes sometimes enclose small vesicles, in other organisms the elements of the photosynthetic apparatus appear in cross section as groups of flattened sack-like structures or thylakoids.

The photochemistry and probably most of the electron transport of photosynthesis is carried on in the thylakoids. The enzymes that catalyze the carbon chemistry associated with photosynthesis are soluble components of the chloroplast; if all or some of these are normally part of the lamellae *in vivo*, they are easily removed. In any event, the photochemical and electron transport segments of the plastid can be washed free of enzymes of carbon metabolism. The unresolved problems of organization for photosynthetic activity begin at this point.

According to current views the plastid lamellae are not smooth membranes, but may at least contain some particles embedded in them or, in the extreme view, are composed entirely of closely associated particles. These problems are being pursued by electron microscopy and low-angle X-ray diffraction.

Attempts have been made to fragment lamellae by ultrasonic radiation and detergent treatment. Lamellar portions have been recovered by differential centrifugation of preparations of disintegrated thylakoids and the amount and kind of residual photosynthetic activity has been determined. The most readily lost manifestation of photosynthesis is probably the S, or slow, ESR signal; the most persistent feature is the rapid, or R, signal. Experiments by M. B. Allen and co-workers (12), indicate that the latter may be fractionable by disruption of chloroplast lamellae of *Chlorella*. Hill reaction activity, which includes a large part of photosynthesis including the mechanism for oxygen release, is shown by some of the smallest lamellar fragments recovered.

Correlations between sublamellar fragments obtained by disruptive treatments and features of the ultrastructure *in situ* are not yet satisfactory.

Studies of the course of plastid development have by now provided a moderately complete over-all outline of these processes, but the course of formation of the functional units is not known. The time course of appearance in the plant of certain capacities related to photosynthesis has been examined in several laboratories but the manner in which pigments, structural proteins, and enzymes are brought or held together remains to be worked out.

Finally, breeding data, which have implied that plastids may have some hereditary independence, have begun to attract more attention as knowledge has advanced in the areas of molecular genetics, nucleic acid metabolism, and protein synthesis. Evidence that plastids contain DNA and that it is qualitatively different from that in the nucleus now appears to be unequivocal. The presence of distinctive plastid ribosomes and at least some independent RNA metabolism are both well established. The extent of interdependence, or independence, of plastids, nuclei, and other subcellular units in a single cell has not yet been defined in a single case. Closely related is the elucidation of mechanisms which control plastid maturation.

Problems in plastid biology are beginning to be defined. They will probably be no more difficult to resolve than similar questions about whole organisms.

Figures 4, 9–11, and 14–18 are reproduced by permission of The Rockefeller University Press from *The Journal of Cell Biology*.

REFERENCES

1. Allen, M. B., and Murchio, J. C. In *Photosynthetic Mechanisms of Green Plants*, Natl. Acad. Sci.–Natl. Res. Council (U.S.) Publ. 1145, Washington, D.C., 1963a, p. 486.
2. Allen, M. M., Murchio, J. C., Jeffery, S. W., and Bendix, S. A., In *Microalgae and Photosynthetic Bacteria*, Ed. Japanese Society of Plant Physiologists, The University of Tokyo Press, Tokyo, 1963b, p. 407.
3. Allen, M. B., Whatley, F. R., Rosenberg, L. L., Capindale, J. B., and Arnon, D. I., In *Research in Photosynthesis*, Ed. H. Gaffron, C. S. French, R. Livingston, E. I. Rabinowitch, B. L. Strehler, and N. E. Tolbert, Interscience Publishers, Inc., New York, 1957, p. 288.

4. Anderson, J. M., and Boardman, N. K., *Australian J. Biol. Sci. 17*, 93 (1964).
5. Androes, G. M., Singleton, M. F., and Calvin, M., *Proc. Natl. Acad. Sci. U.S. 48*, 1022 (1962).
6. Arnon, D. I., Allen, M. B., and Whatley, F. R., *Nature 174*, 394 (1954).
7. Beinert, H., and Kok, B., *Biochim. Biophys. Acta 88*, 278 (1964).
8. Bishop, N. I., *Proc. Natl. Acad. Sci. U.S. 45*, 1696 (1960).
9. Blois, M. S., Jr., and Weaver, E. C., In *Photophysiology*, Ed. A. C. Giese, Academic Press, New York, Vol. I, 1964, p. 35.
10. Boardman, N. K., *Biochim. Biophys. Acta 62*, 63 (1962a).
11. Boardman, N. K., *Biochim. Biophys. Acta 64*, 279 (1962b).
12. Boardman, N. K., and Anderson, J. M., *Nature 203*, 166 (1964).
13. Boardman, N. K., and Wildman, S. G., *Biochim. Biophys. Acta 59*, 222 (1962).
14. Boardman, N. K., Francki, R. I. B., and Wildman, S. G., *Biochemistry 4*, 872 (1965).
15. Bogorad, L., and Jacobson, A. B., *Biochem. Biophys. Res. Commun. 4*, 113 (1964).
16. Bogorad, L., and Jacobson, A. B., *Fed. Proc. 24*, 664 (1965).
17. Bogorad, L., Mercer, F. V., and Mullens, R., In *Photosynthetic Mechanisms in Green Plants*, Nat'l. Acad. Sci.–Nat'l. Res. Council (U.S.) Publ. 1145, Washington, D.C., 1963, p. 560.
18. Brawerman, G., and Eisenstadt, J. M., *J. Mol. Biol. 10*, 403 (1964).
19. Butler, W. L., *Arch. Biochem. Biophys. 92*, 287 (1961a).
20. Butler, W. L., *Arch. Biochem. Biophys. 93*, 413 (1961b).
21. Butler, W. L., *Biochem. Biophys. Acta 102*, 1 (1965).
22. Chance, B., and Bonner, W. D., Jr., In *Photosynthetic Mechanisms in Green Plants*, Natl. Acad. Sci.–Natl. Res. Council (U.S.) Publ. 1145, Washington, D.C., 1963, p. 66.
23. Chibnall, A. C., *Protein Metabolism in the Plant*, Yale University Press, New Haven, 1939.
24. Chun, E. H. L., Vaughn, M. H., and Rich, A., *J. Mol. Biol. 7*, 130 (1963).
25. Clark, M. F., Matthews, R. E. F., and Ralph, R. K., *Biochim. Biophys. Acta 91*, 289 (1964).
26. Duysens, L. M. N., Thesis, University of Utrecht (1952).
27. Edelman, M., Schiff, J. A., and Epstein, H. T., *J. Mol. Biol. 11*, 769 (1965).
28. Eilam, Y., and Klein, S., *J. Cell Biol. 14*, 169 (1962).
29. Eisenstadt, J. M., and Brawerman, G., *J. Mol. Biol. 10*, 392 (1964).
30. Emerson, R., and Arnold, A., *J. Gen. Physiol. 16*, 191 (1932).
31. Eriksson, G., Kahn, A., Walles, B., and von Wettstein, D., *Ber. deutch bot. Ges. 74*, 221, (1961).
32. Eversole, R. A., and Wolken, J. J., *Science 127*, 1287 (1958).
33. Frey-Wyssling, A., and Steinmann, E., *Vierteljahresschr. Naturforsch. Ges. Zurich 98*, 20 (1953).
34. Gassman, M., and Bogorad, L., *Plant Physiol. 40*, lii (1965).
35. Gibbs, S. P., *J. Ultrastructure Res. 7*, 418 (1962).

36. Gibor, A., and Granick, S., *J. Cell Biol. 15*, 599 (1962).
37. Gibor, A., and Izawa, M., *Proc. Natl. Acad. Sci. U.S. 50*, 1164 (1963).
38. Granick, S., *Am. J. Bot. 25*, 558 (1938).
39. Granick, S., In *Encyclopedia of Plant Physiology*, Ed. W. Ruhland, Springer Verlag, Berlin, 1955, Vol. I, p. 507.
40. Granick, S., *Plant Physiol. 34*, xviii (1959).
41. Granick, S., and Porter, K., *Am. J. Bot. 34*, 545 (1947).
42. Gross, J. A., Becker, M. J., and Shefner, A. M., *Nature 203*, 1263 (1964).
43. Heitz, E., *Exptl. Cell Res. 7*, 606 (1954).
44. Holt, A. S., and French, C. S., In *Photosynthesis in Plants*, Ed. J. Franck and W. E. Loomis, Interscience Publishers, Inc., New York, 1949, p. 277.
45. Jacobson, A. B., Swift, H., and Bogorad, L., *J. Cell Biol. 17*, 557 (1963).
46. Kellenberger, E., Ryter, A., and Sechaud, J., *J. Biophys. Biochem. Cytol. 4*, 671 (1958).
47. Kirk, J. T. O., *Biochim. Biophys. Acta 76*, 417 (1963).
48. Kirk, J. T. O., *Biochem. Biophys. Res. Commun. 16*, 233 (1964).
49. Kislev, N., Swift, H., and Bogorad, L., *J. Cell Biol. 25*, 327 (1965).
50. Klein, S., Bryan, G., and Bogorad, L. *J. Cell Biol. 22*, 433 (1964).
51. Kok, B., *Biochim. Biophys. Acta 48*, 527 (1961).
52. Leff, J., Mandel, M., Epstein, H. T., and Schiff, J. A., *Biochem. Biophys. Res. Commun. 13*, 126 (1963).
53. Leyon, A., *Exptl. Cell Res. 7*, 609 (1954).
54. Lyman, H., Epstein, H. T., and Schiff, J. A., *Biochim. Biophys. Acta 50*, 301 (1961).
55. Lyttleton, J. W., *Biochem. J. 74*, 82 (1960).
56. Lyttleton, J. W., *Exptl. Cell Res. 26*, 312 (1962).
57. Mans, R. J., and Novelli, G. D., *Biochim. Biophys. Acta 91*, 186 (1964).
58. Margulies, M. M., *Plant Physiol. 37*, 473 (1962).
59. Margulies, M. M., *Plant Physiol. 39*, 579 (1964).
60. McCalla, D. R., and Allan, R. K., *Nature 201*, 504 (1964).
61. Mego, J. L., and Jagendorf, A. T., *Biochim. Biophys. Acta 53*, 237 (1961).
62. Menke, W., *Z. Physiol. Chem. 257*, 43 (1938).
63. Menke, W., In *Photosynthetic Mechanisms in Green Plants*, Natl. Acad. Sci.–Natl. Res. Council (U.S.) Publ. 1145, Washington, D.C., 1963a, p. 537.
64. Menke, W., *Z. Naturforsch. 18b*, 821 (1963b).
65. Menke, W., and Menke, G., *Protoplasma 46*, 535 (1956).
66. Mercer, F. V., Bogorad, L., and Mullens, R., *J. Cell Biol. 13*, 393 (1962).
67. Mitrakos, K. *Physiol. Plantarum 14*, 497 (1961).
68. Muhlethaler, K., and Frey-Wyssling, A., *J. Cell Biol. 6*, 507 (1959).
69. Olson, R. A., In *Mechanisms of Photosynthesis in Green Plants*, Natl. Acad. Sci.–Natl. Res. Council (U.S.) Publ. 1145, Washington, D.C., 1963, p. 545.
70. Park, R. B., and Biggins, J., *Science 144*, 1009 (1964).

71. Park, R. B., and Pon, N. G., *J. Mol. Biol. 3*, 1 (1961).
72. Pogo, B. G. T., and Pogo, A. O., *J. Cell Biol. 22*, 296 (1964).
73. Price, L., and Klein, W. H., *Plant Physiol. 36*, 733 (1961).
74. Rabinowitch, E. I., *Photosynthesis and Related Processes*, Interscience Publishers, Inc., New York, 1945, 1951, 1956, Vol. I., Vol. II, 1, Vol. II, 2.
75. Ray, D. S., and Hanawalt, P. C., *J. Mol. Biol. 9*, 812 (1964).
76. Ray, D. S., and Hanawalt, P. C., *J. Mol. Biol. 11*, 760 (1965).
77. Rhoades, M. M., In *Encyclopedia of Plant Physiology*, Ed. W. Ruhland, Springer Verlag, Berlin, 1955, Vol. I, p. 19.
78. Ris, H., and Plaut, W., *J. Cell Biol. 13*, 383 (1962).
79. Sager, R., and Ishida, M. R., *Proc. Natl. Acad. Sci. U.S. 50*, 725 (1963).
80. Sauer, K., and Calvin, M., *J. Mol. Biol. 4*, 451 (1962).
81. Schiff, J. A., Lyman, H., and Epstein, H. T., *Biochim. Biophys. Acta 50*, 310 (1961).
82. Semal, J., Spencer, D., Kim, Y. T., and Wildman, S. G., *Biochim. Biophys. Acta 91*, 205 (1964).
83. Shibata, K., *J. Biochem.* (Tokyo) *44*, 147 (1957).
84. Sissakian, N. M., Filippovich, I. I., Svetailo, E. N., and Aliyev, K. A., *Biochim. Biophys. Acta 95*, 474 (1965).
85. Smillie, R. M., *Can. J. Bot. 41*, 123 (1963).
86. Smith, E. L., and Pickels, E. G., *Proc. Natl. Acad. Sci. U.S. 26*, 272 (1940).
87. Smith, E. L., and Pickels, E. G., *J. Gen. Physiol. 24*, 753 (1941).
88. Smith, J. H. C., In *Comparative Biochemistry of Photoreactive Systems*, Ed. M. B. Allen, Academic Press, New York, 1960, p. 257.
89. Smith, J. H. C., and French, C. S., *Ann. Rev. Plant Physiol. 14*, 181 (1963).
90. Steinmann, E., *Exptl. Cell Res. 3*, 267 (1952).
91. Stocking, C. R., and Gifford, E. M., *Biochem. Biophys. Res. Commun. 1*, 159 (1959).
92. Thomas, J. B., Blaauw, O. H., and Duysens, L. N. M., *Biochim. Biophys. Acta 10*, 230 (1953).
93. Virgin, H. I., *Physiol. Plantarum 8*, 630 (1955).
94. Virgin, H. I., Kahn, A., and von Wettstein, D., *Photochem. Photobiol. 2*, 83 (1963).
95. Wehrmeyer, W., *Planta 62*, 272 (1964).
96. Weier, T. E., Stocking, C. R., Thomson, W. W., and Drever, H. J., *J. Ultrastructure Res. 8*, 122 (1963).
97. Wessels, J. S. C., *Proc. Roy. Soc. London, Ser. B. 157*, 345 (1963).
98. von Wettstein, D., *Brookhaven Symp. Biol. 11*, 138 (1958).
99. von Wettstein, D., and Kahn, A., *Proc. European Conf. Electron Microscopy, Delft 2*, 1051 (1960).
100. Withrow, R. B., Wolff, J. B., and Price, L., *Plant Physiol. 31*, xiii (1956).
101. Wolken, J. J., *Brookhaven Symp. Biol. 11*, 87 (1958).
102. Wollgeihn, R., and Mothes, K., *Naturwiss. 50*, 95 (1963).

7

THE ORGANIZATION OF VERTEBRATE VISUAL RECEPTORS

John E. Dowling

The study of vision and the mechanisms by which light and form are perceived has long fascinated biologists, physiologists, and physicists. With the development of new techniques such as electron microscopy, we now can focus closely on the visual receptors and begin to examine them on a molecular level. In this article, we will review briefly what we know of the fine structure of the vertebrate receptor cells and discuss experimental attempts to correlate this structure with the chemistry of vision.

STRUCTURE OF VISUAL CELLS

In most vertebrate retinas we find two types of visual cells: rods and cones. The rods are dim-light receptors and do not perceive color; the cones function in bright light and mediate color vision. Figure 1 shows a light micrograph of the rods and cones in the human retina. Ordinarily, rods and cones may be distinguished by the shapes of their inner and outer segments, as shown here. The rod outer segments are longer, thinner, and cylindrical; whereas the cones are fatter and distinctly conical. (This is not always the case, however. Foveal cones, for example, are very rod-like in gross appearance and are the longest receptor cells in the mammalian retina.) The inner segments of rods and cones differ also in size and shape, the cone inner segments being much stouter. The inner segments of both types of receptor connect by a short stalk with their nuclei, which are packed together below the mosaic

Contribution No. 4 from the Augustus C. Long Laboratories, Alan C. Woods Research Building. Supported in part by Research to Prevent Blindness Inc. and U.S. Public Health Service Grant No. 05336–01.

of rods and cones; they then connect by a longer fiber with the receptor feet or pedicles, where the cells make synaptic contact with the second-order neurons of the retina—the bipolar and horizontal cells.

With the electron microscope, one can examine the internal structure of the visual cell. Figure 2 shows a low-power electron micrograph of cone cells in the ground squirrel retina. The ground squirrel is an interesting animal because its retina contains only cone cells. As one might expect, this animal is highly diurnal, seldom venturing out at night. At the top of the micrograph the densely staining outer segments are shown. (In the ground squirrel, the outer segments are particularly short and not markedly conical.) Between the outer segments extend processes from the overlying pigment epithelial cells. These processes contain densely staining pigment granules, which presumably serve to shield the receptor outer segments from stray light.

Connecting the inner and outer segments is a thin, tenuous-looking structure that on higher magnification closely resembles a cilium (Fig. 4) (9,38). It contains nine pairs of double filaments, arranged radially around its circumference; but it lacks the central pair of filaments ordinarily found in motile cilia. The connecting cilium terminates in the inner segment in a typical basal body or centriole, and a second centriole is usually found nearby at right angles. From the basal body, a rootlet is frequently seen to extend deeper into the inner segment. From such electron microscopic observations, it has become clear that the outer segments of all vertebrate visual cells are cilial derivatives. Cilia or cilium-like structures also appear closely allied with many other receptors found in organisms including the coclear hair cells (21),

---

FIG. 1. Rods and cones in the human retina. The overlying pigment epithelium (top) contains many dense pigment granules which obscure the tips of the rods (R) and cones (C). The nuclei (N) of the receptors, stacked below the inner segments, connect by a long, laterally displaced fiber with the receptor feet or pedicles (P), where the receptors make synaptic contact with the second-order neurons of the retina. The dense line between the receptor inner segments and nuclei is the external limiting membrane (elm; see Fig. 2). Phase micrograph × 2,000.

FIG. 2. Low-power electron micrograph of the inner (IS) and outer (OS) segments of the all-cone retina of the ground squirrel. The pigment epithelial cell processes extending between the outer segments contain densely staining melanin granules (mg). Joining the inner and outer segments is the tenuous connecting cilium (CC). Just below this junction, numerous mitochondria (m) are squeezed into the distal portion of the inner segment. At the base of the inner segment, densities between the glial (Müller) cells (G) and inner segments give the appearance in the light microscope (Fig. 1) of a membrane running transversely between inner segments and nuclei (the so-called external limiting membrane). From the glial cells fine processes extend distally, surrounding the base of the inner segment. × 7,500.

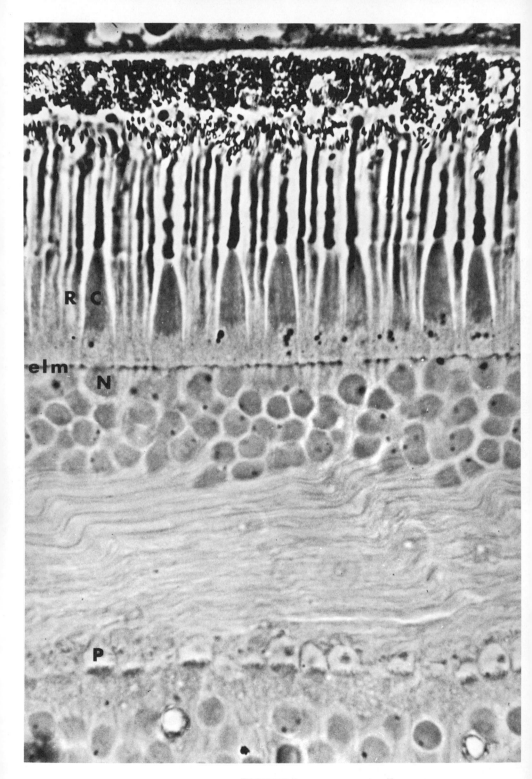

FIGURE 1

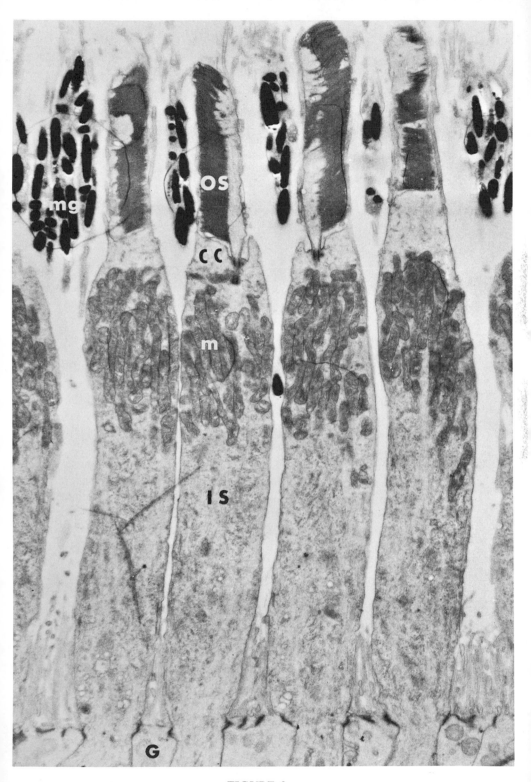

FIGURE 2

and olfactory epithelium (3). Thus, cilia seem to underly the structure and function of many types of receptor.

The inner segment contains most of the typical cytoplasmic organelles of the receptor cells (Fig. 2). Mitochondria are numerous and, especially in cones, are squeezed into the upper portion of the segment, close to the outer segment. The significance of this is not clear, but it is thought to be related perhaps to an energy-requiring process in the outer segment. Outer segments do not contain mitochondria or other cytoplasmic organelles such as ribosomes, and they are believed to depend on the inner segments for their metabolic needs.

The process of photoreception begins in the outer segment, where the light-sensitive visual pigments are located. Figure 3 shows an electron micrograph of a cone outer segment from the ground squirrel. The outer segment consists of many transverse, membrane-limited, flattened discs enclosing a less-dense inner space (34). In a typical outer segment there may be 500 to 1,000 such discs, piled one atop the other like a stack of coins. The membranes of the discs are derived from the plasma membrane of the outer segment. Continuity of disc and plasma membrane is visible in the developing outer segment (19,29,38); but in the adult mammalian receptor most of the discs appear to pinch off from the plasma membrane and to have no discernible contact with the plasma membrane or with each other (6,12,13,28,30). In favorably oriented sections it is possible to follow single discs across the entire width of the segment, and they appear entirely free-floating (Fig. 5).

At the base of the mammalian cone outer segment, however, continuity is still retained between disc and plasma membrane, even in the adult; and the structure may appear, in part, as one continuously folded membrane (arrows, Fig. 3) (6). In cone cells of lower vertebrates such as the frog (28), perch (36), and mudpuppy (5), continuity between disc and plasma membrane is retained in the mature cone throughout the entire length of the segment. In these outer segments, the discs never appear to pinch off and to become free-floating.

This is an important point, for if the discs do retain contact with the plasma membrane, the interior of the disc could be continuous with the extracellular space; and this might have important implications for the problem of visual excitation. If the interior of the disc is extracellular, one could reasonably postulate a differential ion distribution across the disc membrane and suggest the possibility of ion flow across the disc during light absorption by the visual pigment, similar to the local potential recorded in the rods of the squid retina (23). It has therefore been crucial to determine whether discs retain any continuity with the plasma membrane. The best evidence, outlined above, is that most discs of rod and (mammalian) cone outer segments do not contact the plasma membrane and are free-floating. It is possible that there are very fine, narrow connections somewhere along the circumference of the disc (34,35); but such continuities have not been seen in well-oriented segments in which it is possible to follow discs across their entire width. Continuity is also not visible in cross sections, except in instances in which continuity is seen in longitudinal section. To unequivocally demonstrate that such connections do not exist may require the serial sectioning of a rod or cone outer segment, but this has not yet been done.

The fine structure of the discs of rods and cones is quite similar, but certain differences may be noted. Perhaps the clearest difference involves the edge of the disc. In rods there is a circular button-like ending at the edge of the disc, frequently appearing more densely stained than the membranes in the interior of the disc (Fig. 5). In cones, the disc membranes may be slightly farther apart at the edge of the disc, but there is apparently no circular button ending. A second difference between rod and cone discs, perhaps the most significant, involves the spacing of the disc membranes from one another. In the literature, comparisons of rod and cone disc dimensions vary widely, with no clear evidence as to the true spacing (29). The lack of agreement may exist because the discs are osmotically very sensitive and may readily swell or shrink before or during fixation (10). In our experience, primarily with mammalian receptors, the rods appear to be more sensitive osmotically than the cones; and the rods often vary considerably in comparison to the cones. In our best osmium-fixed preparations, we find the rod discs consistently thicker than the cone discs (12). In the monkey, for example, the cone discs appear about 140 Å thick, whereas the rods are about 180 Å thick. Most of the difference in

---

FIG. 3.   Outer segment of a cone from the ground squirrel retina. The outer segment consists of a stack of flattened, membrane-limited discs. Toward the base of the segment, continuity of disc and plasma membrane is clearly seen (thin arrows), and at the very base the structure appears as one continuously folded membrane (thick arrow). Thin processes from the inner segment (IS) extend distally along the length of the outer segment (P). × 75,000.

FIG. 4.   The junction between inner and outer segment, showing connecting cilium (CC), basal bodies (BB), and rootlet (R). In the insert, a cross section of a connecting cilium shows the nine pairs of double filaments arranged radially around the circumference. The two central filaments, found in motile cilia, are absent here in the connecting cilium. In the outer segment, the double filaments become singlets (arrow, inset), and in the case of the rat, run along the incision of the rod. (15). × 62,000.

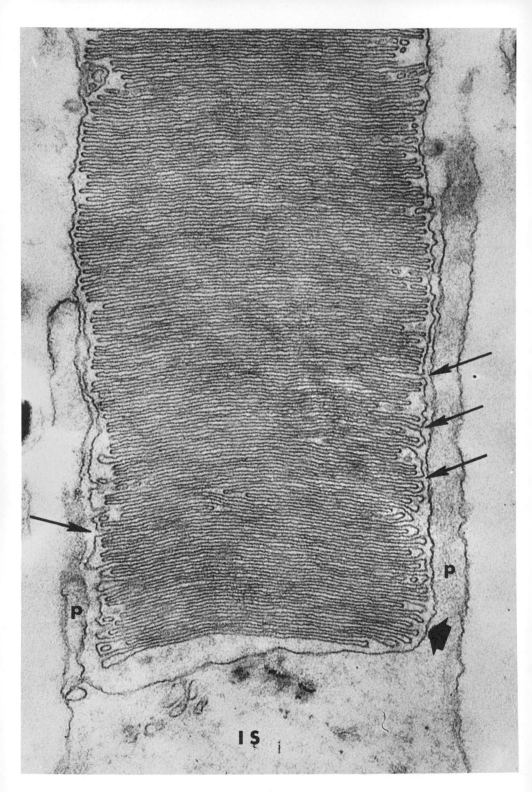

FIGURE 3

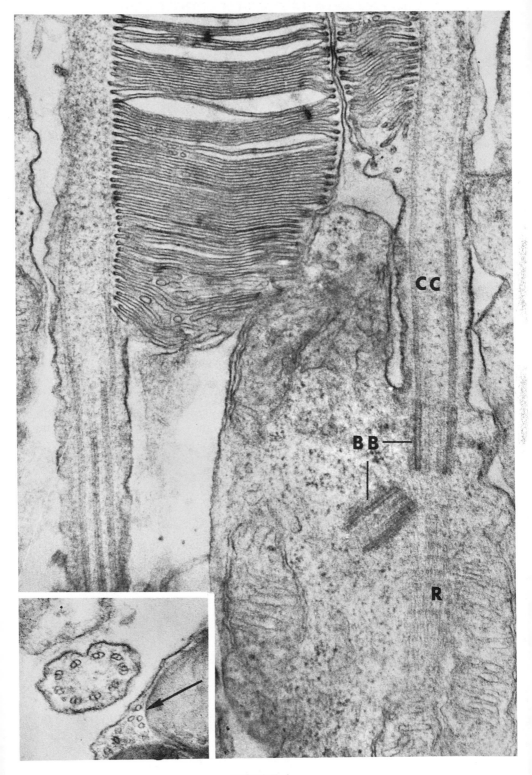

FIGURE 4

thickness is due to an increased intradisc space, although in osmium-fixed material the disc membranes often appear slightly thinner in rod outer segments (Fig. 5) (12,36). However, recent work with glutaralde-hyde-fixed material has not confirmed this observation (39). Apparently, the disc membranes of rods and cones have the same thickness, which is also the dimension of the plasma membrane (Fig. 6).

The rod illustrated in Fig. 6 was fixed with glutaraldehyde in phosphate buffer (6% glutaraldehyde in 0.05 M buffer), which acts as a hypertonic fixative. The osmotic sensitivity of the discs is well demon-strated in this micrograph, because here the discs have in most cases collapsed tightly; thus there often is no intradisc space. The obliteration of the intradisc space with hypertonic fixation also demonstrates that there is probably no structural material contained within the discs. In this high-resolution picture the membranes of the disc may be resolved into the typical triple-layered structure of the unit membrane (33). In those discs that have collapsed, the two inner lines of the unit mem-brane are seen as one very dense membrane running in the middle of the disc. Elsewhere, the disc membranes are sometimes separated in per-haps the truer relation, and in these places the disc membranes appear similar to the plasma membrane (30). Occasionally, globular cross bands or bridges are seen extending across the unit membrane (29). These cross bands are also seen along the plasma membrane. In high-resolution electron microscopy, membranes from a variety of sources often appear globular and exhibit cross bridges (37), so that we cannot ascribe special significance to this inner structure of the unit membrane seen here in the receptor.

The collapsing of the rod discs with hypertonic fixation raises one further point regarding the continuity of disc with extracellular space. If intradisc space does represent extracellular space, with hypertonic solution we might expect the discs to pull apart as the intracellular space shrinks. The opposite result is observed, however, suggesting that the interior of the discs is not extracellular. The converse of this experi-ment has also been done. Rods fixed with hypotonic fixative exhibit swollen discs, which is consistent with the idea that the interior of the disc is intracellular (10).

CHEMISTRY OF OUTER SEGMENTS

As yet, we know almost nothing of the molecules that make up the outer segment of a rod or cone, except for the light-sensing visual pigment molecules. In a single outer segment, however, there are enormous numbers of visual pigment molecules. A recent calculation shows that there are about 30–40 million visual pigment molecules in a mammalian rod (7,40); other estimates indicate that some 15–30% of the dry weight of rods is visual pigment (24,40). The visual pigment molecule must therefore make up a large portion of the structure we observe under the electron microscope.

The rod pigment, rhodopsin, has a molecular weight of about 40,000 (24). Wald (40) has calculated that a molecule of this molecular weight would have a diameter of 45 Å if spherical, or 36 Å if cubical. Such dimensions are easily resolvable in the electron microscope, but as yet no one has observed particles of these dimensions related *specifically* to rod disc membranes. As noted above, globular particles are seen in disc membranes (20,30); but this has been a general finding in membranes. It does seem likely that the visual pigment molecules are part of the disc membranes; if so, what happens to the rod structure when the visual pigment is altered?

In recent years, we have come to know something of the structure of the visual pigments and how they are affected by light (41,42). Figure 7 is a diagram summarizing the reactions the rod pigment, rhodopsin, undergoes during the photoreceptor process. It is likely that this same scheme applies to all vertebrate visual pigments, both rod and cone. In short, rhodopsin bleaches or breaks down in light into its component parts, protein (opsin) and all-trans retinene (vitamin A aldehyde, retinal, retinaldehyde). Retinene is reduced to vitamin A in the eye by an enzyme similar to liver alcohol dehydrogenase (ADH), working with the coenzyme triphosphopyridine nucleotide (TPN) (22).

For the resynthesis of rhodopsin, another isomeric configuration

---

FIG. 5. Longitudinal section of rat rod (a) and monkey foveal cone (b). In these micrographs the discs may be followed across the entire width of the outer segment. No continuities of the discs with the plasma membrane or with each other are obvious. × 50,000. Portions of outer segments of rod (c) and cone (d) from the same preparation of monkey retina. The rods consistently exhibit a wider intradisc space as compared with the cones, and also demonstrate a characteristic button-like ending at the edge of the disc (arrow) (12). × 150,000.

FIG. 6. Glutaraldehyde-fixed monkey rod. The triple-layered nature of the unit membrane is well demonstrated in this micrograph. The hypertonic fixative caused most of the discs to collapse, obliterating the intradisc space. The two inner lines of the unit membrane are seen as one very dense membrane running in the middle of the disc. Globular cross bands or bridges are seen extending across the unit membrane in places (arrows, inset) in both the disc and plasma membranes. No differences between disc and plasma membranes have been detected (39). × 165,000; inset × 257,000.

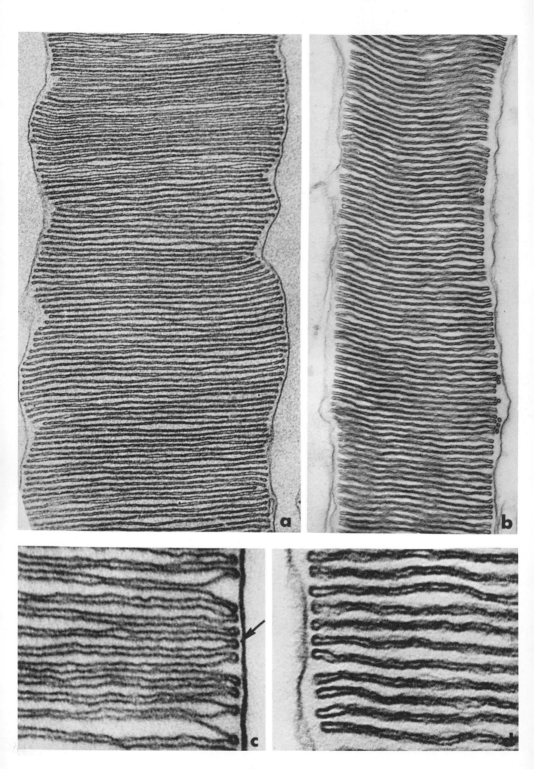

FIGURE 5

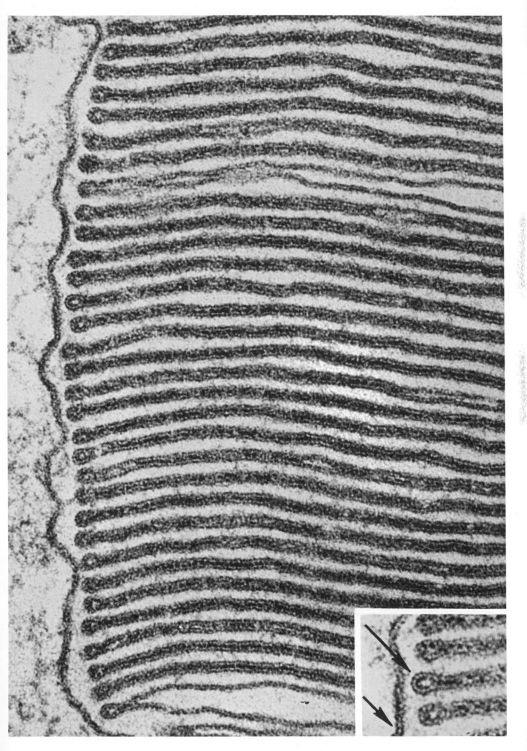

FIGURE 6

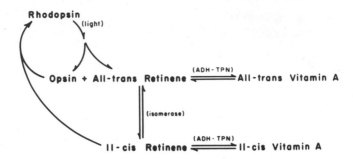

FIG. 7. A summary diagram of the chemistry of the visual pigment, rhodopsin (modified from 41).

of retinene is required, the 11-cis form. Thus all-trans retinene must be isomerized to 11-cis retinene before rhodopsin regeneration can occur. (11-cis retinene may also be reduced to vitamin A by ADH and TPN.) The 11-cis retinene combines spontaneously with opsin to reform rhodopsin, completing the visual cycle.

Light adaptation results in the loss of the retinene chromophore from the visual pigment, a relatively small loss of material from the molecule (less than 1% of the molecular weight). Thus, we might expect not to see changes in the outer segment structure after light adaptation; and although some claims have been made (20,43), such changes have not been convincingly demonstrated. However, with loss of the visual protein, opsin, we would expect to see changes in outer segment structure.

When animals are raised on vitamin A-deficient diets, rhodopsin levels in the eye gradually decline as vitamin A levels in the eye decline. This results in loss of visual sensitivity, known as night blindness. Initially this is a simple lack of the vitamin A chromophore and is readily reversible when vitamin A is administered (16). However, if animals are maintained on deficient diets for prolonged periods, the protein, opsin, will begin to degenerate; and gross structural deterioration of the visual cell occurs. With prolonged vitamin A deficiency, tissue deterioration in an animal is often widespread; but it can be confined to the visual system by maintaining the animal with vitamin A acid (17). Vitamin A acid keeps animals that are on vitamin A-deficient diets healthy and growing, but the acid is not converted to vitamin A or vitamin A aldehyde, the forms of the vitamin required for the visual cycle. Under these circumstances, animals remain systemically healthy but lose their visual pigment and become entirely blind. In such animals it is possible to study the progressive changes in fine structure as visual pigment is gradually lost (17).

In rats raised on a vitamin A-deficient diet there is no detectable change in the outer segment structure until opsin levels begin to deteriorate. With opsin loss, structural changes do occur. The first changes seen are swelling and fragmentation of the disc membranes into distended vesicles and tubules (Fig. 8). Gradually the entire structure becomes filled with vesicles and tubules, and the outer segment loses its normal cylindrical shape, becoming spherical. It is important to note here that the plasma membrane does not (at least initially) seem to undergo the changes that take place in the disc membrane. The plasma membrane appears to remain intact and to competently enclose the fragmented disc membranes. Eventually the outer segments do disappear completely, but the mechanism by which this occurs is not clear.

If feeding of vitamin A to deficient animals is resumed, the outer segments can be regenerated. There appears to be a close correlation between the levels of rhodopsin (or opsin) in the eye and the amount of disc membrane in either a normally developing or a regenerating outer segment (15). Figure 9 compares the quantity of rhodopsin extracted from rat retinas, during development of the visual cells, with the length of the outer segment. (The length of outer segment closely reflects the number of discs present in a receptor.) The correlation is clear, although rods do not develop synchronously, and (especially with the light microscope) one tends to measure only the longest rods, distorting the true mean length of the outer segments. This may be the reason such a correlation was previously not found (4); but on the basis of both light- and electron-microscopic measurements of developing rods, we believe a close correlation does exist.

A genetic abnormality affecting retinal development in rats lends further support to the idea that rhodopsin is correlated with the disc membranes (15). Rats with an inherited retinal dystrophy demonstrate an overabundance of rhodopsin in the early stages of the disease, so that at 18–30 days of age they may have twice as much visual pigment in the eye as do normal animals. Coupled with this increase of visual pigment in the eye is the accumulation of disc-like membranes between the outer segments and the pigment epithelium. These membranes are often paired, as in the normal outer segment disc; but they are not organized into cylindrical, rod-like structures. The membranes appear continuous for great lengths and are frequently seen as giant, whorled structures (Fig. 10). These membranes are not enclosed within a plasma membrane, and they appear to be truly extracellular. How these membranes arise is not clear, but they are already present at a very early stage during the development of the visual cells of the dystrophic animals. Direct extraction of these extracellular lamellae shows that they contain the extra rhodopsin of the abnormal retinas.

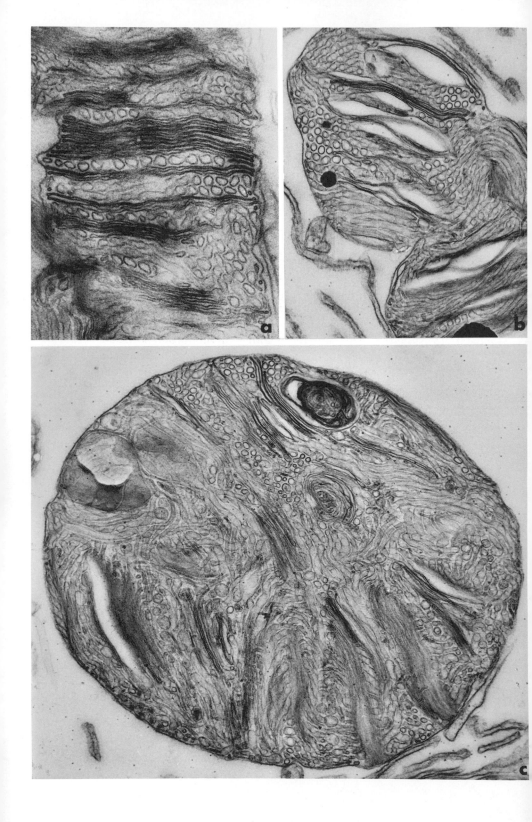

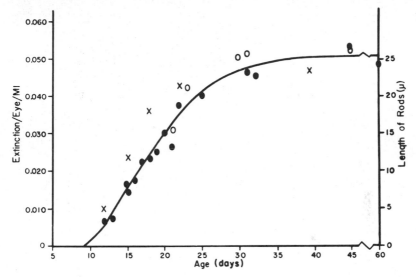

FIG. 9.   Increase of rhodopsin content of the rat eye with age (circles) compared with increase of outer segment length (crosses). Filled circles: animals raised under ordinary laboratory conditions of illumination; open circles: animals raised in darkness (15).

In summary, it appears clear that the visual pigment in the visual cell is closely related to the disc membranes, and is probably an integral part of the membrane. If the pigment is destroyed, as in vitamin A deficiency, the disc membranes fragment and break up. Also, it is possible to correlate the amount of disc membrane with the amount of rhodopsin, both in normal and abnormal retinas. Unfortunately, the examination of the outer segment disc membrane under high resolution has not revealed definite differences between the disc membranes and the plasma membrane or other cellular membranes, although during vitamin A deficiency the disc and plasma membranes appear to respond differently: that is, early in the degeneration, the disc membranes fragment, whereas the plasma membranes do not. I think we must conclude that our techniques are not sufficiently refined at present to distinguish morphologically these membranous structures of presumed different chemical composition.

FIG. 8.   The effect of vitamin A deficiency on the structure of rod outer segments of the rat. Initially, a few of the discs begin to swell and fragment into distended vesicles and tubules (a). Gradually the entire structure becomes filled with vesicles and tubules (b) and the outer segment loses its normal cylindrical shape, becoming spherical (13). × 45,000.

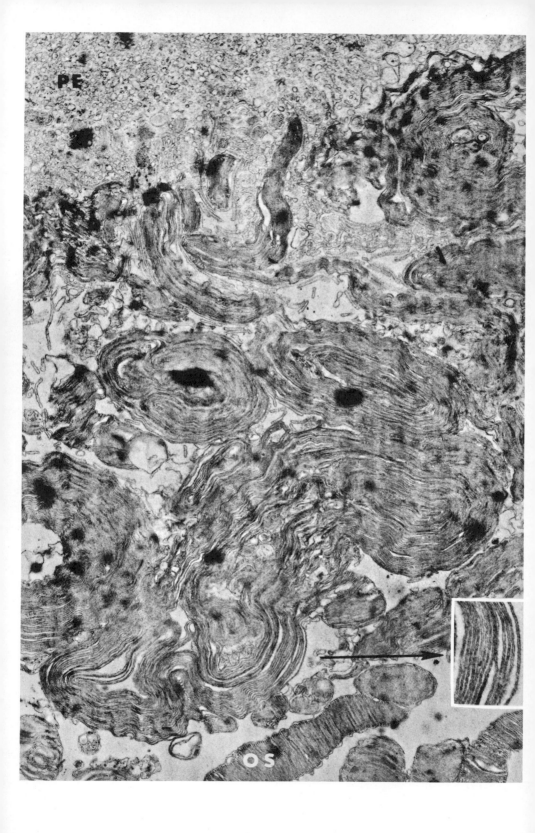

RELATION OF THE PIGMENT EPITHELIUM

The retinal pigment epithelium overlies the outer segments of the visual cells and is in intimate contact with them by means of villous processes extending between the outer segments (Figs. 1 and 2). For almost a century it has been realized that the pigment epithelium plays a vital role in the chemistry of vision. In 1878, Kuhne showed that for visual pigment to regenerate in a frog, the retina must be in contact with the pigment epithelium (27).

The exact role the pigment epithelium plays in the visual cycle is not well understood, but it is known that exchange of vitamin A occurs between retina and pigment epithelium during light and dark adaptation (11,26). Figure 11 shows an experiment demonstrating this exchange. During light adaptation, retinene levels in the retina rapidly decline as the retinene is released from rhodopsin and is reduced to vitamin A. The vitamin A level in the retina at first rapidly increases, but after a few minutes it falls again as most of the vitamin A migrates out of the outer segments into the pigment epithelium. After 1 hr of light adaptation, about 80% of the retinal vitamin A is found in the pigment epithelium. During dark adaptation, vitamin A migrates back into the outer segments of the retina as retinene is reformed and bound into rhodopsin.

The function of the vitamin A exchange between retina and pigment epithelium during adaptation is not clear. However, as noted above, the synthesis of rhodopsin requires that vitamin A be oxidized to retinene and isomerized to the 11-cis configuration. The only enzyme isolated thus far that promotes the isomerization of retinene has been found both in the outer segments and pigment epithelium (25), which suggests that the pigment epithelium may play a role in the isomerization of vitamin A. A difficulty with this concept is that this enzyme acts only on retinene, and retinene is not exchanged with or found in the pigment epithelium (11).

Recent experiments by Droz (18) and Young (45) suggest that the outer segments of mammalian visual cells are continually being

---

FIG. 10. Extracellular disc-like lamellae found between normal-appearing outer segments (OS) and pigment epithelium (PE). Associated with these membranes is an overabundance of rhodopsin in the eye. The membranes are paired, as in the normal outer segment (inset), but are not organized into typical rods. The membranes appear continuous for great lengths and are seen frequently in giant whorled configurations (15). × 14,000.

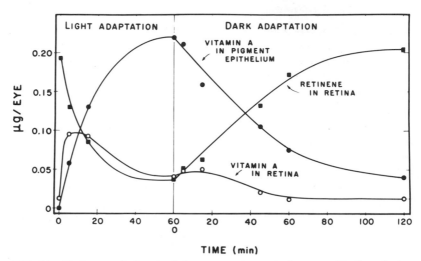

FIG. 11. Exchange of vitamin A between retina and pigment epithelium during light and dark adaptation. During light adaptation, the retinene content of the eye falls as the retinene liberated as rhodopsin is bleached is reduced to vitamin A. Vitamin A in the retina rises for a time, and then declines as most of the vitamin A moves into the pigment layers. During dark adaptation these processes are reversed. The retinene content of the eye increases as rhodopsin is reformed; and reciprocally the vitamin A in the pigment layers and retina declines (11).

renewed. Soon after injection of radioactive amino acids into rats, autoradiographic activity in the eye is localized in the inner segments of the visual cells, particularly near the junction of inner and outer segment. Within 24 hr, radioactivity is detected in the proximal portion of the outer segment; thereafter the radioactivity is gradually displaced distally along the outer segment. The radioactivity is found in the distal portion of the outer segment within a week and then disappears gradually during the next few weeks. These experiments suggest a continuous synthesis of outer segment material at the junction of inner and outer segment, which gradually moves distally along the outer segment. Apparently, material is being continually lost at the distal end of the outer segment, for the outer segments do not continue to lengthen in the mature animal.

In the apical portion of the pigment epithelial cells in mammals, there are numerous characteristic inclusion particles (Fig. 12) (2,14). Many of these are morphologically similar to the lysosome (8) or cytolosome (31) particles of hepatic and other cells that are believed to have the function of ingesting cellular organelles and digesting them (1). In many of the lysosome-like particles of the pigment epithelium, tightly packed membranes similar to disc membranes are found. In large particles within pigment epithelial cells, membranous bodies are occasionally seen that are clearly outer segment fragments. The process involved here, I think, is probably the continual removal and digestion of outer segment fragments by the lysosome-like particles of the pigment epithelium. If outer segments are lost in a retina, as in vitamin A deficiency, the lysosome-like particles of the pigment epithelium no longer contain membranes; and this is consistent with the idea that the membranes in the particles are derived from the outer segments.

Thus, the pigment epithelium may play an important role in the regulation of outer segment growth, for it seems responsible for assimilation and digestion of outer segment membranes and other material. This raises the interesting possibility that the accumulation of membranes in rats with inherited retinal dystrophy may occur because of failure of the pigment epithelium to assimilate outer segment material properly, combined perhaps with an increased synthesis of outer segment substance in the diseased eye. In the pigment epithelial cells of dystrophic animals, lysosome-like particles are seen and they occasionally contain membranous material. These cells do not, however, seem to be taking up the extracellular membranes applied tightly to their apical processes (Fig. 10), which perhaps indicates an inability of these cells to digest outer segment materials.

Finally, we find in the pigment epithelial cells of lower vertebrates such as the frog or turtle a second type of particle, called a myeloid body (32,44), which is distinctly different from the lysosome-like particles described above. These are large particles, 5μ or so in length; they are often diamond-shaped and not surrounded by a membrane. These bodies consist of a stack of membranous plates that, when

---

FIG. 12. Characteristic inclusion particles found in apical portions of pigment epithelial cells. The smaller particles appear morphologically similar to lysosomes, but characteristically contain dark-staining material and membranes (a). In the larger particles, tightly packed membranes similar to the disc membranes are frequently seen (b, c, d, e). The process involved here may be the digestion of ingested outer segment fragments by these lysosome-like particles. Micrographs a–d are from rat specimens, e from human (14). $\times$ 50,000.

FIG. 13. Myeloid bodies (MB) in pigment epithelial cell of frog. The membranes of the myeloid bodies are clearly derived from the endoplasmic reticulum (arrows), but the over-all appearance is strongly reminiscent of the outer segment structure. A lysosome-like particle, similar to those described in Fig. 12, is seen in the upper portion of the micrograph (LP). The dark-staining material to the right is probably a lipid inclusion body (L). A portion of the nucleus (N) is shown in the upper right-hand corner of the micrograph. $\times$ 40,000.

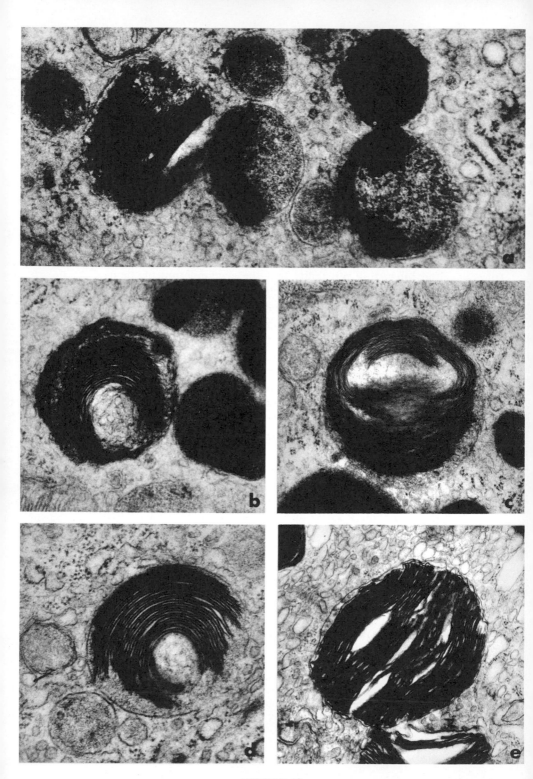

FIGURE 12

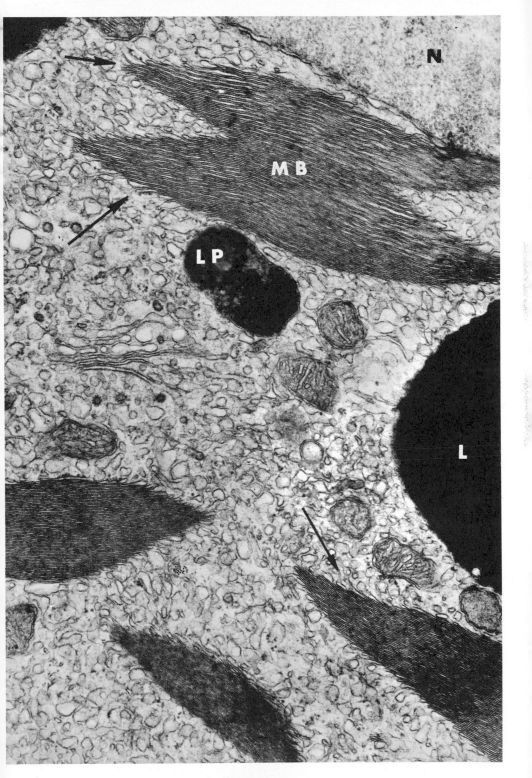

FIGURE 13

properly oriented, appear similar to the outer segment structure. The membranes of the myeloid bodies, though, are clearly derived from the endoplasmic reticulum, not the plasma membrane of the cell (arrows in Fig. 13).

The function of these particles is not yet known; but it may be that the myeloid bodies are related to (and perhaps the photoreceptor for) the migration of the melanin granules that occurs along the villous processes of the pigment epithelial cells during light and dark adaptation. In mammals, melanin granule migration does not occur; and myeloid bodies are not present in the pigment epithelial cells (14,44). Wherever melanin granule migration does occur, however, myeloid bodies are seen, which supports the idea that they are related to pigment migration. Thus, pigment epithelial cells not only play a vital role in the function and metabolism of the visual cell outer segments but may, themselves, contain a photoreceptor, the myeloid body.

SUMMARY

The outer segments of vertebrate visual cells consist of membrane-limited discs piled one on top of the other. The membranes of the discs are derived from the plasma membrane of the visual cell; but in the mature animal, most of the discs lose continuity with the plasma membrane and behave as intracellular organelles. Chemical studies suggest that a substantial portion of the disc membrane may be visual pigment; but one cannot distinguish the disc membranes morphologically from the plasma or other cellular membranes. The outer segment appears to undergo a constant metabolic turnover, with material migrating from the junction with the inner segment to the distal end of the outer segment in the course of a few weeks. The apical portion of the pigment epithelial cells gives cytological evidence of digestion of outer-segment fragments, which suggests that the pigment cells play a role in the regulation of outer segment growth and metabolism.

Figures 4, 9, 10, and 12 are reproduced by permission of The Rockefeller University Press from *The Journal of Cell Biology*.

REFERENCES

1. Ashford, T. P., and Porter, K. R., *J. Cell Biol. 12*, 198 (1962).
2. Bairati, A., and Orzalesi, N., *J. Ultrastructure Res. 9*, 484 (1963).

3. Bloom, G., *Z. Zellforsch. u. Mikr. Anat. 41*, 89 (1954).
4. Bonting, S. L., Caravaggio, L. L., and Gouras, P. *Exptl. Eye Res. 1*, 14 (1961).
5. Brown, P. K., Gibbons, I. R., and Wald, G., *J. Cell Biol. 19*, 79 (1963).
6. Cohen, A. I., *Exptl. Eye Res. 1*, 128 (1961).
7. Cone, R. A., *J. Gen. Physiol. 46*, 1267 (1963).
8. De Duve, C., In *Subcellular Particles*, Ed. T. Hayashi, Ronald Press, New York, 1959, p. 128.
9. De Robertis, E., *J. Biophys. Biochem. Cytol. 2*, 209 (1956).
10. De Robertis, E., and Lasansky, A. In *The Structure of the Eye*, Ed. G. K. Smelser, Academic Press, New York, 1961, p. 29.
11. Dowling, J. E., *Nature 188*, 114 (1960).
12. Dowling, J. E., *Science 147*, 57 (1965).
13. Dowling, J. E., and Gibbons, I. R., In *The Structure of the Eye*, Ed. G. K. Smelser, Academic Press, New York, 1961, p. 85.
14. Dowling, J. E., and Gibbons, I. R., *J. Cell Biol. 14*, 4 (1962).
15. Dowling, J. E., and Sidman, R. L., *J. Cell Biol. 14*, 73 (1962).
16. Dowling, J. E., and Wald, G., *Proc. Natl. Acad. Sci. U.S. 44*, 648 (1958).
17. Dowling, J. E., and Wald, G., *Proc. Natl. Acad. Sci. U.S. 46*, 587 (1960).
18. Droz, B., *Anat. Rec. 145*, 157 (1963).
19. Eakin, R. M., and Westfall, J. A., *Embryologia 6*, 84 (1961).
20. Fernández-Morán, H., In *The Structure of the Eye*, Ed. G. K. Smelser, Academic Press, New York, 1961, p. 521.
21. Flock, A., Kimura, R., Lundquist, P. G., and Wersall, J., *J. Acoust. Soc. Am. 34*, 1351 (1962).
22. Futterman, S., *J. Biol. Chem. 238*, 1145 (1963).
23. Hagins, W. A., Zonana, H. V., and Adams, R. G., *Nature 194*, 844 (1962).
24. Hubbard, R., *J. Gen. Physiol. 37*, 381 (1953–54).
25. Hubbard, R., *J. Gen. Physiol. 39*, 935 (1955–56).
26. Jansco, N. von, and Jansco, H. von, *Biochem. Ztschr. 287*, 289 (1936).
27. Kuhne, W., *On the Photochemistry of the Retina and on Visual Purple*, Ed. M. Foster, Macmillan, London, 1878.
28. Moody, M. F., and Robertson, J. D., *J. Biophys. Biochem. Cytol. 7*, 87 (1960).
29. Nilsson, S. E. G., *J. Ultrastruct. Res. 11*, 581 (1964).
30. Nilsson, S. E. G., *J. Ultrastruct. Res. 12*, 207 (1965).
31. Novikoff, A. B., In *Developing Cell Systems and Their Control*. Ed. D. Rudnick, The Ronald Press, New York, 1960, p. 167.
32. Porter, K. R., and Yamada, E., *J. Biophys. Biochem. Cytol. 8*, 181 (1960).
33. Robertson, J. D., *Biochem. Soc. Symp.* (Cambridge, Eng.) *16*, 3 (1959).
34. Sjöstrand, F. S., *J. Cell Comp. Physiol. 42*, 15 (1953).
35. Sjöstrand, F. S., *Rev. Mod. Physics 31*, 301 (1959).
36. Sjöstrand, F. S., In *The Structure of the Eye*, Ed. G. K. Smelser, Academic Press, New York, 1961, p. 1.
37. Sjöstrand, F. S., *J. Ultrastruct. Res. 9*, 340 (1963).

38. Tokuyasu, K., and Yamada, E., *J. Biophys. Biochem. Cytol. 6*, 225 (1959).
39. Tormey, J. Mc. D., and Dowling, J. E., Unpublished observations.
40. Wald, G., *Science 119*, 887 (1954).
41. Wald, G., *Am. J. Ophthal. 40*, 18 (1955).
42. Wald, G., In *Light and Life*, Ed. W. D. McElroy and B. Glass, The Johns Hopkins Press, Baltimore, 1961, p. 724.
43. Wolken, J. J., In *The Structure of the Eye*, Ed. G. K. Smelser, Academic Press, New York, 1961, p. 173.
44. Yamada, E., In *The Structure of the Eye*, Ed. G. K. Smelser, Academic Press, New York, 1961, p. 73.
45. Young, R. W., *Anat. Rec. 151*, 484 (1965).

8

THE ORGANIZATION OF CILIA AND FLAGELLA

I. R. Gibbons

This article will be concerned with the cilia and flagella of higher organisms (eukaryotes). These organelles form a homologous group with a remarkable uniformity of structural organization. It is important not to confuse them with bacterial flagella, which are quite different.

Typical cilia and flagella are motile hair-like organelles projecting from the free surface of cells. They occur in most groups of animals and plants, except the crustacea, angiosperms, and gymnosperms. Their length varies greatly in different organisms from as little as 2μ in some flagellates, up to as much as several millimeters in ctenophores and in some insect sperm. Their diameter is relatively constant, about 0.2μ.

In recent years the electron microscope has revealed in cilia and flagella a complex internal structure consisting of longitudinal fibers arranged in a precise pattern. This pattern of organization is remarkably uniform in all cilia and flagella no matter what animal or plant they come from, and such deviations from it as have been described are of a clearly secondary nature. Full accounts of the structural features have been given by Fawcett and Porter (10), Gibbons and Grimstone (17), Fawcett (8), Sleigh (28), and others.

Examples of cilia and flagella from various organisms are illustrated by electron micrographs in Figs. 1 to 7. The typical cilium or flagellum consists of a complex bundle of fibers (or "axoneme") embedded in a matrix and enclosed by a membrane (Fig. 8). The ciliary membrane is continuous with the plasma membrane of the cell, and it shows the same triple-layered fine structure. A principal feature of the axoneme is the bundle of nine double outer fibers and two central fibers that runs continuously along its length (Figs. 3 and 7). The two central fibers are

FIG. 1.   Transverse sections through flagella of *Pseudotrichonympha* (17). × 95,000.

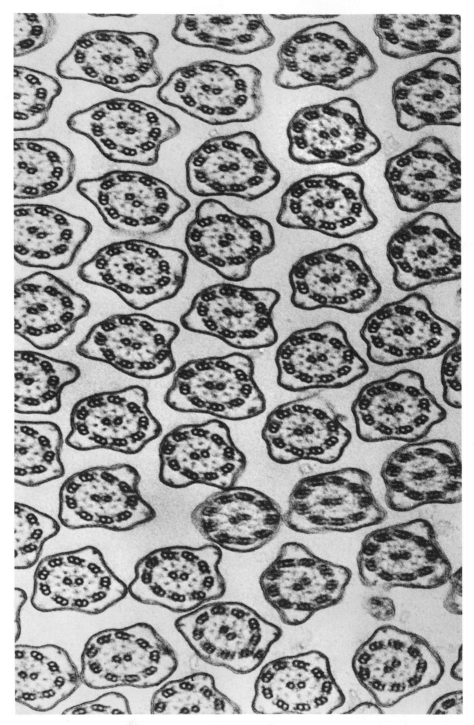

FIGURE 1

FIG. 2. Transverse sections through lateral cilia on gill epithelium of *Anodonta cataracta*. The plane of beat of the cilia lies up and down in the figure, with the effective stroke toward the top (11,12). ×85,000.

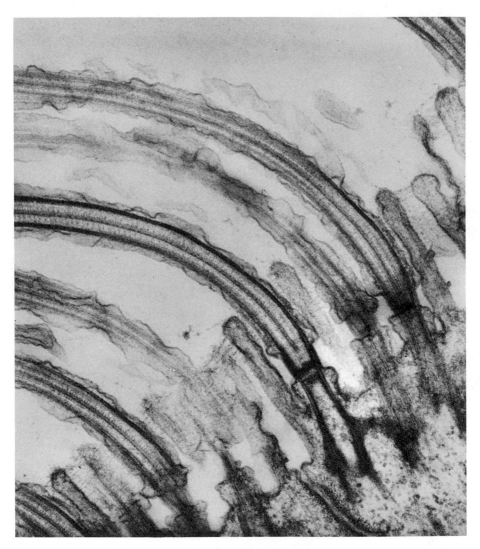

FIG. 3.   Median longitudinal section of lateral cilia and basal bodies on gill epithelium of *Anodonta cataracta* (11,12). × 42,000.

circular in cross section, about 240 Å in diameter and 360 Å apart (center to center). They have a tubular form, with a dense wall about 45 Å thick surrounding a less dense interior. The two fibers are enclosed by a central sheath that appears in cross section as a moderately dense line running out from one fiber and curving around to join the other (Fig. 8).

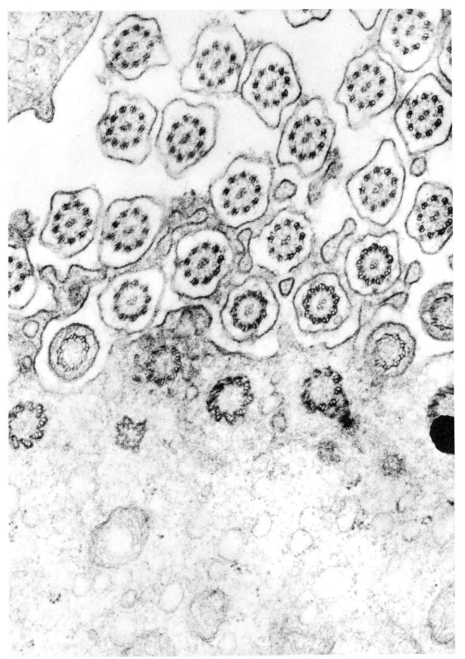

FIG. 4.   Transverse section of cilia and basal bodies in tracheal epithelium of rat. × 65,000.

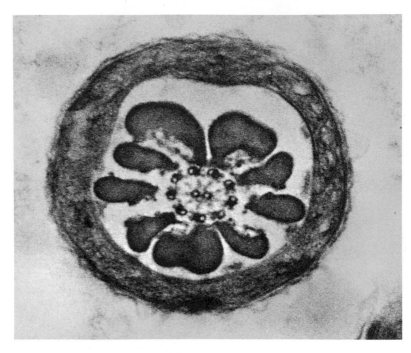

FIG. 5.   Transverse section of midpiece of a rat sperm tail. × 95,000.

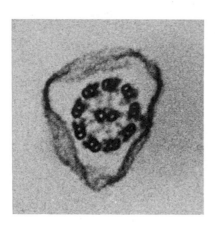

FIG. 6.   Transverse section of a sea urchin sperm tail. × 95,000.

Each of the nine outer fibers appears as a dense figure-of-eight in cross section, and measures about 370 × 250 Å over all. They can be considered to be composed of two subfibers, designated as A and B (17). Subfiber A is slightly smaller, and lies slightly closer to the center of the cilium than subfiber B. Each of the subfibers has a tubular form with

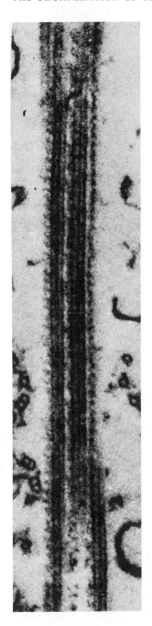

FIG. 7. Tangential longitudinal section of a cilium isolated from *Tetrahymena pyriformis*. Parts of three outer fibers are visible. Arms are seen most clearly along the fiber at the left. × 120,000.

a dense wall 45 Å thick. The thickness (45 Å) and density of the partition between the two subfibers appears the same as that of other portions of the wall.

From subfiber A of each outer fiber there arise short projections,

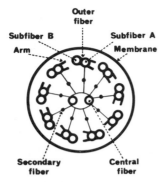

FIG. 8. Diagram showing the structures visible in transverse section of a typical cilium (modified from 17).

which have been termed arms (1). In transverse section two of these are usually visible on each outer fiber. Each arm measures about 50 Å thick and 150 Å long. As shown in Fig. 8, the arms usually point in the same direction on all the fibers in a cilium. This arrangement gives the cilium an enantiomorphic asymmetry. In all cilia and flagella in which it has been studied it has been found that the arms point in the same (clockwise) direction as seen by an observer looking from base to tip (12). In longitudinal sections of cilia, the arms can be identified as approximately rectangular structures about 150 Å long by 70 Å thick, and spaced 170 to 220 Å apart (Fig. 7).

The outer and the central fibers are held together at frequent intervals along their length by radially oriented links, or "spokes," that extend from the A subfibers to the central sheath. The spokes frequently have a thicker and denser region near their middle. These dense regions in the spokes have been interpreted as cross sections of a further set of nine secondary fibers running longitudinally (17). In longitudinal sections of cilia, the secondary fibers appear either as a zigzagging moniliform line or as a series of grains joined by lines, in the manner of a knotted cord (2). The structures in this region are particularly difficult to preserve, and the exact degree of longitudinal continuity in the secondary fibers remains open to some question (for example, 9).

The above descriptions have been based on material prepared by the thin-sectioning technique. Some further details, particularly concerning the substructure of the outer and central fibers, are revealed by the negative-contrast technique of Brenner and Horne (4) and Huxley (21). At low magnification (Fig. 9) the two subfibers of each outer

FIG. 9. Sea urchin (*Arbacia*) sperm tail prepared by the negative-contrast technique, using potassium phosphotungstate. Under these conditions the arms, spokes, and central sheath become dispersed, and only the outer and the central fibers remain. × 100,000.

doublet appear to have dense centers, which illustrates that the negative-contrasting medium is able to penetrate the lumen of the fibers. This confirms the tubular nature of the fibers. In some areas it can be seen that the wall of each fiber is composed of a number of longitudinal protofilaments, 45–50 Å in diameter (3,13,26). These protofilaments are shown more clearly in micrographs at higher magnification (Fig. 10), in which there usually appear to be five or six of them present in each subfiber. Since the negative-contrast technique only shows up one surface of the fiber, the total number of protofilaments is probably between 10 and 13 per subfiber. Each protofilament has a beaded appearance along its length with a periodicity of about 45 Å, suggesting that it may consist of a chain of globular subunits. Figure 11 illustrates a tentative model for the structure of the central and the outer fibers composed of these globular subunits, 45–50 Å in diameter. This model, and the somewhat similar one suggested by Randall (27), can account for the fine structure seen in negative-contrasted preparations such as Figs. 10 and 11, but they are probably oversimplified. In preparations of isolated cilia, it has been demonstrated that the arms can be removed and then put back in their original position by controlling the ionic environment (see Fig. 19), so that there must be specific binding sites for them on subfiber A. This is not explained by the simple model.

The basic features of the axonemal structure described above are common to all typical cilia and flagella. In finer detail, some minor differences between the cilia of different organisms can sometimes be found. For example, in the mussel-gill cilia (Fig. 2), one particular pair of outer fibers always appears joined by a bridge (11,14). In some cases, subfiber A of each doublet does not have its usual hollow appearance (Figs. 2 and 5). Sperm tails show more variation in structure than cilia, but for the most part these variations consist of extra structures added to the normal axoneme rather than changes in the axoneme itself. Mammalian sperm tails (Fig. 5) contain an extra set of nine coarse fibers arranged around the periphery of a typical axoneme (8). The significance of these variations from the usual axonemal structure remains largely obscure.

The fine structure of cilia and flagella has become well known as a result of many studies with the electron microscope. However, functional interpretation of the structure has been held back by lack of knowledge regarding the chemistry of the constituents. The energy for the motility of cilia can be provided by adenosine triphosphate (ATP) (5,20), and the isolated organelles possess adenosine triphosphatase activity (5,6,7,25,29), but until recently the detailed study of ciliary proteins was handicapped by their apparent insolubility at neutral pH (7,32).

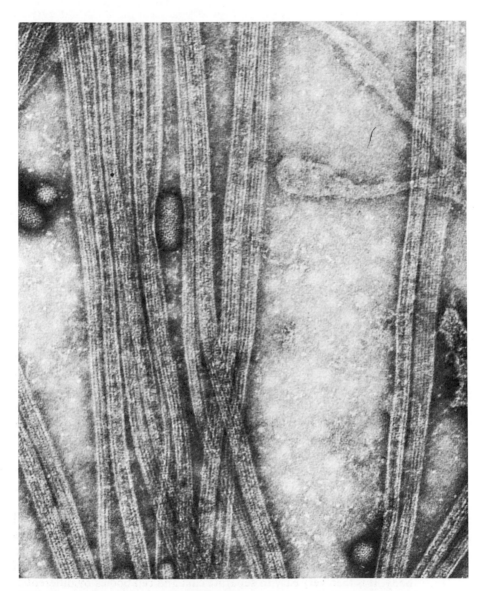

FIG. 10. Flagellum from protozoan in the gut of the termite *Zootermopsis*. Prepared by the negative-contrast technique using potassium phosphotungstate. Only the outer doublet fibers and occasional pieces of debris are present. The walls of the outer fibers are formed by longitudinal protofilaments. Each protofilament has a beaded appearance as if it were made of a chain of globular subunits approximately 45 Å in diameter. (Unpublished micrograph kindly provided by Dr. A. V. Grimstone, University of Cambridge.) × 170,000.

FIG. 11. A tentative model for the central fibers and the outer fibers composed of globular subunits 45–50 Å in diameter. The model is probably oversimplified (see text). The number of protofilaments in ciliary fibers is not known exactly but probably lies between 10 and 13. Ledbetter and Porter (23) have demonstrated 13 protofilaments in cytoplasmic microtubules of *Juniperus*.

I would now like to describe some work that has been done recently on cilia isolated from *Tetrahymena pyriformis*. This has shown that the apparent insolubility reported by previous workers is due to the membrane around the cilium, and that after disruption of the membrane the remaining protein is soluble in salt solutions at neutral pH. The principal structural components of the cilium have been separated by exploiting their differing solubilities. The ciliary adenosine triphosphatase protein, named "dynein," has been isolated and partially characterized. Differential extraction and reconstitution of the ciliary structure, combined with electron microscopy, have made it possible to locate the probable site of dynein in the cilium.

The cilia were isolated by the method of Watson and Hopkins (33), as modified by Gibbons (15). The principle of this method is to suspend the *Tetrahymena* in a solution containing about 9% ethanol, 2.5 mM EDTA, and Tris buffer, pH 8.2. The cells remain alive and motile in this medium. Addition of excess $CaCl_2$ (12 mM) causes immediate detachment of the cilia. The point of breakage is between the cilium and the basal body, so that the basal body remains with the cell body. It is then very easy to separate cilia and cell bodies by differential centrifugation. Beginning with a 40-liter culture of *Tetrahymena*, one obtains a yield of about 400 mg of cilia.

Examination of the isolated cilia in the electron microscope shows that the isolation procedure causes little structural distortion (Fig. 12). The membrane and all the usual components of the axoneme are still present. In occasional cilia the membrane is swollen, or the matrix is abnormally dense.

The differing solubility of the various structural components makes it possible to fractionate them and study them separately. For example, by first dialyzing the cilia against EDTA and then extracting with 0.6 M KCl one obtains a preparation of pure ciliary membranes (Fig. 13). Another procedure is to extract the intact cilia with digitonin; under suitable conditions this selectively removes the membrane leaving a preparation of pure axonemes (Fig. 14). This preparation of axonemes can be further fractionated by dialyzing it against EDTA at low ionic strength. Approximately one-third of the axonemal protein (Fraction 1) passes into solution during this dialysis.

TABLE I. *Distribution of Ciliary Protein and Adenosine Triphosphatase Activity*

			% Protein	% Adenosine Triphosphatase Activity
Membrane-bound protein			22	26[b]
Soluble matrix protein			28 (26[a])	
Axonemal protein—Fraction 1			18	70[b]
	30S dynein	7		
	14S dynein	3		
(non-adenosine-triphosphatase)	4S protein	8		
Axonemal protein—Fraction 2			32 (31[a])	4[b]
Total			100	100

[a] These represent independent values given by the data.
[b] Values obtained under standard assay conditions with Mg^{++} activation (cf. 15).

Examination of the insoluble residue (Fraction 2) in the electron microscope shows that it consists of a fairly pure preparation of the outer fibers (Fig. 15); the other structural components, including the arms on the outer fibers, have been almost completely removed.

Results of a typical experiment in which these various fractions were assayed for protein and for adenosine triphosphatase activity are given in Table I. This shows that most of the adenosine triphosphatase

FIG. 12.   Cilia freshly isolated from *Tetrahymena pyriformis*. In most sections the membrane is tightly applied to the axoneme. The swollen membrane present on a few cilia represents the beginning of the rounding-up process that occurs on storage (15). × 65,000; inset × 100,000.

FIG. 13.   The membrane fraction obtained by dialyzing cilia against Tris-EDTA and then extracting with 0.6 M KCl (15). × 55,000.

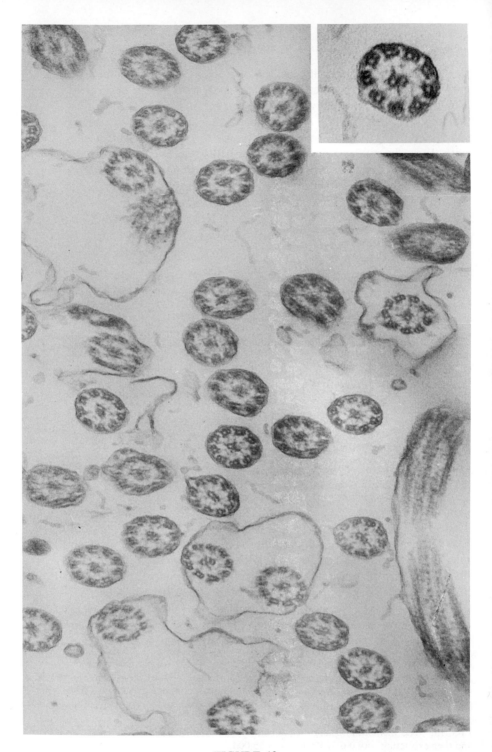

FIGURE 12

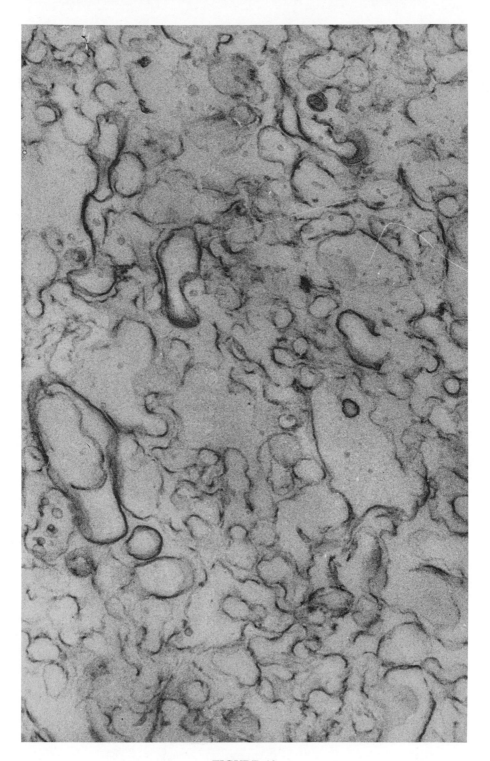

FIGURE 13

activity of the cilia is in the axoneme fraction, with just a small amount
associated with the membranes. Essentially all the axonemal adenosine
triphosphatase activity passes into Fraction 1 of the axonemal protein.

Examination of Fraction 1 in the analytical centrifuge shows three
principal components (Fig. 16). These three components can be separated by zonal centrifugation through a sucrose density gradient (Fig. 17).
The two fast components represent two forms of the axonemal adenosine triphosphatase protein, and they have been named 14S dynein and
30S dynein on the basis of their sedimentation constant $(s_{20,w})$ (18). The
slow (4S) component has no adenosine triphosphatase activity. The
contents of the tubes corresponding to each peak are pooled, and used
for further experiments. The purity of 14S and 30S dynein prepared in
this way has been examined by running the preparations in the analytic
centrifuge (Fig. 18). The purified 30S dynein gave a sharp symmetrical
peak indicating there was no appreciable contamination with 4S or 14S
components. The 14S dynein gave a somewhat skewed peak indicating
the presence of a small amount of aggregated material. Preliminary
characterization of the 14S and 30S forms of dynein has suggested that
they are related as monomer and polymer (see below), and that the 14S
dynein arises from partial breakdown of the 30S form during preparation.

The differential-extraction procedure provides evidence that the
dynein forms part of the ciliary axoneme. Moreover, since the dynein
passes into Fraction 1 it must be located in one of the structural
components that are solubilized during dialysis, and not in the outer
fibers (Fraction 2). A more positive localization is provided by reconstitution experiments in which the purified dynein is made to recombine
with outer fibers. This recombination is performed simply by adding
14S or 30S dynein to a suspension of outer fibers in the presence of
Mg^{++}. (The relative amounts of the two components should be the
same as those obtained from intact cilia.) The results of a typical
experiment (Table II) show that most of the 30S dynein recombines
with the outer fibers, but that only a small fraction of the 14S dynein
does so. Electron micrographs of this experiment (Fig. 19), show that
recombination with 30S dynein restores arms to many of the outer
fibers. The arms appear to have returned with a remarkable degree of
precision to the same position that they had in intact cilia, with one or
a pair of arms on subfiber A of most outer fibers. A count of the
average number of arms visible after recombination with 30S dynein
indicated that around 60% of the original number were present. The
preparation of outer fibers that had been treated with 14S dynein did
not appear significantly different from the control.

The results of this reconstitution experiment show that adding back purified 30S dynein restores the arms on the outer fibers. It seems very probable, therefore, that the arms consist of 30S dynein. However, the evidence available at present does not prove that all the dynein occurs in the arms, and there could be some dynein associated also with the two central fibers. The fact that only the 30S form of dynein is capable of recombining and restoring the arms indicates that it is the more "physiologically" active form under these conditions, and is in agreement with evidence that only 30S dynein restores the sensitivity of the light-scattering properties to ATP (16).

TABLE II.   *Recombination of 14S and 30S Dynein with Fraction 2[a]*

	Concentration of Fraction 2 (mg/ml)	Concentration of Dynein Added (mg/ml)	% Added Dynein that Became Bound to Fraction 2
30S Dynein	1.2	0.26	66
14S Dynein	2.1	0.15	15
Control	4.6	None	—

[a] 14S and 30S dynein were prepared by dialysis of whole cilia against Tris-EDTA-5KCl solution (1 mM Tris buffer, 0.1 mM EDTA, 5 mM KCl, pH 8.3 at 0°C), followed by density gradient fractionations (Fig. 17 shows the analysis of this same preparation). Fraction 2 was prepared from a second batch of cilia by extracting with digitonin, and dialyzing against Tris-EDTA solution containing 3 mM KCl. Recombination was carried out for 90 min at 0°C in a medium containing 2.5 mM MgSO₄, 10 mM KCl, 15 mM Tris-HCl buffer, pH 8.3. Pellets from the centrifugation were fixed for electron microscopy (see Fig. 19). All concentrations are the final ones in the recombination mixture. Dynein preparation was 5 days old (from isolation of cilia). Fraction 2 preparation was 1 day old (from isolation of cilia).

Preliminary characterization of the 14S and 30S dynein by electron microscopic, physico-chemical, and enzymatic techniques suggests that the two forms are related as monomer and polymer (18).

Electron micrographs of 30S dynein, shadow-cast with platinum by the method of Hall (19), show that it consists of rod-like particles of

FIG. 14.   The axoneme fraction obtained by extracting cilia with digitonin (15). × 50,000; inset × 100,000.

FIG. 15.   Preparation of outer fibers (Fraction 2 of axonemal protein), obtained by dialyzing axonemes against Tris-EDTA solution (15). × 65,000.

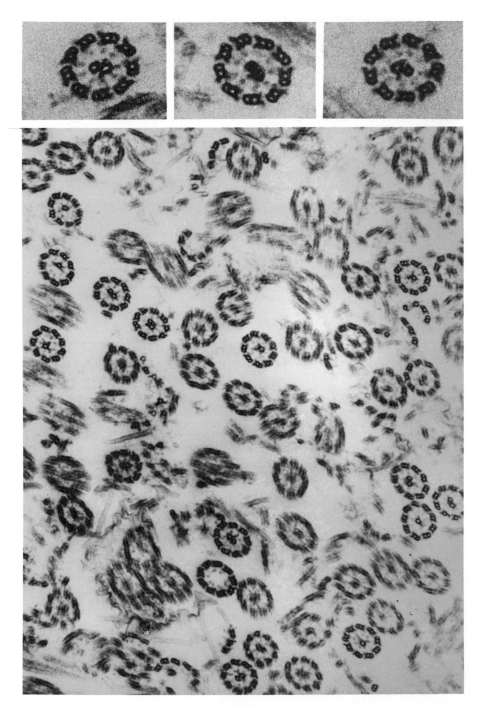

FIGURE 14

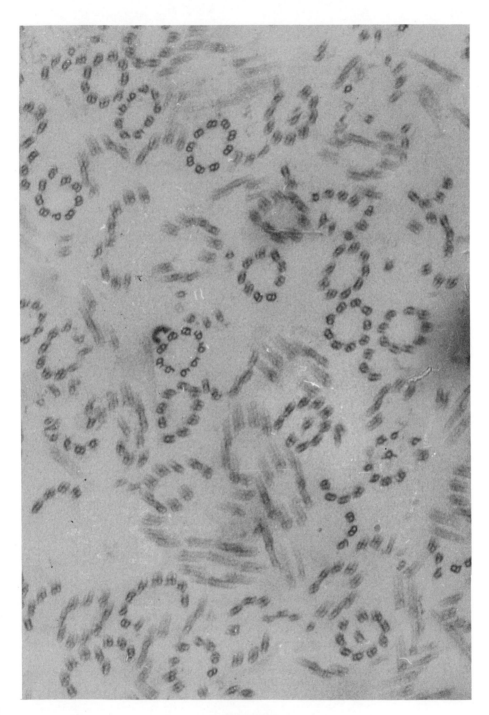

FIGURE 15

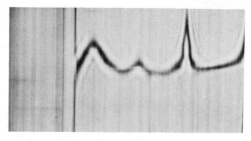

FIG. 16. Analytical ultracentrifugation of the supernatant fraction. Cilia were dialyzed 48 hr against Tris-EDTA-5KCl solution and centrifuged. Supernatant fluid consists of Fraction 1 of axonemal protein plus some matrix protein (15).

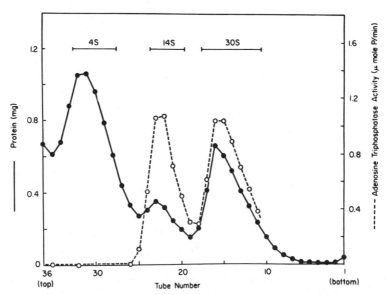

FIG. 17. Purification of dynein by centrifugation through a sucrose density gradient. Whole cilia were dialyzed 48 hr against Tris-EDTA-5KCl solution and centrifuged. Supernatant fluid was concentrated to 1 ml, layered onto a 5–30% sucrose gradient, and centrifuged 24 hr at 25,000 rpm in SW 25 rotor of Spinco Model L centrifuge at 4°C. Contents of centrifuge tube were collected in samples of 13 drops each. The samples corresponding to the 4S, 14S, and 30S components were pooled separately and used for further experiments.

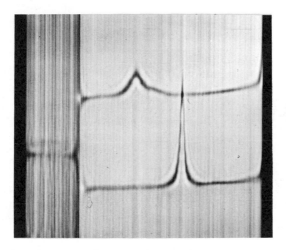

FIG. 18. Analytical ultracentrifugation of 14S and 30S dynein purified by density gradient centrifugation. Two cells were run; one cell had a 1° positive wedge window to displace the trace upward. The upper trace shows 14S dynein (1.2 mg/ml); lower trace shows 30S dynein (1.8 mg/ml) (18).

variable length (Figs. 20 and 21). The particle height is 70–90 Å. The lengths of the particles in a typical preparation ranged between 400 and 5000 Å, with a weight-average length of 1700 Å. When the particles lie obliquely with respect to the direction of shadowing, a repeating globular structure (period about 140 Å) can often be seen along their length (Fig. 21). Composite pictures obtained by linear translation and superimposition (24) reveal this periodicity even more clearly.

Electron micrographs obtained by shadow-casting 14S dynein show globular particles (Fig. 22). The heights are in the range 70–100 Å, and the widths in the range 90–140 Å. These dimensions suggest that the 14S dynein molecule can be approximated as an ellipsoid with axes 85, 90, and 140 Å (18).

Molecular weights of several preparations of dynein have been determined by centrifugation using the methods of Klainer and Kegeles (22) and van Holde and Baldwin (31). The accuracy of these determinations has so far been limited by heterogeneity, but approximate values of 600,000 and 5,400,000 have been obtained for 14S and 30S dynein, respectively.

The enzymatic properties of 14S and 30S dynein are similar. Their adenosine triphosphatase activity can be activated by either Ca^{++} or Mg^{++}, and it is inhibited by an excess of EDTA. With Ca^{++} activation both forms have about the same specific activity, 1.7 ± 0.4 μmole

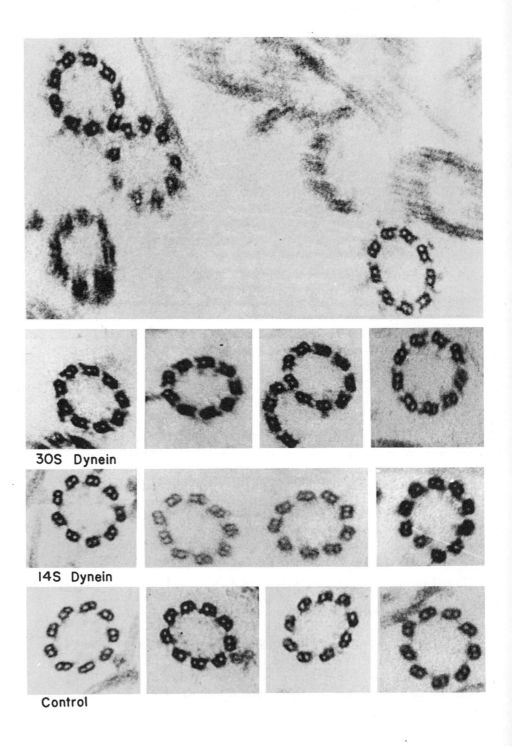

30S Dynein

14S Dynein

Control

FIG. 20. Electron micrograph of 30S dynein shadow-cast with platinum by the method of Hall (18). × 18,000.

P/(mg protein × min) at 20°C. The activity of both forms is moderately specific for ATP, other nucleoside triphosphates being hydrolyzed at only around 10% of the rate of ATP. There is no appreciable hydrolysis of AMP, sodium pyrophosphate, or p-nitrophenyl phosphate.

FIG. 19. "Reconstituted" cilia obtained by mixing purified 14S and 30S dynein with Fraction 2 in the presence of Mg^{++}. Recombination with 30S dynein restored arms to many of the outer fibers. The preparation treated with 14S dynein does not appear significantly different from the control. See Table II for further details (15). Top × 115,000; remainder × 100,000.

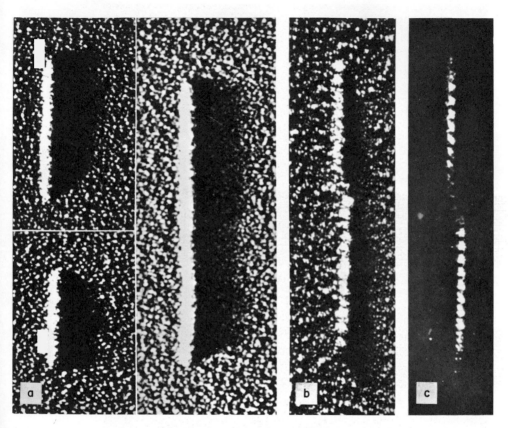

FIG. 21.   Selected particles of 30S dynein at higher magnification. (a) Three particles shadowed approximately normal to their long axis; (b) two particles shadowed obliquely; (c) same particles as (b) with six images superimposed, translating through a distance equivalent to 140 Å between each exposure (taken in part from 18). × 225,000.

The evidence that 30S dynein is a linear polymer of 14S dynein units is as follows: (a) electron microscopy reveals that 30S dynein consists of a string of globular subunits indistinguishable in size from 14S dynein molecules; (b) both 14S and 30S dynein are broken down in alkali to a form sedimenting at about 10S (14); (c) the enzymatic properties of the two forms are closely similar. This hypothesis, however, can only be finally proved by a demonstration that the two forms can be interconverted under mild conditions.

The repeat distance between subunits in 30S dynein is comparable with that shown by the arms on the outer fibers in longitudinal sections

FIG. 22.   Electron micrograph of 14S dynein shadow-cast with platinum. × 150,000.

of cilia (170–220 Å), which supports the previous evidence that the arms consist of dynein. (In view of the likelihood of shrinkage during drying, the somewhat smaller periodicity—140 Å—observed in shadow-cast preparations of purified dynein is not surprising.) It seems probable, therefore, that the 14S dynein molecules form the individual units of the arms, and that these units are linked in the longitudinal plane of the cilium. The breaking of links between 14S units at random places during preparation would give rise to the observed scatter of lengths among the 30S particles.

It is interesting to consider the relationship of dynein to the adenosine triphosphatase proteins found in other motile systems. Myosin from skeletal muscle has about the same molecular weight as 14S dynein, but it is a highly asymmetric molecule (axial ratio about 80), whereas the dynein monomer is nearly globular. Myosin-adenosine-triphosphatase is activated by Ca^{++} but not by Mg^{++}, and it shows little specificity for any particular nucleoside triphosphate: dynein-adenosine-triphosphatase, on the other hand, is activated by either Ca^{++} or Mg^{++}, and it is relatively quite specific for ATP. The other fibrillar muscle-proteins are not comparable to dynein at all, for they have a much lower molecular weight and no adenosine triphosphatase activity. Thus, from the evidence available at present, it must be concluded that dynein shows little similarity to any of the contractile proteins of skeletal muscle.

However, there is a striking resemblance between dynein and the protein "myxomyosin" associated with protoplasmic streaming in slime molds, and also some similarity to the protein of the mitotic apparatus (34). Myxomyosin, which has been characterized in some detail by Ts'o *et al.* (30), is an adenosine triphosphatase, has a sedimentation constant of 30S, and consists of rod-like particles of variable length (up to 7000 Å) having a diameter of 60–80 Å. These properties are all very close to those of 30S dynein. This comparison, although necessarily based on fragmentary evidence, suggests that ciliary dynein is one of a class of proteins of widespread occurrence in association with cell motility, but distinct from the contractile proteins related to actomyosin.

Figures 1, 2, 3, and 8 are reproduced by permission of The Rockefeller University Press from *The Journal of Biophysical and Biochemical Cytology.*

REFERENCES

1. Afzelius, B., *J. Biophys. Biochem. Cytol. 5*, 269 (1959).
2. André, J., *J. Ultrastruct. Res. 5*, 86 (1961).
3. André, J., and Thiéry, J.-P., *J. Micros. 2*, 71 (1963).
4. Brenner, S., and Horne, R. W., *Biochim. Biophys. Acta 34*, 103 (1959).
5. Brokaw, C. J., *Exptl. Cell Res. 22*, 151 (1961).
6. Burnasheva, S. A., Yefremenko, M. V., and Lubimova, M. N., *Biokhimiya 28*, 547 (1963).
7. Child, F. M., In *Progress in Protozoology*, Proceedings of the 1st Int. Cong. Protozoology, Ed. J. Ludvik and J. Vavra, Prague, p. 415 (1961).
8. Fawcett, D. W., In *The Cell*, Ed. J. Brachet and A. E. Mirsky, Academic Press, New York, 1961, Vol. 2, p. 217.
9. Fawcett, D. W., and Ito, S., *Am. J. Anat. 116*, 567 (1965).
10. Fawcett, D. W., and Porter, K. R., *J. Morphol. 94*, 221 (1954).
11. Gibbons, I. R., *J. Biophys. Biochem. Cytol. 11*, 179 (1961a).
12. Gibbons, I. R., *Nature 190*, 1128 (1961b).
13. Gibbons, I. R., Paper presented at 5th Int. Cong. for Elec. Micr., Philadelphia (1962).
14. Gibbons, I. R., *Proc. Natl. Acad. Sci. U.S. 50*, 1002 (1963).
15. Gibbons, I. R., *Arch. Biol. (Liège) 76*, 317 (1965a).
16. Gibbons, I. R., *J. Cell Biol. 26*, 707 (1965b).

17. Gibbons, I. R., and Grimstone, A. V., *J. Biophys. Biochem. Cytol. 7*, 697 (1960).
18. Gibbons, I. R., and Rowe, A. J., *Science 149*, 424 (1965).
19. Hall, C. E., *J. Biophys. Biochem. Cytol. 7*, 613 (1960).
20. Hoffmann-Berling, H., *Biochim. Biophys. Acta 16*, 146 (1955).
21. Huxley, H. E., *J. Mol. Biol. 7*, 281 (1963).
22. Klainer, S. M., and Kegeles, G., *J. Phys. Chem. 59*, 952 (1955).
23. Ledbetter, M. C., and Porter, K. R., *Science 144*, 872 (1964).
24. Markham, R., Hitchborn, J. H., Hills, G. J., and Frey, S., *Virology 22*, 342 (1964).
25. Nelson, L., *Biol. Bull. 109*, 295 (1955).
26. Pease, D. C., *J. Cell Biol. 18*, 313 (1963).
27. Randall, J. T., paper presented at International Congress for Cell Biology, Providence (1964).
28. Sleigh, M. A., *The Biology of Cilia and Flagella*, Pergamon Press, Oxford, 1962.
29. Tibbs, J., *Biochim. Biophys. Acta 33*, 220 (1959).
30. Ts'o, P. O. P., Eggman, L., and Vinograd, J., *Biochim. Biophys. Acta 25*, 532 (1957).
31. van Holde, K. E., and Baldwin, R. L., *J. Phys. Chem. 62*, 734 (1958).
32. Watson, M. R., Alexander, J. B., and Silvester, N. R., *Exptl. Cell Res. 33*, 112 (1964).
33. Watson, M. R., and Hopkins, J. M., *Exptl. Cell Res. 28*, 280 (1962).
34. Zimmerman, A. M., *Exptl. Cell Res. 20*, 529 (1960).

INDEX

1930